Alfred Plummer

The epistles of St. John

with notes, introduction and appendices

Alfred Plummer

The epistles of St. John
with notes, introduction and appendices

ISBN/EAN: 9783337728946

Printed in Europe, USA, Canada, Australia, Japan

Cover: Foto ©Lupo / pixelio.de

More available books at **www.hansebooks.com**

The Cambridge Bible for Schools and Colleges.

GENERAL EDITOR:—J. J. S. PEROWNE, D.D.
DEAN OF PETERBOROUGH.

THE EPISTLES OF

S. JOHN,

WITH NOTES, INTRODUCTION AND APPENDICES

BY

THE REV. A. PLUMMER, M.A. D.D.
MASTER OF UNIVERSITY COLLEGE, DURHAM,
FORMERLY FELLOW AND TUTOR OF TRINITY COLLEGE, OXFORD.

EDITED FOR THE SYNDICS OF THE UNIVERSITY PRESS.

Cambridge:
AT THE UNIVERSITY PRESS.
1890

PREFACE
BY THE GENERAL EDITOR.

THE General Editor of *The Cambridge Bible for Schools* thinks it right to say that he does not hold himself responsible either for the interpretation of particular passages which the Editors of the several Books have adopted, or for any opinion on points of doctrine that they may have expressed. In the New Testament more especially questions arise of the deepest theological import, on which the ablest and most conscientious interpreters have differed and always will differ. His aim has been in all such cases to leave each Contributor to the unfettered exercise of his own judgment, only taking care that mere controversy should as far as possible be avoided. He has contented himself chiefly with a careful revision of the notes, with pointing out omissions, with suggesting occasionally a reconsideration of some question, or a fuller treatment of difficult passages, and the like.

Beyond this he has not attempted to interfere, feeling it better that each Commentary should have its own individual character, and being convinced that freshness and variety of treatment are more than a compensation for any lack of uniformity in the Series.

DEANERY, PETERBOROUGH.

CONTENTS.

		PAGES
I.	INTRODUCTION.	
	Chapter I. The Last Years of S. John	9—28
	Chapter II. The First Epistle of S. John	28—49
	Chapter III. The Second Epistle	49—59
	Chapter IV. The Third Epistle	59—62
	Chapter V. The Text of the Epistles	63—68
	Chapter VI. The Literature of the Epistles	68—70
II.	TEXT AND NOTES	71—195
	APPENDICES.	
	A. The Three Evil Tendencies in the World	196
	B. Antichrist	198
	C. The Sect of the Cainites	202
	D. The Three Heavenly Witnesses	204
	E. John the Presbyter or the Elder	213
III.	INDICES	217—220

*** The Text adopted in this Edition is that of Dr Scrivener's *Cambridge Paragraph Bible*. A few variations from the ordinary Text, chiefly in the spelling of certain words, and in the use of italics, will be noticed. For the principles adopted by Dr Scrivener as regards the printing of the Text see his Introduction to the *Paragraph Bible*, published by the Cambridge University Press.

INTRODUCTION.

CHAPTER I.

THE LAST YEARS OF S. JOHN.

A SKETCH of the life of S. John as a whole has been given in the Introduction to the Fourth Gospel. Here it will not be necessary to do more than retouch and somewhat enlarge what was there said respecting the closing years of his life, in which period, according to all probability, whether derived from direct or indirect evidence, our three Epistles were written. In order to understand the motive and tone of the Epistles, it is requisite to have some clear idea of the circumstances, local, moral, and intellectual, in the midst of which they were written.

(i) *The Local Surroundings—Ephesus.*

Unless the whole history of the century which followed upon the destruction of Jerusalem is to be abandoned as chimerical and untrustworthy, we must continue to believe the almost universally accepted statement that S. John spent the last portion of his life in Asia Minor, and chiefly at Ephesus. The sceptical spirit which insists upon the truism that well-attested facts have nevertheless not been demonstrated with all the certainty of a proposition in Euclid, and contends that it is therefore right to doubt them, and lawful to dispute them, renders history impossible. The evidence of S. John's residence at Ephesus is too strong to be shaken by conjectures. It will be worth while to state the main elements of it.

(1) The opening chapters of the Book of Revelation are written in the character of the Metropolitan of the Churches of Asia Minor. Even if we admit that the Book is possibly not written by S. John, at least it is written by some one who knows that S. John held that position. Had S. John never lived in Asia Minor, the writer of the Apocalypse would at once have been detected as personating an Apostle of whose abode and position he was ignorant.

(2) Justin Martyr (c. A.D. 150) probably within fifty years of S. John's death writes: "*Among us* also a certain man named John, one of the Apostles of Christ, prophesied in a Revelation made to him, that the believers of our Christ shall spend a thousand years in Jerusalem." These words occur in the *Dialogue with Trypho* (LXXXI.), which Eusebius tells us was held at Ephesus: so that 'among us' naturally means at or near Ephesus.

(3) Irenaeus, the disciple of Polycarp, the disciple of S. John, writes thus (c. A.D. 180) in the celebrated Epistle to Florinus, of which a portion has been preserved by Eusebius (*H. E.* v. xx. 4, 5): "These doctrines those presbyters who preceded us, who also were conversant with the Apostles, did not hand down to thee. For when I was yet a boy I saw thee in lower Asia with Polycarp, distinguishing thyself in the royal court, and endeavouring to have his approbation. For I remember what happened then more clearly than recent occurrences. For the experiences of childhood, growing up along with the soul, become part and parcel of it: so that I can describe both the place in which the blessed Polycarp used to sit and discourse, and his goings out and his comings in, the character of his life and the appearance of his person, and the discourses which he used to deliver to the multitude; and how he recounted *his close intercourse with John*, and with the rest of those who had seen the Lord." That Polycarp was Bishop of Smyrna, where he spent most of his life and suffered martyrdom, is well known. And this again proves S. John's residence in Asia Minor. Still more plainly Irenaeus says elsewhere (*Haer.* III. i. 1): "Then John, the disciple of the Lord, who also leaned back on His breast, he

EPHESUS. 11

too published a gospel *during his residence at Ephesus* in Asia."

(4) Polycrates, Bishop of Ephesus, in his Epistle to Victor Bishop of Rome (A.D. 190—200) says: "And moreover John also that leaned back upon the Lord's breast, who was a priest bearing the plate of gold, and a martyr and a teacher,—he lies asleep *at Ephesus.*"

(5) Apollonius, sometimes said to have been Presbyter of Ephesus, wrote a treatise against Montanism (c. A.D. 200), which Tertullian answered; and Eusebius tells us that Apollonius related the raising of a dead man to life by S. John *at Ephesus (H.E.* v. xviii. 14).

There is no need to multiply witnesses. That S. John ended his days in Asia Minor, ruling 'the Churches of Asia' from Ephesus as his usual abode, was the uniform belief of Christendom in the second and third centuries, and there is no sufficient reason for doubting its truth. We shall find that S. John's residence there harmonizes admirably with the tone and contents of these Epistles.

Ephesus was situated on high ground in the midst of a fertile plain, not far from the mouth of the Cayster. As a centre of commerce its position was magnificent. Three rivers drain western Asia Minor, the Maeander, the Cayster, and the Hermes, and of these three the Cayster is the central one, and its valley is connected by passes with the valleys of the other two. The trade of the eastern Aegean was concentrated in its port. Through Ephesus flowed the chief of the trade between Asia Minor and the West. Strabo, the geographer, who was still living when S. John was a young man, had visited Ephesus, and as a native of Asia Minor must have known the city well from reputation. Writing of it in the time of Augustus he says: "Owing to its favourable situation, the city is in all other respects increasing daily, for it is the greatest place of trade of all the cities of Asia west of the Taurus." The vermilion trade of Cappadocia, which used to find a port at Sinope, now passed through Ephesus. What Corinth was to Greece and the Adriatic, and Marseilles to Gaul and the western Mediterranean, that Ephesus was to Asia Minor and the Aegean. And its home products were considerable: corn in abundance grew in its plains, and wine and oil on its surrounding hills. Patmos, the scene of the Revelation, is only a day's sail from Ephesus, and it has been reasonably conjectured that the gorgeous description of the merchandise of 'Babylon,' given in the Apocalypse (xviii. 12, 13) is derived from S. John's own experiences in Ephesus: 'Merchandise of gold, and silver, and precious stone, and pearls, and fine linen, and purple, and silk, and scarlet; and all thyine wood, and every vessel of ivory, and every vessel made of most precious wood, and of brass, and iron, and marble; and cinnamon, and spice, and incense, and ointment, and frankincense, and wine and oil, and fine flour, and wheat, and cattle, and sheep; and merchandise of horses and chariots and slaves; and souls of men.' The last two items give us in terrible simplicity the traffic in human beings which treated them as body and soul the property of their purchaser. Ephesus was the place at which Romans visiting the East commonly landed. Among all the cities of the Roman province of Asia it ranked as 'first of all and greatest,' and was called 'the Metropolis of Asia.' In his Natural History Pliny speaks of it as *Asiae lumen*. It is quite in harmony with this that it should after Jerusalem and Antioch become the third great home of Christianity, and after the death of S. Paul be chosen by S. John as the centre whence he would direct the Churches of Asia. It is the first Church addressed in the Apocalypse (i. 11, ii. 1). If we had been entirely without information respecting S. John's life subsequent to the destruction of Jerusalem, the conjecture that he had moved to Asia Minor and taken up his abode in Ephesus would have been one of the most reasonable that could have been formed. With the exception of Rome, and perhaps of Alexandria, no more important centre could have been found for the work of the last surviving Apostle. There is nothing either in his writings or in traditions respecting him to connect S. John with Alexandria; and not much, excepting the tradition about the martyrdom near the Porta Latina (see p. 22), to connect him with Rome. If S. John ever was in Rome, it was probably with S. Peter at the time of S. Peter's death. Some have thought that Rev. xiii. and xviii. are influenced by recollections of the horrors of the persecution in which S. Peter suffered. It is not improbable that the death of his companion Apostle (Luke xxii. 8; John xx. 2; Acts iii. 1, iv. 13, viii. 14) may have been one of the circumstances which led to S. John's settling in Asia Minor. The older friend, whose destiny it was to wander and to suffer, was dead; the younger friend, whose lot was 'that he abide,' was therefore free to choose the place where his abiding would be of most use to the Church.

The Church of Ephesus had been founded by S. Paul about A.D. 55, and some eight years later he had written the Epistle which now bears the name of the Ephesians, but which was apparently a circular letter addressed to other Churches as well as to that at Ephesus. Timothy was left there by S. Paul, when the latter went on to Macedonia (1 Tim. i. 3) to endeavour to keep in check the presumptuous and even heretical theories in which some members of the Ephesian Church had begun to indulge. Timothy was probably at Rome at the time of S. Paul's death (2 Tim. iv. 9, 21), and then returned to Ephesus, where, according to tradition, he suffered martyrdom during one of the great festivals in honour of 'the great goddess Artemis,' under Domitian or Nerva. It is not impossible that 'the angel of the Church of Ephesus' praised and blamed in Rev. ii. 1—7 is Timothy, although Timothy is often supposed to have died before the Apocalypse was written. He was succeeded, according to Dorotheus of Tyre (c. A.D. 300), by Gaius (Rom. xvi. 23; 1 Cor. i. 14); but Origen mentions a tradition that this Gaius became Bishop of Thessalonica.

These particulars warrant us in believing that by the time that S. John settled in Ephesus there must have been a considerable number of Christians there. The labours of Aquila and Priscilla (Acts xviii. 19; 2 Tim. iv. 19), of S. Paul for more than two years (Acts xix. 8—10), of Trophimus (Acts xxi. 29), of the family of Onesiphorus (2 Tim. i. 16—18, iv. 9), and of Timothy for a considerable number of years, must have resulted in the conversion of many Jews and heathen. Besides which, after the destruction of Jerusalem not a few Christians would be likely to settle there from Palestine. A Church which was already organised under presbyters in S. Paul's day, as his own speech to them and his letters to Timothy shew, must have been scandalously mismanaged and neglected, if in such a centre as Ephesus, it had not largely increased in the interval between S. Paul's departure and S. John's arrival.

(ii) *The Moral Surroundings—Idolatry.*

If there was one thing for which the Metropolis of Asia was more celebrated than another in the apostolic age, it was for the magnificence of its idolatrous worship. The temple of Artemis, its tutelary deity, which crowned the head of its harbour, was one of the wonders of the world. Its 127 columns, 60 feet high, were each one the gift of a people or a prince. In area it was considerably larger than Durham Cathedral and nearly as large as S. Paul's; and its magnificence had become a proverb. 'The gods had one house on earth, and that was at Ephesus.' The architectural imagery of S. Paul in the First Epistle to the Corinthians (iii. 9—17), which was written at Ephesus, and in the Epistles to the Ephesians (ii. 19—22), and to Timothy (1 Tim. iii. 15, vi. 19; 2 Tim. ii. 19, 20), may well have been suggested by it. The city was proud of the title 'Temple-keeper of the great Artemis' (Acts xix. 35), and the wealthy vied with one another in lavishing gifts upon the shrine. The temple thus became a vast treasure-house of gold and silver vessels and works of art. It was served by a college of priestesses and of priests. "Besides these there was a vast throng of dependents, who lived by the temple and its services,—*theologi*, who may have expounded sacred legends, *hymnodi*, who composed hymns in honour of the deity, and others, together with a great crowd of *hierodulae*, who performed more menial offices. The making of shrines and images of the goddess occupied many hands.... But perhaps the most important of all the privileges possessed by the goddess and her priests was that of *asylum*. Fugitives from justice or vengeance who reached her precincts were per-

IDOLATRY.

fectly safe from all pursuit and arrest. The boundaries of the space possessing such virtue were from time to time enlarged. Mark Antony imprudently allowed them to take in part of the city, which part thus became free of all law, and a haunt of thieves and villains.....Besides being a place of worship, a museum, and a sanctuary, the Ephesian temple was a great bank. Nowhere in Asia could money be more safely bestowed than here" (P. Gardner). S. Paul's advice to Timothy to 'charge them that are rich' not to amass, but to 'distribute' and 'communicate' their wealth, 'laying up in store for themselves a good foundation,' for 'the life which is life indeed' (1 Tim. vi. 17—19), acquires fresh meaning when we remember this last fact. In short, what S. Peter's and the Vatican have been to Rome, that the temple of Artemis was to Ephesus in S. John's day.

It was in consequence of the scandals arising out of the abuse of sanctuary, that certain states were ordered to submit their charters to the Roman Senate (A.D. 22). As Tacitus remarks, no authority was strong enough to keep in check the turbulence of a people which protected the crimes of men as worship of the gods. The first to bring and defend their claims were the Ephesians. They represented "that Diana and Apollo were not born at Delos, as was commonly supposed; the Ephesians possessed the Cenchrean stream and the Ortygian grove where Latona, in the hour of travail, had reposed against an olive-tree, still in existence, and given birth to those deities; and it was by the gods' command that the grove had been consecrated. It was there that Apollo himself, after slaying the Cyclops, had escaped the wrath of Jupiter: and again that father Bacchus in his victory had spared the suppliant Amazons who had occupied his shrine" (Tac. *Ann.* III. 61).

We have only to read the first chapter of the Epistle to the Romans (21—32), or the catalogue of vices in the Epistles to the Galatians (v. 19—21) and Colossians (iii. 5—8) to know enough of the kind of morality which commonly accompanied Greek and Roman idolatry in the first century of the Christian era; especially when, as in Ephesus, it was mixed up with the wilder rites of Oriental polytheism, amid all the seductiveness of Ionian luxury, and in a climate which, while it enflamed the passions, unnerved the will. Was it not with the idolatry of Ephesus and all its attendant abominations in his mind that the Apostle of the Gentiles wrote Eph. v. 1—21?

A few words must be said of one particular phase of superstition, closely connected with idolatry, for which Ephesus was famous;—its magic. "It was preeminently the city of astrology, sorcery, incantations, amulets, exorcisms, and every form of magical imposture." About the statue of the Ephesian Artemis were written unintelligible inscriptions to which mysterious efficacy was attributed. 'Ephesian writings,' or charms ('Εφέσια γράμματα) were much sought after, and seem to have been about as senseless as Abracadabra. In the epistles of the pseudo-Heraclitus the unknown writer explains why Heraclitus of Ephesus was called "the weeping philosopher." It was because of the monstrous idiotcy and vice of the Ephesian people. Who would not weep to see religion made the vehicle of brutal superstition and nameless abominations? There was not a man in Ephesus who did not deserve hanging. (See Farrar's *Life of S. Paul*, Vol. II. p. 18.) Wicked folly of this kind had tainted the earliest Christian community at Ephesus. They had accepted the Gospel and still secretly held fast their magic. Hence the bonfire of costly books of charms and incantations which followed upon the defeat of the sons of Sceva when they attempted to use the name of Jesus as a magical form of exorcism (Acts xix. 13—20).

Facts such as these place in a very vivid light S. John's stern insistence upon the necessity of holding steadfastly the true faith in the Father and the incarnate Son, of keeping oneself pure, of avoiding the world and the things in the world, of being on one's guard against lying spirits, and especially the sharp final admonition, 'Guard yourselves from the idols.'

(iii) *The Intellectual Surroundings—Gnosticism.*

It is common to speak of the Gnostic heresy or the Gnostic heresies; but such language, though correct enough, is apt to be misleading. We commonly think of heresy as a corrupt

GNOSTICISM.

growth out of Christian truth, or a deflection from it; as when we call Unitarianism, which so insists upon the Unity of God as to deny the Trinity, or Arianism, which so insists upon the Primacy of the Father as to deny the true Divinity of the Son, heretical systems or heresies. These and many other corruptions of the truth grew up inside the bosom of the Church. They are one-sided and exaggerated developments of Christian doctrines. But corruption may come from without as well as from within. It may be the result of impure elements imported into the system, contaminating and poisoning it. It was in this way that the Gnostic heresies found their way into the Church. The germs of Gnosticism in various stages of development were in the very air in which Christianity was born. They had influenced Judaism; they had influenced the religions of Greece and of the East: and the Christian Church had not advanced beyond its infancy when they began to shew their influence there also. While professing to have no hostility to the Gospel, Gnosticism proved one of the subtlest and most dangerous enemies which it has ever encountered. On the plea of interpreting Christian doctrines from a higher standpoint it really disintegrated and demolished them; in explaining them it explained them away. With a promise of giving to the Gospel a broader and more catholic basis, it cut away the very foundations on which it rested—the reality of sin, and the reality of redemption.

It is not easy to define Gnosticism. Its name is Greek, and so were many of its elements; but there was much also that was Oriental in its composition; and before long, first Jewish, and then Christian elements were added to the compound. It has been called a 'philosophy of religion.' It would be more true perhaps to call it a philosophy of being or of existence; an attempt to explain the seen and the unseen universe. But this again would be misleading to the learner. Philosophy with us presupposes a patient investigation of facts: it is an attempt to rise from facts to explanations of their relations to one another, and their causes, efficient and final. In Gnosticism we look almost in vain for any appeal to facts. Imagination takes the place of investigation, and what may be conceived is made the test, and sometimes almost the only test, of what is. Gnosticism, though eminently philosophic in its aims and professions, was yet in its method more closely akin to poetry and fiction than to philosophy. While it professed to appeal to the intellect, and in modern language would have called itself rationalistic, yet it perpetually set intelligence at defiance, both in its premises and in its conclusions. We may describe it as a series of imaginative speculations respecting the origin of the universe and its relation to the Supreme Being.

Gnosticism had in the main two ground principles which run through all the bewildering varieties of Gnostic systems: A. The supremacy of the intellect, and the superiority of enlightenment to faith and conduct. This is the *Greek* element in Gnosticism. B. The absolutely evil character of matter and everything material. This is the *Oriental* element.

A. In the N. T. *knowledge* or *gnosis* means the profound apprehension of Christian truth. Christianity is not the Gospel of stupidity. It offers the highest satisfaction to the intellectual powers in the study of revealed truth; and theology in all its branches is the fruit of such study. But this is a very different thing from saying that the intellectual appreciation of truth is the main thing. Theology exists for religion, and not religion for theology. The Gnostics made knowledge the main thing, indeed the only thing of real value. Moreover, as the knowledge was difficult of attainment, they completely reversed the principle of the Gospel and made 'the Truth' the possession of the privileged few, instead of being open to the simplest. The historical and moral character of the Gospel, which brings it within the reach of the humblest intellectual power, was set on one side as valueless, or fantastically explained away. Spiritual excellence was made to consist, not in a holy life, but in knowledge of an esoteric kind open only to the initiated, who " knew the depths" and could say "this is profound." (Tert. *Adv. Valent.* I. 37.) In the fragment of a letter of Valentinus preserved by Epiphanius this Gnostic teacher says: "I come to speak to you of things ineffable, secret, higher than the heavens, which cannot be understood by principalities or powers, nor by

GNOSTICISM.

anything beneath, nor by any creature, unless it be by those whose intelligence can know no change" (Epiph. *Contra Haer. adv. Valent.* I. 31). This doctrine contained three or four errors in one. (1) Knowledge was placed above virtue. (2) This knowledge treated the facts and morality of the Gospel as matter which the ordinary Christian might understand literally, but which the Gnostic knew to mean something very different. Besides which, there was a great deal of the highest value that was not contained in the Scriptures at all. (3) The true meaning of Scripture and this knowledge over and above Scripture being hard to attain, the benefits of Revelation were the exclusive property of a select band of philosophers. (4) To the poor, therefore, the Gospel (in its reality and fulness) could *not* be preached.

B. That the material universe is utterly evil and impure in character is a doctrine which has its source in Oriental Dualism, which teaches that there are two independent Principles of existence, one good and the other bad, which are respectively the origin of all the good and all the evil that exists. The material world, on account of the manifest imperfections and evils which it contains, is assumed to be evil and to be the product of an evil power. This doctrine runs through almost all Gnostic teaching. It involves the following consequences: (1) The world being evil, a limitless gulf lies between it and the Supreme God. He cannot have created it. Therefore (2) The God of the O. T., who created the world, is not the Supreme God, but an inferior, if not an evil power. (3) The Incarnation is incredible; for how could the Divine Word consent to be united with an impure material body? This last difficulty drove many Gnostics into what is called Docetism, i.e. the theory that Christ's body was not a real one, but only *appeared* (δοκεῖν) to exist; in short, that it was a phantom. The gulf between the material world and the Supreme God was commonly filled by Gnostic speculators with a series of beings or aeons emanating from the Supreme God and generating one from another, in bewildering profusion and intricacy. It is this portion of the Gnostic theories which is so repugnant to the modern student. It seems more like a nightmare than sober speculation; and one feels that to call such things 'fables and endless genealogies, the which minister questionings rather than a dispensation of God' (1 Tim. i. 4) is very gentle condemnation. But we must remember (1) that these were not mere wanton flights of an unbridled imagination. They were attempts to bridge the chasm between the finite and the Infinite, between the evil world and the Supreme God, attempts to explain the origin of the universe and with it the origin of evil. We must remember (2) that in those days any hypothesis was admissible which might conceivably account for the facts. The scientific principles, that hypotheses must be *capable* of verification, that existences must not rashly be multiplied, that imaginary causes are unphilosophical, and the like, were utterly unknown. The unseen world might be peopled with any number of mysterious beings; and if their existence helped to explain the world of sense and thought, then their existence might be asserted. If the Supreme God generated an aeon inferior to Himself, and that aeon other inferior aeons, we might at last arrive at a being so far removed from the excellence of God, that his creation of this evil world would not be inconceivable. Thus the Gnostic cosmogony was evolution inverted: it was not an ascent from good to better, but a descent from best to bad. And the whole was expressed in a chaotic imagery, in which allegory, symbolism, mythology and astronomy were mixed up in a way that sets reason at defiance.

These two great Gnostic principles, the supremacy of knowledge, and the impurity of matter, produced opposite results in ethical teaching; asceticism, and antinomian profligacy. If knowledge is everything, and if the body is worthless, then the body must be beaten down and crushed, in order that the emancipated soul may rise to the knowledge of higher things: "the soul must live by ecstasy, as the cicada feeds on dew." On the other hand, if knowledge is everything and the body worthless, the body may rightly be made to undergo every kind of experience, no matter how shameless and impure, in order that the soul may increase its store of knowledge. The body

GNOSTICISM.

cannot be made more vile than it is, and the soul of the enlightened is incapable of pollution.

Speculations such as these were rife in Asia Minor, both among Jews and Christians. That S. John would offer the most uncompromising opposition to them is only what we should expect. While professing to be Christian and to be a sublime interpretation of the Gospel, they struck at the very root of all Christian doctrine and Christian morality. They contradicted the O. T., for they asserted that all things were made, not 'very good,' but very evil, and that the Maker of them was not God. They contradicted the N. T., for they denied the reality of the Incarnation and the sinfulness of sin. Morality was undermined when knowledge was made of far more importance than conduct: it was turned upside down when men were taught that crimes which enlarged experience were a duty.

The fantastic speculations of the Gnostics as to the origin of the universe have long since perished, and cannot be revived. Nor is their tenet as to the evil nature of everything material much in harmony with modern thought. With us the danger is the other way;—of deifying matter, or materialising God. But the heresy of the supremacy of knowledge is as prevalent as ever. We still need an Apostle to teach us that mere knowledge will not raise the quality of men's moral natures any more than light without food and warmth will raise the quality of their bodies. We still need a Bishop Butler to assure us that information is "really the least part" of education, and that religion "does not consist in the knowledge and belief even of fundamental truth," but rather in our being brought "to a certain temper and behaviour." The philosophic Apostle of the first century and the philosophic Bishop of the eighteenth alike contend, that light without love is moral darkness, and that not he that can 'know all mysteries and all knowledge,' but only 'he who *doeth* righteousness is righteous.' If the *Sermons* of the one have not become obsolete, still less have the Epistles of the other.

(iv) *The Traditions respecting S. John.*

The century succeeding the persecution under Nero (A.D. 65 —165) is a period that is exceedingly tantalizing to the ecclesiastical historian and exceedingly perplexing to the chronologer. The historian finds a very meagre supply of materials: facts are neither abundant nor, as a rule, very substantial. And when the historian has gleaned together every available fact, the chronologer finds his ingenuity taxed to the utmost to arrange these facts in a manner that is at once harmonious with itself and with the evidence of the principal witnesses.

The traditions respecting S. John share the general character of the period. They are very fragmentary and not always trustworthy; and they cannot with any certainty be put into chronological order. The following sketch is offered as a tentative arrangement, in the belief that a clear idea, even if wrong in details, is a great deal better than bewildering confusion. The roughest map gives unity and intelligibility to inadequate and piecemeal description.

S. John was present at the Council of Jerusalem (Acts xv.), which settled for the time the controversy between Jewish and Gentile Christians. He was at Jerusalem as one of the 'pillars' of the Church (Gal. ii. 6), and in all probability Jerusalem had been his usual abode from the Ascension until this date (A.D. 50) and for some time longer. It is by no means improbable that he was with S. Peter during the last portion of his great friend's life and was in Rome when he was martyred (A.D. 64). Here will come in the well-known story, which rests upon the early testimony of Tertullian (*Praescr. Haer.* XXXVI.), and perhaps the still earlier testimony of Leucius, that S. John was thrown into boiling oil near the site of the Porta Latina and was preserved unhurt. Two churches in Rome and a festival in the Calendar (May 6th) perpetuate the tradition. The story, if untrue, may have grown out of the fact that S. John was in Rome during the Neronian persecution. The similar story, that he was offered poison and that the drink became harmless in his hands, may have had a similar origin. In paintings S. John is often represented with a cup from which poison in the form of a viper is departing.

It is too soon to take S. John to Ephesus immediately after S. Peter's death. Let us suppose that he returned to Jerusalem (if he had ever left it) and remained there until A.D. 67, when large numbers of people left the city just before the siege. If the very questionable tradition be accepted, that after leaving Jerusalem he preached to the Parthians, we must place the departure from Judaea somewhat earlier. Somewhere in the next two years (A.D. 67—69) we may perhaps place the Revelation, written during the exile, enforced or voluntary, in Patmos. This exile over, S. John went, or more probably returned, to Ephesus, which henceforth becomes his chief place of abode until his death in or near the year A.D. 100.

Most of the traditions respecting him are connected with this last portion of his life and with his government of the Churches of Asia as Metropolitan Bishop. Irenaeus, the disciple of Polycarp, the disciple of S. John, says: "All the presbyters, who met John the disciple of the Lord in Asia, bear witness that John has handed on to them this tradition. For he continued with them until the times of Trajan" (A.D. 98—117). And again: "Then John, the disciple of the Lord, who also leaned back on His breast, he too published a gospel during his residence at Ephesus." And again: "The Church in Ephesus founded by Paul, and having John continuing with them until the times of Trajan, is a truthful witness of the tradition of Apostles" (*Haer.* II. xxii. 5; III. i. 1, iii. 4). Here, therefore, he remained "a priest," as his successor Polycrates tells us, "wearing the plate of gold;" an expression which some people consider to be merely figurative. "John, the last survivor of the Apostolate, had left on the Church of Asia the impression of a pontiff from whose forehead shone the spiritual splendour of the holiness of Christ" (Godet). And here, according to the anti-Montanist writer Apollonius, he raised a dead man to life (Eus. *H. E.* v. xviii. 14).

It would be in connexion with his journeys through the Churches of Asia that the beautiful episode commonly known as

'S. John and the Robber' took place. The Apostle had commended a noble-looking lad to the local Bishop, who had instructed and baptized him. After a while the lad fell away and became a bandit-chief. S. John on his next visit astounded the Bishop by asking for his 'deposit;' for the Apostle had left no money in his care. "I demand the young man, the soul of a brother:" and then the sad tale had to be told. The Apostle called for a horse and rode away to the haunts of the banditti. The chief recognised him and fled. But S. John went after him, and by his loving entreaties induced him to return to his old home and a holy life (Clement of Alexandria in Eus. *H. E.* III. xxxiii.).

The incident of S. John's rushing out of a public bath, at the sight of Cerinthus, crying, "Let us fly, lest even the bath fall on us, because Cerinthus, the enemy of the truth, is within," took place at Ephesus. Doubt has been thrown on the story because of the improbability of the Apostle visiting a public bath, and because Epiphanius, in his version of the matter, substitutes Ebion for Cerinthus. But Irenaeus gives us the story on the authority of those *who had heard it from Polycarp:* and it must be admitted that such evidence is somewhat strong. If Christians of the second century saw nothing incredible in an Apostle resorting to a public bath, we cannot safely dogmatize on the point. The incident may doubtless be taken as no more than "a strong metaphor by way of expressing marked disapproval." But at any rate, when we remember the downright wickedness involved in the teaching of Cerinthus, we may with Dean Stanley regard the story "as a living exemplification of the possibility of uniting the deepest love and gentleness with the sternest denunciation of moral evil." The charge given to the elect lady (2 John 10, 11) is a strong corroboration of the story. Late versions of it end with the sensational addition that when the Apostle had gone out, the bath fell in ruins, and Cerinthus was killed.

Another and far less credible story comes to us through Irenaeus (*Haer.* v. xxxiii. 3) on the authority of the uncritical and (if Eusebius is to be believed) not very intelligent Papias, the companion of Polycarp.—The elders who had seen John, the disciple of the Lord, relate that they heard from him how the Lord used to teach about those times and say, "The days will come in which vines shall grow, each having 10,000 stems, and on each stem 10,000 branches, and on each branch 10,000 shoots, and on each shoot 10,000 clusters, and on each cluster 10,000 grapes, and each grape when pressed shall give 25 firkins of wine. And when any saint shall have seized one cluster, another shall cry, I am a better cluster, take me; through me bless the Lord." In like manner that a grain of wheat would produce 10,000 ears, and each ear would have 10,000 grains, and each grain 5 double pounds of clear, pure flour: and all other fruit-trees, and seeds, and grass, in like proportion. And all animals feeding on the products of the earth would become peaceful and harmonious one with another, subject to man with all subjection. And he added these words: "These things are believable to believers." And he says that when Judas the traitor did not believe and asked, "How then shall such production be accomplished by the Lord?" the Lord said, "They shall see who come to those [times]."

This extraordinary narrative is of great value as shewing the kind of discourse which pious Christians of the second century attributed to Christ, when they came to inventing such things. Can we believe that those who credited the Lord with millenarian utterances of this kind could have written a single chapter of the Gospels with nothing but their own imagination to draw upon? Even with the Gospels before them they can do no better than this. Possibly the whole is only a grotesque enlargement of Matt. xxvi. 29.

Of S. John's manner of life nothing trustworthy has come down to us. That he never married may be mere conjecture; but it looks like history. S. Paul certainly implies that most, if not all, of the Apostles did 'lead about a wife' (1 Cor. ix. 5). But the tradition respecting S. John's virginity is early and general. In a Leucian fragment (Zahn, *Acta Johannis*, p. 248) the Lord is represented as thrice interposing to prevent John from marrying. We find the tradition in Tertullian (*De Monog.* XVII.), Ambrose, Augustine, Jerome, and Epiphanius. It may well be true that (as Jerome expresses it) to a virgin Apostle the Virgin Mother was committed. Epiphanius (A.D. 375) is much too late to be good authority for S. John's rigid asceticism. It is mentioned by no earlier writer, and would be likely enough to be assumed; especially as S. James, brother of the Lord and Bishop of Jerusalem, was known to have led a life of great rigour. The story of S. John's entering a public bath for the purpose of bathing is against any extreme asceticism.

We may conclude with two stories of late authority, but possibly true. Internal evidence is strongly in favour of the second. Cassian (A.D. 420) tells us that S. John used sometimes to amuse himself with a tame partridge. A hunter expressed surprise at an occupation which seemed frivolous. The Apostle in reply reminded him that hunters do not keep their bows always bent, as his own weapon at that moment shewed. It is not improbable that Cassian obtained this story from the writings of Leucius, which he seems to have known. In this case the authority for the story becomes some 250 years earlier. In a Greek fragment it is an old priest who is scandalized at finding the Apostle gazing with interest on a partridge which is rolling in the dust before him (Zahn, p. 190).

The other story is told by Jerome (*In Gal.* VI. 10). When the Apostle became so infirm that he could not preach he used to be carried to church and content himself with the exhortation, "Little children, love one another." And when his hearers wearied of it and asked him, "Master, why dost thou always speak thus?" "Because it is the Lord's command," he said, "and if only this be done, it is enough."

Of his death nothing is known; but the Leucian fragments contain a remarkable story respecting it. On the Lord's Day, the last Sunday of the Apostle's life, "after the celebration of the divine and awful mysteries and the breaking of the bread," S. John told some of his disciples to take spades and follow him. Having led them out to a certain place he told them to dig a grave, in which, after prayer, he placed himself, and they buried him up to the neck. He then told them to place a cloth over his face and complete the burial. They wept much but

TRADITIONS. 27

obeyed him and returned home to tell the others what had taken place. Next day they all went out in prayer to translate the body to the great church. But when they had opened the grave they found nothing therein. And they called to mind the words of the Christ to Peter, 'If I will that he abide till I come, what is that to thee?' (Zahn, p. 191; comp. p. 162.) The still stranger story, which S. Augustine is disposed to believe[1], that the earth over his grave moved with his breathing and shewed that he was not dead but sleeping,—is another, and probably a later outgrowth, of the misunderstood saying of Christ respecting S. John. Such legends testify to the estimation in which the last man living who had seen the Lord was held. After he had passed away people refused to believe that no such person remained alive. The expectations respecting Antichrist helped to strengthen such ideas. If Nero was not dead, but had merely passed out of sight for a time, so also had the beloved Apostle. If the one was to return as Antichrist to vex the Church, so also would the other to defend her. (See Appendix B.)

One point in the above sketch requires a few words of explanation,—the early date assigned to the Book of Revelation. This sets at defiance the express statement of Irenaeus, that the vision "was seen almost in our own days, at the end of the reign of Domitian" (*Haer.* V. xxx. 1), who was killed A.D. 97. The discussion of this point belongs to the commentary on Revelation. Suffice to say that the present writer shares the opinion which seems to be gaining ground among students, that only on one hypothesis can one believe that the Fourth Gospel, First Epistle, and Apocalypse are all by the same author; viz., that the Apocalypse was written first, and that a good many years elapsed before the Gospel and Epistle were written. The writer of the Apocalypse has not yet learned to write Greek. The writer of the Gospel and Epistle writes Greek, not indeed elegantly, but with ease and correctness.

[1] Viderint enim qui locum sciunt, utrum hoc ibi faciat vel patiatur terra quod dicitur, quia et re vera non a levibus hominibus id audivimus (*Tract.* CXXIV. in Johann. XXI. 19).

CHAPTER II.

THE FIRST EPISTLE OF S. JOHN.

THE First Epistle of S. John has an interest which is unique. In all probability, as we shall hereafter find reason for believing, it contains the last exhortations of that Apostle to the Church of Christ. And as he long outlived all the rest of the Apostles, and as this Epistle was written near the end of his long life, we may regard it as the farewell of the Apostolic body to the whole company of believers who survived them or have been born since their time. The Second and Third Epistles may indeed have been written later, and probably were so, but they are addressed to individuals and not to the Church at large. An Introduction to this unique Epistle requires the discussion of a variety of questions, which can most conveniently be taken separately, each under a heading of its own. The first which confronts us is that of its genuineness. Is the Epistle the work of the Apostle whose name it bears?

(i) *The Authorship of the Epistle.*

Eusebius (*H. E.* III. xxv.) is fully justified in reckoning our Epistle among those canonical books of N. T. which had been universally received (ὁμολογούμενα) by the Churches. The obscure sect, whom Epiphanius with a scornful *double entendre* calls the Alogi ('devoid of [the doctrine of] the Logos,' or 'devoid of reason') probably rejected it, for the same reason as they rejected the Fourth Gospel; because they distrusted S. John's teaching respecting the Word or Logos. And Marcion rejected it, as he rejected all the Gospels, excepting an expurgated S. Luke, and all the Epistles, excepting those of S. Paul; not because he believed the books which he discarded to be spurious, but because they contradicted his peculiar views. Neither of these rejections, therefore, need have any weight with us. The objectors did not contend that the Epistle was

FIRST EPISTLE—AUTHORSHIP.

not written by an Apostle, but that some of its contents were doctrinally objectionable.

On the other hand, the evidence that the Epistle was received as Apostolic from the earliest times is abundant and satisfactory. It begins with those who knew S. John himself and goes on in an unbroken stream which soon becomes full and strong.

POLYCARP, the disciple of S. John, in his Epistle to the Philippians writes in a way which needs only to be placed side by side with the similar passage in our Epistle to convince any unprejudiced mind that the two passages cannot have become so like one another accidentally, and that of the two writers it is Polycarp who borrows from S. John and not *vice versâ*.

1 John.	Polycarp, *Phil.* vii.
Every spirit which confesseth Jesus Christ as come in the flesh is of God: and every spirit which confesseth not Jesus is not of God: and this is the spirit of Antichrist (iv. 2, 3). He that doeth sin is of the devil (iii. 8).	Every one that confesseth not that Jesus Christ is come in the flesh is Antichrist: and whosoever confesseth not the witness of the Cross is of the devil.

When we remember that the expression 'Antichrist' in N.T. is peculiar to S. John's Epistles, that it is not common in the literature of the sub-Apostolic age, and that 'confess,' 'witness,' and 'to be of the devil' are also expressions which are very characteristic of S. John, the supposition that Polycarp knew and accepted our Epistle seems to be placed beyond reasonable doubt. Therefore about fifty years after the date at which the Epistle, if genuine, was written we have a quotation of it by a man who was the friend and pupil of its reputed author. Could Polycarp have been ignorant of the authorship, and would he have made use of it if he had doubted its genuineness? Would he not have denounced it as an impudent forgery?

Eusebius tells us (*H. E.* III. xxxix. 16) that PAPIAS (c. A.D. 140) "made use of testimonies from the First Epistle of John." Irenaeus tells us that Papias was "a disciple of John and a companion of Polycarp." Thus we have a second Christian writer among the generation which knew S. John, making use of this Epistle. When we consider how little of the literature of that age has come down to us, and how short this Epistle is, we may well be surprised at having two such early witnesses.

Eusebius also states (*H. E.* v. viii. 7) that IRENAEUS (c. A.D. 140—202) "mentions the First Epistle of John, citing very many testimonies from it." In the great work of Irenaeus on Heresies, which has come down to us, he quotes it twice. In III. xvi. 5 he quotes 1 John ii. 18—22, expressly stating that it comes from the Epistle of S. John. In III. xvi. 8 he quotes 2 John 7, 8, and by a slip of memory says that it comes from "the Epistle before mentioned" (*praedictâ epistolâ*). He then goes on to quote 1 John iv. 1—3. This evidence is strengthened by two facts. 1. Irenaeus, being the disciple of Polycarp, is in a direct line of tradition from S. John. 2. Irenaeus gives abundant testimony to the authenticity of the Fourth Gospel; and it is so generally admitted by critics of all schools that the Fourth Gospel and our Epistle are by the same hand, that evidence to the genuineness of the one may be used as evidence to the genuineness of the other.

CLEMENT OF ALEXANDRIA (fl. A.D. 185—210) makes repeated use of the Epistle and in several places mentions it as S. John's.

TERTULLIAN (fl. 195—215) quotes it 40 or 50 times, repeatedly stating that the words he quotes are S. John's[1].

The MURATORIAN FRAGMENT is a portion of the earliest attempt known to us to catalogue those books of N.T. which were recognised by the Church. Its date is commonly given as c. A.D. 170—180; but some now prefer to say A.D. 200 —215. It is written in barbarous and sometimes scarcely intelligible Latin, having been copied by an ignorant and very careless scribe. It says: "The Epistle of Jude however and two Epistles of the John who has been mentioned above are received in the Catholic (Church)," or "are reckoned among the

---

[1] The frequency with which Clement and Tertullian quote this Epistle is sufficient answer to the empty argument, that the Catholic Epistles are not often quoted by early writers, and that therefore the fact that 1 John v. 7 is *never* quoted is no proof of its spuriousness.

Catholic (Epistles)." It is uncertain what 'two Epistles' means. But if, as is probably the case (see p. 52), the Second and Third are meant, we may be confident that the First was accepted also and included in the catalogue. The opening words of the Epistle are quoted in the Fragment in connexion with the Fourth Gospel. We know of no person or sect that accepted the Second and Third Epistles and yet rejected the First.

ORIGEN (fl. A.D. 220—250) frequently cites the Epistle as S. John's. DIONYSIUS OF ALEXANDRIA, his pupil (fl. A.D. 235—265), in his masterly discussion of the authenticity of the Apocalypse argues that, as the Fourth Gospel and First Epistle are by S. John, the Apocalypse (on account of its very different style) cannot be by him (Eus. *H. E.* VII. xxv). CYPRIAN, ATHANASIUS, EPIPHANIUS, JEROME, and in short all Fathers, Greek and Latin, accept the Epistle as S. John's.

The Epistle is found in the Old Syriac Version, which omits the Second and Third as well as other Epistles.

In the face of such evidence as this, the suspicion that the Epistle may have been written by some careful imitator of the Fourth Gospel does not seem to need serious consideration. A guess, not supported by any evidence, has no claim to be admitted as a rival to a sober theory, which is supported by all the evidence that is available, that being both plentiful and trustworthy.

The student must, however, be on his guard against uncritical overstatements of the case in favour of the Epistle. Some commentators put forward an imposing array of references to Justin Martyr, the Epistle of Barnabas, the Shepherd of Hermas, and the Ignatian Epistles. This is altogether misleading. All that such references prove is that early Christian writers to a large extent used similar language in speaking of spiritual truths, and that this language was influenced by the *writers* (not necessarily the *writings*) of the N.T.

Where the resemblance to passages in the N.T. is very slight and indistinct (as will be found to be the case in these references), it is at least as possible that the language comes from the oral teaching of Apostles and Apostolic men as from the writings contained in N.T.

The author of the Epistle to Diognetus knew our Epistle; but the date of that perplexing treatise, though probably ante-Nicene, is uncertain.

That the *internal* evidence in favour of the Apostolic authorship of the Epistle is also very strong, will be seen when we consider in Sections iv. and v. its *relation to the Gospel* and its *characteristics*.

(ii) *The Persons addressed.*

The Epistle is rightly called *catholic* or *general*, as being addressed to the Church at large. It was probably written with special reference to the Church of Ephesus and the other Churches of Asia, to which it would be sent as a circular letter. The fact of its containing no quotations from the O.T. and not many allusions to it, as also the warning against idolatry (v. 21), would lead us to suppose that the writer had converts from heathenism specially in his mind.

S. Augustine in the heading[1] to his ten homilies on the Epistle styles it 'the Epistle of John to the Parthians' (*ad Parthos*), and he elsewhere (*Quaest. Evang.* II. xxxix.) gives it the same title. In this he has been followed by other writers in the Latin Church. The title occurs in some MSS. of the Vulgate. The Venerable Bede states that "Many ecclesiastical writers, and among them Athanasius, Bishop of the Church of Alexandria, witness that the First Epistle of S. John was written to the Parthians" (Cave *Script. Eccles. Hist. Lit.* ann. 701). But Athanasius and the Greek Church generally seem to be wholly ignorant of this superscription; although in a few modern Greek MSS. 'to the Parthians' occurs in the subscription of the *second* Epistle. Whether the tradition that S. John once preached in Parthia grew out of this Latin superscription, or the latter produced the tradition, is uncertain. More probably the title

---

[1] This heading is by some considered not to be original: it occurs in the *Indiculus Operum S. Augustini* of his pupil Possidius.

originated in a mistake and then gave birth to the tradition. Gieseler's conjecture respecting the mistake seems to be reasonable, that it arose from a Latin writer finding the letter designated 'the Epistle of John *the Virgin*' (τοῦ παρθένου) and supposing that this meant 'the Epistle of John *to the Parthians*' (πρὸς πάρθους). From very early times S. John was called 'virgin' from the belief that he never married. *Johannes aliqui Christi spado*, says Tertullian (*De Monogam.* XVII). In the longer and probably interpolated form of the Ignatian Epistles (*Philad.* IV.) we read "Virgins, have Christ alone before your eyes, and His Father in your prayers, being enlightened by the Spirit. May I have pleasure in your purity as that of Elijah...... as of *the beloved disciple*, as of Timothy......who departed this life in chastity." But there is reason for believing that *Ad Virgines* (πρὸς παρθένους) was an early superscription for the *second* Epistle. Some transcriber, thinking this very inappropriate for a letter addressed to a lady with children, may have transferred the heading to the first Epistle, and then the corruption from 'virgins' (παρθένους) to 'Parthians' (πάρθους) would be easy enough.

Other variations or conjectures are *Ad Spartos, Ad Pathmios,* and *Ad sparsos.* None are worth much consideration.

(iii) *The Place and Date.*

Neither of these can be determined with any certainty, the Epistle itself containing no intimations on either point. Irenaeus tells us that the Fourth Gospel was written in Ephesus, and Jerome writes to the same effect. In all probability the Epistle was written at the same place. Excepting Alexandria, no place was so distinctly the home of that Gnosticism, which S. John opposes in both Gospel and Epistle, as Asia Minor, and in particular Ephesus. We know of no tradition connecting S. John with Alexandria, whereas tradition is unanimous in connecting him with Ephesus. In the next section we shall find reason for believing that Gospel and Epistle were written near about the same time; and this in itself is good reason for believing that they were written at the same place. Excepting occasional visits to the other Churches of Asia, S. John probably rarely moved from Ephesus.

As to the date also we cannot do more than attain to probability. (1) Reason has been given above why as long an interval as possible ought to be placed between the Apocalypse on the one hand and the Gospel and Epistle on the other. If then the Apocalypse was written about A.D. 68, and S. John died about A.D. 100, we may place Gospel and Epistle between A.D. 85 and 95. (2) Moreover, the later we place these two writings in S. John's lifetime, the more intelligible does the uncompromising and explicit position, which characterizes both of them in reference to Gnosticism, become. (3) Again, the tone of the Epistles is that of an old man, writing to a younger generation. We can scarcely fancy an Apostle, still in the prime of life, writing thus to men of his own age. But those who see in this forcible and out-spoken letter, with its marvellous combination of love and sternness, signs of senility and failing powers, have read either without care or with prejudice. 'The eye' of the Eagle Apostle is 'not dim, nor his natural force abated.' (4) No inference can be drawn from 'it is the last hour' (ii. 18): these words cannot refer to the destruction of Jerusalem (see note *in loco*). And perhaps it is not wise to dwell much on the fact that the introductory verses seem to imply that the seeing, hearing, and handling of the Word of Life took place in the remote past. This will not help us to determine whether S. John wrote the Epistle forty or sixty years after the Ascension.

(iv) *The Object of the Epistle: its Relation to the Gospel.*

The Epistle appears to have been intended as a *companion to the Gospel*. No more definite word than 'companion' seems to be applicable, without going beyond the truth. We may call it "a preface and introduction to the Gospel," or a "second part" and "supplement" to it; but this is only to a very limited extent true. The Gospel has its proper introduction in its first 18 verses, and its supplement in its last chapter. It is nearer the

RELATION TO THE GOSPEL. 35

truth to speak of the Epistle as a comment on the Gospel, "a sermon with the Gospel for its text." References to the Gospel are scattered thickly over the whole Epistle.

If this theory respecting its connexion with the Gospel be correct, we shall expect to find that the object of Gospel and Epistle is to a large extent one and the same. This is amply borne out by the facts. The object of the Gospel S. John tells us himself; 'these have been written *that ye may believe that Jesus is the Christ, the Son of God, and that believing ye may have life in His name*' (xx. 31). The object of the Epistle he tells us also; 'These things have I written unto you, *that ye may know that ye have eternal life*, even *unto you that believe on the name of the Son of God*' (v. 13). The Gospel is written to shew the way to eternal life through belief in the incarnate Son. The Epistle is written to confirm and enforce the Gospel; to assure those who believe in the incarnate Son that they *have* eternal life. The one is an historical, the other an ethical statement of the truth. The one sets forth the acts and words which prove that Jesus is the Christ, the Son of God; the other sets forth the acts and words which are obligatory upon those who believe this great truth. Of necessity both writings in stating the truth oppose error: but with this difference. In the Gospel S. John simply states the truth and leaves it: in the Epistle he commonly over against the truth places the error to which it is opposed. The Epistle is often directly polemical: the Gospel is never more than indirectly so.

S. John's Gospel has been called a summary of *Christian Theology*, his first Epistle a summary of *Christian Ethics*, and his Apocalypse a summary of *Christian Politics*. There is much truth in this classification, especially as regards the first two members of it. It will help us to give definiteness to the statement that the Epistle was written to be a companion to the Gospel. They both supply us with the fundamental doctrines of Christianity. But in the Gospel these are given as the foundations of the Christian's *faith;* in the Epistle they are given as the foundation of the Christian's *life*. The one answers the question, 'What must I believe about God and Jesus Christ?'

The other answers the question, 'What is my duty towards God and towards man?' It is obvious that in the latter case the direct treatment of error is much more in place than in the former. If we know clearly what to believe, we may leave on one side the consideration of what *not* to believe. But inasmuch as the world contains many who assert what is false and do what is wrong, we cannot know our duty to God and man, without learning how we are to bear ourselves in reference to falsehood and wrong.

Again, it has been said that in his three works S. John has given us three pictures of the *Divine life* or *life in God*. In the Gospel he sets forth the Divine life as it is exhibited in *the person of Christ*. In his Epistle he sets forth that life as it is exhibited in *the individual Christian*. And in the Apocalypse he sets forth that life as it is exhibited in *the Church*. This again is true, especially as regards the Gospel and Epistle. It is between these two that the comparison and contrast are closest. The Church is the Body of Christ, and it is also the collective body of individual Christians. So far as it comes up to its ideal, it will present the life in God as it is exhibited in Christ Himself. So far as it falls short of it, it will present the Divine life as it is exhibited in the ordinary Christian. It is therefore in the field occupied by the Gospel and Epistle respectively that we find the largest amount both of similarity and difference. In the one we have the perfect life in God as it was realised in an historical Person. In the other we have the directions for reproducing that life as it might be realised by an earnest but necessarily imperfect Christian.

To sum up the relations of the Gospel to the Epistle, we may say that the Gospel is objective, the Epistle subjective; the one is historical, the other moral; the one gives us the theology of the Christ, the other the ethics of the Christian; the one is didactic, the other polemical; the one states the truth as a thesis, the other as an antithesis; the one starts from the human side, the other from the divine; the one proves that the Man Jesus is the Son of God, the other insists that the Son of God is come in the flesh. But the connexion between the two is intimate and organic throughout. The Gospel suggests principles of conduct which the Epistle lays down explicitly; the Epistle implies facts which the Gospel states as historically true.

It would perhaps be too much to say that the Epistle "was written designedly as the supplement to all extant New Testament Scripture, as, in fact, the final treatise of inspired revelation." But it will be well to remember in studying it that as a matter of fact the letter is that final treatise. We can hardly venture to say that in penning it S. John was consciously putting the coping stone on the edifice of the New Testament and closing the Canon. But in it the leading doctrines of Christianity are stated in their final form. The teaching of S. Paul and that of S. James are restated, no longer in apparent opposition, but in intimate and inseparable harmony. They are but two sides of the same truth.

But though S. John's hand was thus guided to gather up and consummate the whole body of evangelical truth, it seems evident that this was not his own intention in writing the Epistle. The letter, like most of the Epistles in N.T., is an *occasional* one. It is written for a special occasion; to meet a definite crisis in the Church. It is a solemn warning against the seductive assumptions and deductions of various forms of Gnostic error; an emphatic protest against anything like a compromise where Christian truth is in question. The nature of God, so far as it can be grasped by man; the nature of Christ; the relation of man to God, to the world, and to the evil one; are stated with a firm hand to meet the shifty theories of false teachers. "I have been very jealous for the Lord God of hosts" (1 Kings xix. 10) is the mental attitude of this polemical element in the Epistle. "We hear again the voice of the 'son of thunder,' still vehement against every insult to the majesty of his Lord."

The connexion between Gospel and Epistle is recognised by the writer of the Muratorian Canon, who probably lived within a century of the writing of both. We have no means of verifying his narrative, but must take it or leave it as it stands. "Of the fourth of the Gospels, John one of the disciples [is the author]. When his fellow-disciples and bishops exhorted him [to write it], he said; 'Fast with me for three days from to-day, and let us relate to each other whatever shall be revealed to each.' On the same night it was revealed to Andrew, one of the Apostles, that, though all should revise, John should write down everything in his own name. And therefore, though various principles are taught in the separate books of the Gospels, yet it makes no difference to the faith of believers, seeing that by one supreme Spirit there are declared in all all things concerning the Birth, the Passion, the Resurrection, the life with His disciples, and His double Advent; the first in humility, despised, which is past; the second glorious in kingly power, which is to come. What wonder, therefore, is it, if John so constantly in his Epistles also puts forward particular [phrases], saying in his own person, *what we have seen with our eyes and heard with our ears, and our hands have handled, these things have we written to you.*"

The following table of parallels between the Gospel and the Epistle will go far to convince anyone; (1) that the two writings are by one and the same hand; (2) that the passages in the Gospel are the originals to which the parallels in the Epistle have been consciously or unconsciously adapted; (3) that in a number of cases the reference to the Gospel is conscious and intentional.

Gospel.	Epistle.
i. 1. In the beginning was the Word.	i. 1. That which was from the beginning...concerning the Word of life.
i. 14. We beheld His glory.	That which we beheld.
xx. 27. Reach hither thy hand, and put it into My side.	And our hands handled.
iii. 11. We speak that we do know, and bear witness of that we have seen.	i. 2. We have seen, and bear witness, and declare unto you.
xix. 35. He that hath seen hath borne witness.	
i. 1. The Word was with God.	The eternal life, which was with the Father.

Gospel.	Epistle.
xvii. 21. That they may all be one; even as Thou, Father, art in Me, and I in Thee, that they also may be in Us.	i. 3. Our fellowship is with the Father, and with His Son Jesus Christ.
xvi. 24. That your joy may be fulfilled.	i. 4. That our joy may be fulfilled.
i. 19. And this is the witness of John.	i. 5. And this is the message which we have heard from Him, God is light, and in Him is no darkness at all.
i. 5. The light shineth in the darkness; and the darkness apprehended it not.	
viii. 12. He that followeth Me shall not walk in darkness, but shall have that light of life.	i. 6. If we say that we have fellowship with Him, and walk in darkness we lie, and do not the truth; but if we walk in light, as He is in the light...
iii. 21. He that doeth the truth, cometh to the light.	
xiv. 16. I will pray the Father and He shall give you another Advocate.	ii. 1. We have an Advocate with the Father, Jesus Christ the righteous.
i. 29. Behold, the Lamb of God, which taketh away the sin of the world.	ii. 1. And not for ours only, but also for the whole world.
iv. 24. The Saviour of the world.	
xiv. 15. If ye love Me, ye will keep my commandments.	ii. 3. Hereby know we that we know Him, if we keep His commandments.
xiv. 21. He that hath My commandments and keepeth them, he it is that loveth Me.	ii. 5. Whoso keepeth His word, in Him verily hath the love of God been perfected.
xv. 5. He that abideth in Me, and I in him, the same beareth much fruit.	ii. 6. He that saith he abideth in Him ought himself also to walk even as He walked.
xiii. 34. A new commandment I give unto you.	ii. 8. A new commandment write I unto you.
i. 9. There was the true light.	The true light already shineth.
v. 17. Even until now.	ii. 9. Even until now.
xi. 9. If a man walk in the day, he stumbleth not, because he	ii. 10. He that loveth his brother abideth in the light, and there

Gospel.	Epistle.
seeth the light of this world.	is none occasion of stumbling in him.
xii. 35. He that walketh in the darkness knoweth not whither he goeth.	ii. 11. He that hateth his brother is in the darkness, and walketh in the darkness, and knoweth not whither he goeth, because the darkness hath blinded his eyes.
xii. 40. He hath blinded their eyes.	
xiii. 33. Little children (τεκνία).	ii. 1, 12, 28. Little children (τεκνία).
i. 1. In the beginning was the Word.	ii. 13. Ye know Him which is from the beginning.
v. 38. Ye have not His word abiding in you.	ii. 14. The word of God abideth in you.
xxi. 5. Children (παιδία).	ii. 18. Little children (παιδία).
vi. 39. This is the will of Him that sent Me, that of all which He hath given Me I should lose nothing.	ii. 19. If they had been of us, they would have abided with us.
vi. 69. The Holy One of God (Christ).	ii. 20. The Holy One (Christ).
xvi. 13. When He, the Spirit of truth, is come, He shall guide you into all truth.	Ye have an anointing from the Holy One, and ye know all things.
xv. 23. He that hateth Me hateth My Father also.	ii. 23. Whosoever denieth the Son, the same hath not the Father. He that confesseth the Son, hath the Father also.
xiv. 9. He that hath seen Me hath seen the Father.	
xiv. 23. If a man love Me, he will keep My word; and My Father will love him, and We will come unto him, and make Our abode with him.	ii. 24. If that which ye heard from the beginning abide in you, ye also shall abide in the Son, and in the Father.
xvii. 2. That whatsoever Thou hast given Him, to them He should give eternal life.	ii. 25. And this is the promise which He promised us, even eternal life.
xvi. 13. When He, the Spirit of truth, is come, He shall guide you into all truth.	ii. 27. As His anointing teacheth you concerning all things.

These are but gleanings out of a couple of chapters, but they are sufficient to shew the relation between the two writings. Some of them are mere reminiscences of particular modes of expressions. But in other cases the passage in the Epistle is a deduction from the passage in the Gospel, or an illustration of it, or a development in accordance with the Apostle's experience in the half century which had elapsed since the Ascension. But the fact that the Epistle at every turn presupposes the Gospel, does not prove beyond all question that the Gospel was *written* first. S. John had delivered his Gospel orally over and over again before writing it: and it is possible, though hardly probable, that the Epistle was written before the Gospel.

In this abundance of parallels between the two writings, especially between the discourses of the Lord in the Gospel and the Apostle's teaching in the Epistle, "it is most worthy of notice that no use is made in the Epistle of the language of the discourses in John iii. and vi."

"Generally it will be found on a comparison of the closest parallels, that the Apostle's own words are more formal in expression than the words of the Lord which he records. The Lord's words have been moulded by the disciple into aphorisms in the Epistle."—Westcott.

(v) *The Plan of the Epistle.*

That S. John had a plan, and a very carefully arranged plan, in writing his Gospel, those who have studied its structure will scarcely be able to doubt. It is far otherwise with the Epistle. Here we may reasonably doubt whether the Apostle had any systematic arrangement of his thoughts in his mind when he wrote the letter. Indeed some commentators have regarded it as the rambling prattle of an old man, "an unmethodised effusion of pious sentiments and reflections." Others, without going quite these lengths, have concluded that the contemplative and undialectical temper of S. John has caused him to pour forth his thoughts in a series of aphorisms without much sequence or logical connexion.

Both these opinions are erroneous. It is quite true to say

with Calvin that the Epistle is a compound of doctrine and exhortation: what Epistle in N. T. is not? But it is a mistake to suppose with him that the composition is confused. Again, it is quite true to say that the Apostle's method is not dialectical. But it cannot follow from this that he has no method at all. He seldom argues; one who sees the truth, and believes that every sincere believer will see it also, has not much need to argue: he merely states the truth and leaves it to exercise its legitimate power over every truth-loving heart. But in thus simply affirming what is true and denying what is false he does not allow his thoughts to come out hap-hazard. Each one as it comes before us may be complete in itself; but it is linked on to what precedes and what follows. The links are often subtle, and sometimes we cannot be sure that we have detected them; but they are seldom entirely absent. This peculiarity brings with it the further characteristic, that the transitions from one section of the subject to another, and even from one main division of it to another, are for the most part very gradual. They are like the changes in dissolving views. We know that we have passed on to something new, but we hardly know how the change has come about.

A writing of this kind is exceedingly difficult to analyse. We feel that there are divisions; but we are by no means sure where to make them, or how to name them. We are conscious that the separate thoughts are intimately connected one with another; but we cannot satisfy ourselves that we have discovered the exact lines of connexion. At times we hardly know whether we are moving forwards or backwards, whether we are returning to an old subject or passing onwards to a new one, when in truth we are doing both and neither; for the old material is recast and made new, and the new material is shewn to have been involved in the old. Probably few commentators have satisfied themselves with their own analysis of this Epistle: still fewer have satisfied other people. Only those who have seriously attempted it know the real difficulties of the problem. It is like analysing the face of the sky or of the sea. There is contrast, and yet harmony; variety and yet order; fixedness, and yet ceaseless change; a monotony which soothes without wearying us, because the frequent repetitions come to us as things that are both new and old. But about one point most students of the Epistle will agree; that it is better to read it under the guidance of any scheme that will at all coincide with its contents, than with no guidance whatever. Jewels, it is true, remain jewels, even when piled confusedly into a heap: but they are then seen to the very least advantage. Any arrangement is better than that. So also with S. John's utterances in this Epistle. They are robbed of more than half their power if they are regarded as a string of detached aphorisms, with no more organic unity than a collection of proverbs. It is in the conviction of the truth of this opinion that the following analysis is offered for consideration. It is, of course, to a considerable extent based upon previous attempts, and possibly it is no great improvement upon any of them. It has, however, been of service to the writer in studying the Epistle, and if it helps any other student to frame a better analysis for himself, it will have served its purpose.

One or two divisions may be asserted with confidence. Beyond all question the first four verses are introductory, and are analogous to the first eighteen verses of the Gospel. Equally beyond question the last four verses, and probably the last nine verses, form the summary and conclusion. This leaves the intermediate portion from i. 5 to v. 12 or v. 17 as the main body of the Epistle: and it is about the divisions and subdivisions of this portion that so much difference of opinion exists.

Again, nearly every commentator seems to have felt that a division must be made somewhere near the end of the second chapter. In the following analysis this generally recognised landmark has been adopted as central. Logically as well as locally it divides the main body of the Epistle into two fairly equal halves. And these two halves may be conveniently designated by the great statement which each contains respecting the Divine Nature—'God is Light' and 'God is Love.' These headings are not merely convenient; they correspond to a very considerable extent with the contents of each half. The first half, especially in its earlier portions, is dominated by the idea of 'light': the second half is still more clearly and thoroughly dominated by the idea of 'love.'

As regards the subdivisions and the titles given to them, all that it would be safe to affirm is this;—that, like trees in a well-wooded landscape, the Apostle's thoughts evidently fall into groups, and that it conduces to clearness to distinguish the groups. But it may easily be the case that what to one eye is only one cluster, to another eye is two or three clusters, and that there may also be a difference of opinion as to where each cluster begins and ends. Moreover the description of a particular group which satisfies one mind will seem inaccurate to another. The following scheme will do excellent service if it provokes the student to challenge its correctness and to correct it, if necessary, throughout.

An Analysis of the Epistle.

i. 1—4. INTRODUCTION.
 1. The Subject-matter of the Gospel employed in the Epistle (i. 1—3).
 2. The Purpose of the Epistle (i. 4).

i. 5—ii. 28. GOD IS LIGHT.

a. i. 5—ii. 11. **What Walking in the Light involves: the Condition and Conduct of the Believer.**
 1. Fellowship with God and with the Brethren (i. 5—7).
 2. Consciousness and Confession of Sin (i. 8—10).
 3. Obedience to God by Imitation of Christ (ii. 1—6).
 4. Love of the Brethren (ii. 7—11).

b. ii. 12—28. **What Walking in the Light excludes: the Things and Persons to be avoided.**
 1. Threefold Statement of Reasons for Writing (ii. 12—14).
 2. The Things to be avoided;—the World and its Ways (ii. 15—17).
 3. The Persons to be avoided;—Antichrists (ii. 18—26).
 4. (Transitional) The Place of Safety;—Christ (ii. 27, 28).

ii. 29—v. 12. GOD IS LOVE.

ANALYSIS.

c. ii. 29—iii. 24. **The Evidence of Sonship;—Deeds of righteousness before God.**
    1. The Children of God and the Children of the Devil (ii. 29—iii. 12).
    2. Love and Hate; Life and Death (iii. 13—24).

d. iv. 1—v. 12. **The Source of Sonship;—Possession of the Spirit as shewn by Confession of the Incarnation.**
    1. The Spirit of Truth and the Spirit of Error (iv. 1—6).
    2. Love is the Mark of the Children of Him who is Love (iv. 7—21).
    3. Faith is the Source of Love, the Victory over the World, and the Possession of Life (v. 1—12).

v. 13—21. CONCLUSION.
    1. Intercessory Love the Fruit of Faith (v. 13—17).
    2. The Sum of the Christian's Knowledge (v. 18—20).
    3. Final Injunction (v. 21).

Perhaps our first impression on looking at the headings of the smaller sections would be that these subjects have not much connexion with one another, and that the order in which they come is more or less a matter of accident. This impression would be erroneous. *Fellowship with God* involves *consciousness of sin*, and its *confession* with a view to its removal. This implies *obedience to God*, which finds its highest expression in *love*. *Love of God and of the brethren* excludes love of the *world*, which is passing away, as is shewn by the appearance of *antichrists*. He who would not pass away must *abide in Christ*. With the idea of *sonship*, introduced by the expression 'begotten of God,' the Epistle takes a fresh start. This Divine sonship implies *mutual love* among God's children and the *indwelling of Christ* to which the Spirit testifies. The mention of the Spirit leads on to the distinction between *true and false spirits*. By a rather subtle connexion (see on iv. 7) this once more leads to the topic of *mutual love*, and to *faith as the source of love*, especially as shewn in *intercessory prayer*. The whole closes with a *summary of the knowledge* on which the moral principles inculcated in the Epistle are based, and with a warning against idols.

(vi) *The Characteristics of the Epistle.*

"In reading John it is always with me as though I saw him before me, lying on the bosom of his Master at the Last Supper: as though his angel were holding the light for me, and in certain passages would fall upon my neck and whisper something in mine ear. I am far from understanding all I read, but it often seems to me as if what John meant were floating before me in the distance; and even when I look into a passage altogether dark, I have a foretaste of some great, glorious meaning, which I shall one day understand" (Claudius).

Dante expresses the same feeling still more strongly when he represents himself as blinded by the radiance of the beloved disciple (*Paradiso*, xxv. 136—xxvi. 6).

"Ah, how much in my mind was I disturbed,
   When I turned round to look on Beatrice,
   That her I could not see, although I was
   Close at her side and in the Happy World!
   While I was doubting for my vision quenched,
     Out of the flame refulgent that had quenched it
     Issued a breathing, that attentive made me,
   Saying—'Whilst thou recoverest the sense
     Of seeing which in me thou hast consumed,
   'Tis well that speaking thou should'st compensate it.'"

(Longfellow's Translation: see notes.)

Two characteristics of this Epistle will strike every serious reader; the almost oppressive *majesty of the thoughts* which are put before us, and the extreme *simplicity of the language* in which they are expressed. The most profound mysteries in the Divine scheme of Redemption, the spiritual and moral relations between God, the human soul, the world, and the evil one, and the fundamental principles of Christian Ethics, are all stated in words which any intelligent child can understand. They are the words of one who has 'received the kingdom' of heaven into his inmost soul, and received it 'as a little child.' They are the foolish things of the world putting to shame them that are wise. Their ease, and simplicity, and repose irresistibly attract us. Even the unwilling ear is arrested and listens. We are held as by a spell. And as we listen, and stop, and ponder, we find that the simple words, which at first seemed to convey a meaning as simple as themselves, are charged with truths which are not of this world, but have their roots in the Infinite and Eternal. S. John has been so long on the mount in communion with God that his very words, when the veil is taken off them, shine : and, as Dante intimates, to be brought suddenly face to face with his spirit is well-nigh too much for mortal eyes.

Another characteristic of the Epistle, less conspicuous perhaps, but indisputable, is its *finality*. As S. John's Gospel, not merely in time, but in conception and form and point of view, is the last of the Gospels, so this is the last of the Epistles. It rises above and consummates all the rest. It is in a sphere in which the difficulties between Jewish Christian and Gentile Christian, and the apparent discords between S. Paul and S. James, are harmonized and cease to exist. It is indeed no handbook or summary of Christian doctrine; for it is written expressly for those who 'know the truth'; and therefore much is left unstated, because it may be taken for granted. But in no other book in the Bible are so many cardinal doctrines touched, or with so firm a hand. And each point is laid before us with the awe-inspiring solemnity of one who writes under the profound conviction that 'it is the last hour.'

Closely connected with this characteristic of finality is another which it shares with the Gospel;—the tone of *magisterial authority* which pervades the whole. None but an Apostle, perhaps we may almost venture to say, none but the last surviving Apostle, could write like this. There is no passionate claim to authority, as of one who feels compelled to assert himself and ask, 'Am I not an Apostle?' There is no fierce denunciation of those who are opposed to him, no attempt at a compromise, no anxiety about the result. He will not argue the point; he states the truth and leaves it. Every sentence seems to tell of the conscious authority and resistless though unexerted strength of one who has 'seen, and heard, and handled' the Eternal Word, and who 'knows that his witness is true.'

Once more, there is throughout the Epistle a *love of moral and spiritual antitheses*. Over against each thought there is constantly placed in sharp contrast its opposite. Thus light and darkness, truth and falsehood, love and hate, life and death, love of the Father and love of the world, the children of God and the children of the devil, the spirit of truth and the spirit of error, sin unto death and sin not unto death, to do righteousness and to do sin, follow one another in impressive alternation. The movement of the Epistle largely consists of progress from one opposite to another. And it will nearly always be found that the antithesis is not exact, but an advance beyond the original statement or else an expansion of it. 'He that loveth his brother abideth in the light, and there is none occasion of stumbling in him. But he that hateth his brother is in the darkness, and walketh in darkness, and knoweth not whither he goeth because the darkness hath blinded his eyes' (ii. 10, 11). The antithetical structure and rythmical cadence of the sentences would do much to commend them "to the ear and to the memory of the hearers. To Greek readers, familiar with the lyrical arrangements of the Greek Drama, this mode of writing would have a peculiar charm; and Jewish readers would recognise in it a correspondence to the style and diction of their own Prophetical Books" (Wordsworth).

> If we say we have no sin,
> We deceive ourselves,
> And the truth is not in us.
>
> If we confess our sins,
> He is faithful and righteous to forgive us our sins,
> And to cleanse us from all unrighteousness.
>
> If we say that we have not sinned,
> We make Him a liar;
> And His word is not in us.

In this instance it will be noticed that we pass from one opposite to another and back again: but that to which we return covers more ground than the original position and is a distinct advance upon it.

For other characteristics of S. John's style which are common to both Gospel and Epistle see the Introduction to the Gospel, chapter v. Many of these are pointed out in the notes on these Epistles: see in particular the notes on 1 John i. 2, 4, 5, 8, ii. 1, 3, 8, 24, iii. 9, 15, 17, iv. 9, v. 9, 10.

The following characteristic words and phrases are common to Gospel and Epistles;—

abide, Advocate, be of God, be of the truth, be of the world, believe on, children of God, darkness, do sin, do the truth, eternal life, evil one, joy be fulfilled, have sin, keep His commandments, keep His word, lay down one's life, life, light, love, manifest, murderer, new commandment, Only-begotten, pass over out of death into life, true, truth, walk in darkness, witness, Word, world.

The following expressions are found in the Epistles, but not in the Gospel;—

anointing, Antichrist, deceiver, fellowship, lawlessness, lust of the eyes, lust of the flesh, message, presence or *coming* (of the Second Advent), *propitiation, sin unto death, walk in truth.*

CHAPTER III.

THE SECOND EPISTLE.

SHORT as this letter is, and having more than half of its contents common to either the First or the Second Epistle, our loss would have been great had it been refused a place in the Canon, and in consequence been allowed to perish. It gives us a new aspect of the Apostle: it shews him to us as the shepherd of individual souls. In the First Epistle he addresses the Church at large. In this Epistle, whether it be addressed to a local Church, or (as we shall find reason to believe) to a Christian lady, it is certain definite individuals that he has in his mind as he writes. It is for the sake of particular persons about whom he is greatly interested that he sends the letter, rather than for

S. JOHN (EP.) 4

the sake of Christians in general. It is a less formal and less public utterance than the First Epistle. We see the Apostle at home rather than in the Church, and hear him speaking as a friend rather than as a Metropolitan. The Apostolic authority is there, but it is in the background. The letter beseeches and warns more than it commands.

i. *The Authorship of the Epistle.*

Just as nearly all critics allow that the Fourth Gospel and the First Epistle are by one hand, so it is generally admitted that the Second and Third Epistle are by one hand. The question is whether *all four* writings are by the same person; whether 'the Elder' of the two short Epistles is the beloved disciple of the Gospel, the author of the First Epistle. If this question is answered in the negative, then only two alternatives remain; either these twin Epistles were written by a person commonly known as 'John the Elder' or 'the Presbyter John,' a contemporary of the Apostle sometimes confused with him; or they were written by some Elder entirely unknown to us. In either case he is a person who has studiously and with very great success imitated the style of the Apostle.

The External Evidence.

The voice of antiquity is strongly in favour of the first and simplest hypothesis; that all four writings are the work of the Apostle S. John. The evidence is not so full or so indisputably unanimous as for the Apostolicity of the First Epistle; but, when we take into account the brevity and comparative unimportance of these two letters, the amount is considerable.

IRENAEUS, the disciple of Polycarp, the disciple of S. John, says; "*John, the disciple of the Lord*, intensified their condemnation by desiring that not even a 'God-speed' should be bid to them by us; *For*, says he, *he that biddeth him God speed, partaketh in his evil works*" (*Haer.* I. xvi. 3). And again, after quoting 1 John ii. 18, he resumes a little further on; "These are they against whom the Lord warned us beforehand; and *His disciple*, in his Epistle already mentioned, commands us to avoid them, when he says; *Many deceivers are gone forth into this world, who confess not that Jesus Christ is come in the flesh. This is the deceiver and the Antichrist. Look to* them, *that ye lose not* that *which ye have wrought*" (III. xvi. 8). In one or two respects, it will be observed, Irenaeus must have had a different text from ours: but these quotations shew that he was well acquainted with the Second Epistle and believed it to be by the beloved disciple. And though in the second passage he makes the slip of quoting the Second Epistle and calling it the First, yet this only shews all the more plainly how remote from his mind was the idea that the one Epistle might be by S. John and the other not.

CLEMENT OF ALEXANDRIA, and indeed the Alexandrian school generally (A.D. 200—300), testify to the belief that the second letter is by the Apostle. He quotes 1 John v. 16 with the introductory words, "John in his longer Epistle (ἐν τῇ μείζονι ἐπιστολῇ) seems to teach &c." (*Strom.* II. xv), which shews that he knows of at least one other and shorter Epistle by the same John. In a fragment of a Latin translation of one of his works we read, "The Second Epistle of John, which is written to virgins, is very simple: it is written indeed to a certain Babylonian lady, Electa by name; but it signifies the election of the holy Church." Eusebius (*H. E.* VI. xiv. 1) tells us that Clement in his *Hypotyposes* or *Outlines* commented on the 'disputed' books in N. T. viz. "the Epistle of Jude and the other Catholic Epistles."

DIONYSIUS OF ALEXANDRIA in his famous criticism (Eus. *H.E.* VII. xxv.) so far from thinking 'the Elder' an unlikely title to be taken by S. John, thinks that his not naming himself is like the Apostle's usual manner.

Thus we have witnesses from two very different centres, Irenaeus in Gaul, Clement and Dionysius in Alexandria.

CYPRIAN in his account of a Council at Carthage, A.D. 256, gives us what we may fairly consider to be evidence as to the belief of the North African Church. He says that Aurelius, Bishop of Chullabi, quoted 2 John 10, 11 with the observation, "*John the Apostle* laid it down in his Epistle."

The evidence of the MURATORIAN FRAGMENT is by no means clear. We have seen (p. 38) that the writer quotes the First Epistle in his account of the Fourth Gospel, and later on speaks of "two Epistles of the John who has been mentioned before." This has been interpreted in various ways. (1) That these 'two Epistles' are the Second and Third, the First being omitted by the copyist (who evidently was a very inaccurate and incompetent person), or being counted as part of the Gospel. (2) That these two are the First and the Second, the Third being omitted. (3) That the First and the Second are taken together as one Epistle and the Third as a second. And it is remarkable that Eusebius twice speaks of the First Epistle as "the *former* Epistle of John" (*H. E.* III. xxv. 2, xxxix. 16), as if in some arrangements there were only two Epistles. But in spite of this the first of these three explanations is to be preferred. The context in the Fragment decidedly favours it.

ORIGEN knows of the two shorter letters, but says that "not all admit that these are genuine" (Eus. *H. E.* VI. xxv. 10). But he expresses no opinion of his own, and never quotes them. On the other hand he quotes the First Epistle " in such a manner as at least to shew that the other Epistles were not familiarly known " (Westcott).

EUSEBIUS, who was possibly influenced by Origen, classes these two Epistles among the 'disputed' books of the Canon, and suggests (without giving his own view) that they may be the work of a namesake of the Evangelist. "Among the *disputed* (ἀντιλεγόμενα) books, which, however, are well known and recognised by most, we class the Epistle circulated under the name of James, and that of Jude, as well as the Second of Peter, and the so-called second and third of John, whether they belong to the Evangelist, or possibly to another of the same name as he" (*H. E.* III. xxv. 3). Elsewhere he speaks in a way which leaves one less in doubt as to his own opinion (*Dem. Evan.* III. iii. p. 120), which appears to be favourable to the Apostolic authorship; he speaks of them without qualification as S. John's.

The SCHOOL OF ANTIOCH seems to have rejected these two 'disputed' Epistles, together with Jude and 2 Peter.

AUTHORSHIP. 53

JEROME (*Vir. Illust.* ix.) says that, while the First Epistle is approved by all Churches and scholars, the two others are ascribed to John the Presbyter, whose tomb was still shewn at Ephesus as well as that of the Apostle.

The Middle Ages attributed all three to S. John.

From this summary of the external evidence it is apparent that precisely those witnesses who are nearest to S. John in time are favourable to the Apostolic authorship, and seem to know of no other view. Doubts are first indicated by Origen, although we need not suppose that they were first propounded by him. Probably the belief that there had been another John at Ephesus, and that he had been known as 'John the Presbyter' or 'the Elder,' first made people think that these two comparatively insignificant Epistles, written by someone who calls himself 'the Elder,' were not the work of the Apostle. But, as is shewn in Appendix E., *it is doubtful, whether any such person as John the Elder, as distinct from the Apostle and Evangelist, ever existed.* In all probability those writers who attribute the two shorter letters to John the Presbyter, whether they know it or not, are really attributing them to S. John.

The Internal Evidence.

The internal is hardly less strong than the external evidence in favour of the Apostolic authorship of the Second, and therefore of the Third Epistle: for no one can reasonably doubt that the writer of the one is the writer of the other. We have seen in the preceding sections that Apostles were sometimes called Elders. This humbler title would not be likely to be assumed by one who wished to pass himself off as an Apostle; all the less so, because no Apostolic writing in N. T. begins with this appellation, except the Epistles in question. Therefore these Epistles are not like the work of a forger imitating S. John in order to be taken for S. John. On the other hand an ordinary Presbyter or Elder, writing in his own person without any wish to mislead, would hardly style himself '*The* Elder.' Assume, however, that S. John wrote the Epistles, and the title seems to be very appropriate. The oldest member of the Christian Church and the last surviving Apostle might well be called, and call himself, with simple dignity, 'The Elder.'

The following table will help us to judge whether the similarities between the four writings are not most naturally and reasonably explained by accepting the primitive (though not universal) tradition, that all four proceeded from one and the same author.

Gospel and First Epistle.	Second Epistle.	Third Epistle.
1 John iii. 18. Let us not love in word, neither in tongue, but in deed and truth. John viii. 31. If ye abide in My word... ye shall know the truth.	1. The Elder unto the elect lady...whom I love in truth: and not I only, but also all they that know the truth.	1. The Elder unto Gaius the beloved whom I love in truth.
x. 18. This commandment received I from My Father. 1 John iv. 21. This commandment have we from Him.	4. I rejoiced greatly that I have found of thy children walking in truth, even as we received commandment from the Father.	3. I rejoiced greatly when brethren came and bare witness unto thy truth, even as thou walkest in truth.
ii. 7. No new commandment write I unto you, but an old commandment which ye had from the beginning. John xiii. 34. A new commandment I give unto you, that ye love one another.	5. And now I beseech thee, lady, not as though I wrote to thee a new commandment, but that which we had from the beginning, that we love one another.	
xiv. 21. He that hath My commandments, and keepeth them,	6. And this is love, that we should walk after His command-	

Gospel and First Epistle.	Second Epistle.	Third Epistle.
he it is that loveth Me. 1 John v. This is the love of God, that we keep His commandments. ii. 24. Let that abide in you which ye heard from the beginning. iv. 1—3. Many false prophets are gone out into the world. Hereby know ye the Spirit of God: every spirit which confesseth that Jesus Christ is come in the flesh is of God: and every spirit which confesseth not Jesus is not of God: and this is the spirit of the Antichrist. ii. 23. Whosoever denieth the Son, the same hath not the Father: he that confesseth the Son hath the Father also. ii. 29. Every one that doeth righteousness is begotten of Him. iii. 6. Whosoever sinneth hath not seen	ments. This is the commandment, even as ye heard from the beginning, that ye should walk in it. 7. For many deceivers are gone forth into the world, even they that confess not that Jesus Christ cometh in the flesh. This is the deceiver and the Antichrist. 9. Whosoever goeth onward and abideth not in the doctrine of Christ, hath not God: he that abideth in the doctrine, the same hath both the Father and the Son.	 11. He that doeth good is of God: he that doeth evil hath not seen God.

Gospel and First Epistle.	Second Epistle.	Third Epistle.
Him, neither knoweth Him. John xxi. 24. This is the disciple which beareth witness of these things: and we know that his witness is true. xv. 11. That your joy may be fulfilled. 1 John i. 4. That our joy may be fulfilled.	12, 13. Having many things to write unto you, I would not write them with paper and ink: but I hope to come unto you, and to speak face to face that your joy may be fulfilled. The children of thine elect sister salute thee.	12. Yea, we also bear witness; and thou knowest that our witness is true. 13, 14. I had many things to write unto thee, but I am unwilling to write them to thee with ink and pen: but I hope shortly to see thee, and we shall speak face to face. Peace be unto thee. The friends salute thee. Salute the friends by name.

The brevity and comparative unimportance of the two letters is another point in favour of their Apostolicity. What motive could there be for attempting to pass such letters off as the work of an Apostle? Those were not days in which the excitement of duping the literary world would induce anyone to make the experiment. Some years ago the present writer was disposed to think the authorship of these two Epistles very doubtful. Further study has led him to believe that the balance of probability is very greatly in favour of their being the writings, and probably the last writings, of the Apostle S. John.

ii. *The Person or Persons addressed.*

It seems to be impossible to determine with anything like certainty whether the Second Epistle is addressed to *a community*, i.e. a particular Church, or the Church at large, or to *an individual*, i.e. some lady personally known to the Apostle.

In favour of the former hypothesis it is argued as follows: "There is no individual reference to one person; on the contrary, the children 'walk in truth'; mutual love is enjoined; there is an admonition, 'look to yourselves'; and 'the bringing of doctrine' is mentioned. Besides, it is improbable that 'the children of an elect sister' would send a greeting by the writer to an 'elect Kyria and her children.' A sister church might naturally salute another" (Davidson).

A very great deal will depend upon the translation of the opening words (ἐκλεκτῇ κυρίᾳ), which may mean: (1) *To the elect lady;* (2) *To an elect lady;* (3) *To the elect Kyria;* (4) *To the lady Electa.* The first two renderings leave the question respecting a community or an individual open: the last two close it in favour of an individual. But the fourth rendering, though supported by the Latin translation of some fragments of Clement of Alexandria (see p. 51), is untenable on account of ver. 13. It is incredible that there were *two* sisters each bearing the very unusual name of Electa. The third rendering is more admissible. The proper name Kyria occurs in ancient documents. Like Martha in Hebrew, it is the feminine of the common word for 'Lord'; and some have conjectured that the letter is addressed to Martha of Bethany. But, had Kyria been a proper name, S. John would probably (though not necessarily) have written 'to Kyria, the elect,' like 'to Gaius, the beloved.' Moreover, to insist on this third rendering is to assume as certain two things which are uncertain: (1) That the letter is addressed to an individual; (2) that the individual's name was Kyria. We therefore fall back upon one of the first two renderings; and of the two the first seems preferable. The omission of the Greek definite article is quite intelligible, and may be compared with ΑΓΝΩΣΤΩ ΘΕΩ in Acts xvii. 23, which may quite correctly be rendered, 'To *the* Unknown God,' in spite of the absence of the article in the original.

That 'the elect Lady' *may* be a figurative name for a Church, or for *the* Church, must at once be admitted : and perhaps we may go further and say that such a figure would not be unlikely in the case of a writer so fond of symbolism as S. John. But is a sustained allegory of this kind likely in the case of so slight a letter? Is not the form of the First Epistle against it? Is there any parallel case in the literature of the first three centuries? No one doubts that the twin Epistle is addressed to an individual. In letters so similar it is scarcely probable that in the one case the person addressed is to be taken literally, while in the other the person addressed is to be taken as the allegorical representative of a Church. It seems more reasonable to suppose that in both Epistles, as in the Epistle to Philemon, we have precious specimens of the private correspondence of an Apostle. We are allowed to see how the beloved Disciple at the close of his life could write to a Christian lady and to a Christian gentleman respecting their personal conduct.

Adopting, therefore, the literal interpretation as not only tenable but probable, we must be content to remain in ignorance who 'the elect lady' is. That she is Mary the Mother of the Lord is not merely a gratuitous but an incredible conjecture. The Mother of the Lord, during S. John's later years, would be from a hundred and twenty to a hundred and forty years old.

iii. *Place, Date and Contents.*

We can do no more than frame probable hypotheses with regard to place and date. The Epistle itself gives us vague outlines; and these outlines are all that is certain. But it will give reality and life to the letter if we fill in these outlines with details which may be true, which are probably like the truth, and which though confessedly conjectural make the drift of the letter more intelligible.

The Apostle, towards the close of his life—for the letter presupposes both Gospel and First Epistle—has been engaged upon his usual work of supervision and direction among the

THIRD EPISTLE.

Churches of Asia. In the course of it he has seen some children of the lady to whom the letter is addressed, and has found that they are living Christian lives, steadfast in the faith. But there are other members of her family of whom this cannot be said. And on his return to Ephesus the Apostle, in expressing his joy respecting the faithful children, conveys a warning respecting their less steadfast brothers. 'Has their mother been as watchful as she might have been to keep them from pernicious influences? Her hospitality must be exercised with discretion; for her guests may contaminate her household. There is no real progress in advancing beyond the limits of Christian truth. There is no real charity in helping workers of evil to work successfully. On his next Apostolic journey he hopes to see her.' Near the Apostle's abode are some nephews of the lady addressed, but their mother, her sister, is dead, or is living elsewhere. These nephews send their greeting in his letter, and thus shew that they share his loving anxiety respecting the elect lady's household. It was very possibly from them that he had heard that all was not well there.

The letter may be subdivided thus:

1—3. **Address and Greeting.**
4—11. **Main Body of the Epistle.**
    1. Occasion of the Letter (*v.* 4).
    2. Exhortation to Love and Obedience (5, 6).
    3. Warnings against False Doctrine (7—9).
    4. Warnings against False Charity (10, 11).
12, 13. **Conclusion.**

CHAPTER IV.

THE THIRD EPISTLE.

IN this we have another sample of the private correspondence of an Apostle. For beyond all question, whatever we may think of the Second Epistle, this letter is addressed to an individual. And it is not an official letter, like the Epistles to Timothy and

Titus, but a private one, like that to Philemon. While the Second Epistle is mainly one of warning, the Third is one of encouragement. As in the former case, we are conscious of the writer's authority in the tone of the letter; which, however, is friendly rather than official.

i. *The Authorship of the Epistle.*

On this point very little need be added to what has been said respecting the authorship of the Second Epistle. The two Epistles are universally admitted to be by one and the same person. But it must be pointed out that, if the Second Epistle did not exist, the claims of the Third to be Apostolic would be more disputable. Neither the external nor the internal evidence is so strongly in its favour. It is neither quoted nor mentioned so early or so frequently as the Second. It is not nearly so closely akin to the First Epistle and the Gospel. It labours under the difficulty involved in the conduct of Diotrephes: for it must be admitted that "there is something astonishing in the notion that the prominent Christian Presbyter of an Asiatic Church should not only repudiate the authority of St John, and not only refuse to receive his travelling missionary, and prevent others from doing so, but should even excommunicate or try to excommunicate those who did so" (Farrar). Nevertheless, it is impossible to separate these two twin letters, and assign them to different authors. And, as has been seen already, the balance of evidence, both external and internal, strongly favours the Apostolicity of the Second; and this, notwithstanding the difficulty about Diotrephes, carries with it the Apostolicity of the Third.

ii. *The Person Addressed.*

The name Gaius was so common throughout the Roman Empire that to identify any person of this name with any other of the same name requires specially clear evidence. In N.T. there are probably at least three Christians who are thus called.

THIRD EPISTLE. 61

1. *Gaius of Corinth*, in whose house S. Paul was staying when he wrote the Epistle to the Romans (Rom. xvi. 23), who is probably the same as he whom S. Paul baptized (1 Cor. i. 14). 2. *Gaius of Macedonia*, who was S. Paul's travelling-companion at the time of the uproar at Ephesus, and was seized by the mob (Acts xix. 29). 3. *Gaius of Derbe*, who with Timothy and others left Greece before S. Paul and waited for him at Troas (Acts xx. 4, 5). But these three may be reduced to two, for 1 and 3 may possibly be the same person. It is possible, but nothing more, that the Gaius of our Epistle may be one of these. Origen says that the first of these three became Bishop of Thessalonica. The Apostolical Constitutions (vii. 46) mention a Gaius, Bishop of Pergamos, and the context implies that he was the first Bishop, or at least one of the earliest Bishops, of that city. Here again we can only say that he may be the Gaius of S. John. The Epistle leaves us in doubt whether Gaius is at this time a Presbyter or not. Apparently he is a well-to-do layman.

iii. *Place, Date, and Contents.*

The place may with probability be supposed to be Ephesus: the letter has the tone of being written from head-quarters. Its strong resemblance, especially in its opening and conclusion, inclines us to believe that it was written about the same time as the Second Epistle, i.e. after the Gospel and First Epistle, and therefore towards the end of S. John's life. The unwillingness to write a long letter which appears in both Epistles (*vv.* 12, 13) would be natural in an old man to whom correspondence is a burden.

The contents speak for themselves. Gaius is commended for his hospitality, in which he resembles his namesake of Corinth (Rom. xvi. 23); is warned against imitating the factious and intolerant Diotrephes; and in contrast to him is told of the excellence of Demetrius, who is perhaps the bearer of the letter. In his next Apostolic journey S. John hopes to visit him. Meanwhile he and 'the friends' with him send a salutation to Gaius and 'the friends' with him.

The Epistle may be thus analysed.
1. **Address.**
2—12. **Main Body of the Epistle.**
   1. Personal Good Wishes and Sentiments (2—4).
   2. Gaius commended for his Hospitality (5—8).
   3. Diotrephes condemned for his Hostility (9, 10).
   4. The Moral (11, 12).
13, 14. **Conclusion.**

"The Second and Third Epistles of S. John occupy their own place in the sacred Canon, and contribute their own peculiar element to the stock of Christian truth and practice. They lead us from the region of miracle and prophecy, out of an atmosphere charged with the supernatural, to the more average every-day life of Christendom, with its regular paths and unexciting air. There is no hint in these short notes of extraordinary *charismata*. The tone of their Christianity is deep, earnest, severe, devout, but has the quiet of the Christian Church and home very much as at present constituted. The religion which pervades them is simple, unexaggerated, and practical. The writer is grave and reserved. Evidently in the possession of the fulness of the Christian faith, he is content to rest upon it with a calm consciousness of strength....By the conception of the Incarnate Lord, the Creator and Light of all men, and of the universality of Redemption, which the Gospel and the First Epistle did so much to bring home to all who received Christ, germs were deposited in the soil of Christianity which necessarily grew from an abstract idea into the great reality of the Catholic Church. In these two short occasional letters S. John provided two safeguards for that great institution. Heresy and schism are the dangers to which it is perpetually exposed. St John's condemnation of the spirit of *heresy* is recorded in the Second Epistle; his condemnation of the spirit of *schism* is written in the Third Epistle. Every age of Christendom up to the present has rather exaggerated than dwarfed the significance of this condemnation" (Bishop Alexander).

CHAPTER V.

THE TEXT OF THE EPISTLES.

i. *The Greek Text.*

OUR authorities for determining the Greek which S. John wrote are various and abundant. They consist of Greek MSS., Ancient Versions, and quotations from the Epistles in Christian writers of the second, third and fourth centuries. Quotations by writers later than the middle of the fourth century are of little or no value. By that time corruptions of the text had become widely diffused and permanent. The Diocletian persecution had swept away most of the ancient copies of N.T., and a composite text emanating mainly from Constantinople gradually became the text generally accepted.

It will be worth while to specify a few of the principal MSS. and Versions which contain these Epistles or portions of them.

Greek Manuscripts.

CODEX SINAITICUS (ℵ). 4th century. Discovered by Tischendorf in 1859 at the monastery of S. Catherine on Mount Sinai, and now at Petersburg. All three Epistles.

CODEX ALEXANDRINUS (A). 5th century. Brought by Cyril Lucar, Patriarch of Constantinople, from Alexandria, and afterwards presented by him to Charles I. in 1628. In the British Museum. All three Epistles.

CODEX VATICANUS (B). 4th century, but perhaps later than the Sinaiticus. In the Vatican Library. All three Epistles.

CODEX EPHRAEMI (C). 5th century. A palimpsest: the original writing has been partially rubbed out and the works of Ephraem the Syrian have been written over it. In the National Library at Paris. Part of the First and Third Epistles; 1 John i. 1—iv. 2; 3 John 3—15. Of the whole N.T. the only Books entirely missing are 2 John and 2 Thess.

CODEX BEZAE (D). 6th or 7th century. Given by Beza to the University Library at Cambridge in 1581. The Greek text has a parallel Latin translation throughout. The Greek text of the Catholic Epistles is missing, and of the servile Latin translation only 3 John 11—15 remains.

CODEX MOSQUENSIS (K). 9th century. All three Epistles.

Ancient Versions.

VULGATE SYRIAC (Peschito='simple,' meaning perhaps 'faithful'). 3rd century. The First Epistle.

PHILOXENIAN SYRIAC. "Probably the most servile version of Scripture ever made." 6th century. All three Epistles.

VULGATE LATIN (mainly a revision of the Old Latin by Jerome, A.D. 383—385). 4th century. All three Epistles.

THEBAIC or SAHIDIC (Egyptian). 3rd century. All three Epistles.

ARMENIAN. 5th century. All three Epistles.

AETHIOPIC. 5th century. All three Epistles.

ii. *The English Versions.*

It is well known that WICLIF began his work of translating the Scriptures into the vulgar tongue with the Apocalypse; so that S. John was the first inspired writer made known to the English people. A version of the Gospels with a commentary was given next; and then the rest of the N. T. A complete N. T. in English was finished about 1380. This, therefore, we may take as the date at which our Epistle first appeared in the English language. The whole was revised by JOHN PURVEY, about 1388.

But these early English Versions, made from a late and corrupt text of the Latin Vulgate, exercised little or no influence on the later Versions of Tyndale and others, which were made from late and corrupt Greek texts. TYNDALE translated direct from the Greek, checking himself by the Vulgate, the Latin of Erasmus, and the German of Luther. Dr Westcott in his most valuable work on the *History of the English Bible,* from which the material for this section has been mainly taken, often takes the First Epistle of S. John as an illustration of the variations between different versions and editions. The present writer gratefully borrows his statements. Tyndale published his first edition in 1525, his second in 1534, and his third in 1535; each time, especially in 1534, making many alterations and corrections. "Of the thirty-one changes which I have noticed in the later (1534) version of 1 John, about a third are closer approximations to the Greek: rather more are variations in connecting particles or the like designed to bring out the argument of the original more clearly; three new readings are adopted; and in one passage it appears that Luther's rendering has been substituted for an awkward paraphrase. Yet it must be remarked that even in this revision the changes are far more frequently at variance with Luther's renderings than in accordance with them" (p. 185). "In his Preface to the edition of 1534, Tyndale had expressed his readiness to revise his work and adopt any changes in it which might be shewn to be improvements. The edition of 1535, however enigmatic it may be in other respects, is a proof of his sincerity. The text of this exhibits a true revision and differs from that of 1534, though considerably less than the text of 1534 from that of 1525. In 1 John I have noted sixteen variations from the text of 1534 as against thirty-two (thirty-one?) in that of 1534 from the original text" (p. 190). But for the ordinary student the differences between the three editions of Tyndale are less interesting than the differences between Tyndale and the A.V. How much we owe to him appears from the fact that "about *nine-tenths* of the A.V. of the First Epistle of S. John are retained from Tyndale" (p. 211). Tyndale places the three Epistles of S. John between those of S. Peter and that to the Hebrews, S. James being placed between Hebrews and S. Jude. This is the order of Luther's translation, of Coverdale's Bible (1535), of Matthew's Bible (1537), and also of Taverner's (1539).

The GREAT BIBLE, which exists in three typical editions (Cromwell's, April, 1539; Cranmer's, April, 1540; Tunstall's and Heath's, Nov. 1540) is in the N. T. "based upon a careful use of the Vulgate and of Erasmus' Latin Version. An analysis of the variations in the First Epistle of S. John may furnish a type of its general character. As nearly as I can reckon there are seventy-one differences between Tyndale's text (1534) and that of the Great Bible: of these forty-three come directly from Coverdale's earlier revision (and in a great measure indirectly from the Latin): seventeen from the Vulgate where Coverdale before had not followed it: the remaining eleven variations are from other sources. Some of the new readings from the Vulgate are important, as for example the additions in i. 4, 'that *ye may rejoice and that* your joy may be full.' ii. 23, '*he that knowledgeth the Son hath the Father also.*' iii. 1, 'that we should be called *and be indeed* the sons of God.' v. 9, 'this is the witness of God *that is greater.*' All these additions (like v. 7) are marked distinctly as *Latin* readings: of the renderings adopted from Coverdale one is very important and holds its place in our present version. iii. 24, '*Hereby* we know that *he* abideth in us, *even by* the Spirit which he *hath given* us,' for which Tyndale reads: '*thereby* we know that *there* abideth in us *of* the Spirit which he *gave* us.' One strange blunder also is corrected; 'that old commandment which ye *heard*' (as it was in the earlier texts) is replaced by the true reading: 'that old commandment which ye have *had*' (ii. 7). No one of the new renderings is of any moment" (pp. 257, 258).

The revision made by TAVERNER, though superficial as regards the O. T., has important alterations in the N. T. He shews an improved appreciation of the Greek article. "Two consecutive verses of the First Epistle of S. John furnish good examples of his endeavour to find English equivalents for the terms before him. All the other versions adopt the Latin '*advocate*' in 1 John ii. 1, for which Taverner substitutes the Saxon '*spokesman.*' Tyndale, followed by Coverdale, the Great Bible, &c. strives after an adequate rendering of ἱλασμός (1 John ii. 2) in the awkward periphrasis 'he *it is that obtaineth grace* for our sins:' Taverner boldly coins a word which if insufficient is yet worthy of notice: 'he is *a mercystock* for our sins'" (p. 271).

The history of the GENEVA N. T. "is little more than the record of the application of Beza's translation and commentary to Tyndale's Testament......An analysis of the changes in one short Epistle will render this plain. Thus according to as accurate a calculation as I can make more than two-thirds of the new renderings in 1 John introduced into the revision of

1560 are derived from Beza, and two-thirds of these then for the first time. The rest are due to the revisers themselves, and of these only two are found in the revision of 1557" (pp. 287, 288).

The RHEMISH BIBLE, like Wiclif's, is a translation of a translation, being based upon the Vulgate. It furnished the revisers of 1611 with a great many of the words of Latin origin which they employ. It is "simply the ordinary, and not pure, Latin text of Jerome in an English dress. Its merits, and they are considerable, lie in its vocabulary. The style, so far as it has a style, is unnatural, the phrasing is most unrythmical, but the language is enriched by the bold reduction of innumerable Latin words to English service" (p. 328). Dr Westcott gives no examples from these Epistles, but the following may serve as such.

In a few instances the Rhemish has given to the A.V. a word not previously used in English Versions. 'And he is the *propitiation* for our sins' (ii. 2). 'And sent his son a *propitiation* for our sins' (iv. 10). 'But you have the *unction* from the Holy one' (ii. 20). 'These things have I written to you concerning them that *seduce* you' (ii. 26).

In some cases the Rhemish is superior to the A.V. '*Every one that* committeth sin, *committeth* also *iniquity: and* sin is *iniquity*' (iii. 4). The following also are worthy of notice. 'We *seduce* ourselves' (i. 8). 'Let no man *seduce* you' (ii. 6). 'Because many *seducers* are *gone out* into the world' (2 John 7).

But we may be thankful that King James's revisers did not adopt such renderings as these. 'That you also may have *society* with us, and our *society may be* with the Father and with his Son' (i. 3). 'And this is the *annuntiation*' (i. 5, iii. 11). 'That he might *dissolve* the works of the devil' (iii. 8). '*The generation* of God *preserveth* him' (v. 18). 'The *Senior* to the lady elect' (2 John 1). 'The *Senior* to Gaius the *dearest*' (3 John 1). 'Greater *thanke* have I not of them' (3 John 4). 'That we may be *coadjutors* of the truth' (3 John 8).

This is not the place to discuss the REVISED VERSION of 1881. When it appeared the present writer had the satisfaction of finding that a very large proportion of the alterations which he had suggested in notes on S. John's Gospel in this series in 1880 were sanctioned by alterations actually made by the revisers. In the notes on these Epistles it will be found that in a large number of cases he has followed the R. V., of the merits of which he has a high opinion. Those merits seem to consist not so much in skilful and happy treatment of very difficult passages as in careful correction of an enormous number of small errors and inaccuracies. The late Dr Routh, of Magdalen College, Oxford, when some one asked him what he considered to be the best commentary on the N. T., is said to have replied, 'The Vulgate.' If by that he meant that in the Vulgate we have a faithful translation made from a good Greek text, we may say in a similar spirit that the best commentary on the N. T. is now the Revised Version.

CHAPTER VI.

THE LITERATURE OF THE EPISTLES.

ALTHOUGH not so voluminous as that of the Gospel of S. John, the literature of the Epistles is nevertheless very abundant. It would be simply confusing to give anything approaching to an exhaustive list of the numerous works on the subject. All that will be attempted here will be to give the more advanced student some information as to where he may look for greater help than can be given in a handbook for the use of schools.

Of ancient commentaries not a very great deal remains. In his *Outlines* (Ὑποτυπώσεις) CLEMENT OF ALEXANDRIA (c. A.D. 200) commented on detached verses of the First and Second Epistles, and of these comments a valuable fragment in a Latin translation is extant. DIDYMUS, who was placed by S. Athanasius in the catechetical chair of Clement at Alexandria a century and a half later (c. A.D. 360), commented on all the Catholic Epistles; and his notes as translated by Epiphanius Scholasticus survive. "The chief features of his remarks on S.

John's three Epistles are (1) the earnestness against Docetism, Valentinianism, all speculations injurious to the Maker of the world, (2) the assertion that a true knowledge of God is possible without a knowledge of His essence, (3) care to urge the necessity of combining orthodoxy with right action" (W. Bright). The commentary of DIODORUS OF TARSUS (C. A.D. 380) on the First Epistle is lost. We have ten Homilies by S. AUGUSTINE on the First Epistle; but the series ends abruptly in the tenth Homily at 1 John v. 3. They are translated in the *Library of the Fathers*, vol. 29, Oxford 1849. In our own country the earliest commentary is that of the VENERABLE BEDE (C. A.D. 720), written in Latin. Like S. Augustine's, it is doctrinal and hortatory: quotations from both will be found in the notes.

Of the reformers, Beza, Calvin, Erasmus, Luther, and Zwingli have all left commentaries on one or more of these Epistles. Besides these we have the frequently quoted works of Grotius (c. A.D. 1550), of his critic Calovius (c. A.D. 1650), and of Bengel (c. A.D. 1750). Bengel's *Gnomon N. T.* has been translated into English; but those who can read Latin will prefer the epigrammatic terseness of the original.

The following foreign commentaries have been published in an English form by T. and T. Clark, Edinburgh: Braune, Ebrard, Haupt, Huther, Lücke. Of these that of Haupt on the First Epistle may be specially commended.

Among original English commentaries those of Bishop Alexander in *The Speaker's Commentary*, Alford, Jelf, Sinclair, Westcott, and Bishop Wordsworth are well known.

Other works which give valuable assistance are Cox's *Private Letters of S. Paul and S. John*, F. W. Farrar's *Early Days of Christianity*, F. D. Maurice's *Epistles of S. John*, and various articles in the *Dictionary of Christian Biography* edited by Smith and Wace.

The present writer desires to express his obligations, which in some cases are very great, to many of the works mentioned above, as well as to others. His debt to Dr Westcott would no doubt have been still greater had not the whole of this volume been in print before Dr Westcott's invaluable commentary was published: but he has been able to make much use of it both in the way of correction and addition. Almost all that can be said with truth about S. John's writings has already been said, and well said, by some one. The most that a new commentator can hope to do is to collect together what seems to him to be best in other writers, to think it out afresh, and recoin it for his own and others' use. What might have remained unknown, or unintelligible, or unattractive to many, if left in the original author and language, may possibly become better known and more intelligible when reduced to a smaller compass and placed in a new light and in new surroundings. Be this as it may, the writer who undertakes, even with all the helps available, to interpret S. John to others, must know that he incurs serious responsibility. He will not be anxious to be original. He will not be eager to insist upon views which have found no favour among previous workers in the same field. He will not regret that his conclusions should be questioned and his mistakes exposed. He will be content that a dirge should be sung over the results of his own work, if only what is true may prevail.

αἴλινον αἴλινον εἰπέ, τὸ δ' εὖ νικάτω.

THE FIRST EPISTLE GENERAL OF
JOHN.

THE FIRST EPISTLE GENERAL OF ST JOHN] This title exists in very different forms both ancient and modern, and is not original. As we might expect, the oldest authorities are the simplest; thus, 1. *Of John A.*; 2. *First Epistle of John*; 3. *Catholic Epistle of the Holy Apostle John*; 4. *First Epistle of the Evangelist and Apostle John*. So also with the English Versions.

'General' means Catholic or Universal. The Epistle is not addressed to any particular Church or individual, but to the whole Church throughout all ages. It is as suitable to the Church of England in the nineteenth century as to that of Ephesus in the first.

CHAP. I. 1—4. THE INTRODUCTION.

That the first four verses are introductory is generally admitted. They are analogous to the first eighteen verses of the Gospel and to the first three verses of the Revelation. Like the Prologue to the Gospel, this Introduction tells us that what the Apostle purposes to write about is *the Word who is the Life*. At the same time it states the authority with which he writes, an authority derived from the irrefragable evidence of the closest personal experience: and it states also the purpose of the letter,—to complete their joy in the Lord.

1—4. The construction is somewhat involved and prolonged. Such complicated sentences are not common in S. John: but we have similar sentences, extending over three verses, John vi. 22—24, xiii. 2—4. Various ways of connecting the clauses have been suggested, making 'is' understood, or 'handled', the main verb, thus; 'That which was from the beginning *is* that which we have heard', or 'That which was from the beginning, which &c., our hands also *touched*'. But beyond all reasonable doubt 'we declare' is the main verb, and, 'that which' in each case introduces the thing declared. Verse 2 is a parenthesis, and then part of v. 1 is repeated for emphasis and clearness. The complication is due to the crowding of profound thoughts which almost strangle the Apostle's simple command of language.

"S. John throughout this section uses the plural as speaking in the name of the apostolic body of which he was the last surviving representative" (Westcott).

1 *THAT* which was from the beginning, which we have heard, which we have seen with our eyes, which we have looked

1. *That which was from the beginning*] The similarity to the opening of the Gospel is manifest: but the thought is somewhat different. There the point is that the Word existed before the Creation; here that the Word existed before the Incarnation. With the neuter 'that which' comp. John iv. 22, vi. 37, xvii. 2; Acts xvii. 23 (R. V.). The Socinian interpretation, that 'that which' means the *doctrine* of Jesus, and not the Incarnate Word, cannot stand: the verbs, 'have seen', 'beheld', 'handled', are fatal to it. In using the neuter S. John takes the most comprehensive expression to cover the attributes, words and works of the Word and the Life manifested in the flesh.

was] not 'came into existence', but was already in existence. The difference between 'to be' (i. 2) and 'to come to be' or 'become' (ii. 18) must be carefully noted. Christ *was* from all eternity; antichrists *have arisen*, have come into existence in time.

from the beginning] The meaning of 'beginning' must always depend upon the context. Here it is explained by 'was with the Father' in *v*. 2. It does not mean the beginning of the gospel, or even of the world, but a beginning prior to that. It is equivalent to 'from all eternity'. The Gospel is no new-fangled invention, as Jewish and heathen philosophers contended. The same Greek phrase is used in LXX. for 'Art Thou not *from everlasting*, O Lord my God?' (Hab. i. 12), and when this is denied of idols (Wisd. xiv. 3). See on John i. 1.

which we have heard] With this clause we pass from eternity into time. The first clause refers to something prior to the Creation. Here both the Creation and the Incarnation have taken place. The second clause refers to the teaching of all the Prophets and of the Christ. There is no need to make 'which' (better, **that** *which*, to bring out the exact similarity of the first four clauses) in the different clauses refer to different things; e.g. the words, miracles, glory, and body of Christ. Rather, each 'which' indicates that collective whole of Divine and human attributes which is the Incarnate Word of Life.

have seen with our eyes] Note the climax: seeing is more than hearing, and beholding (which requires time) is more than seeing (which may be momentary); while handling is more than all. 'With our eyes' is added for emphasis. The Apostle would have us know that 'see' is no figure of speech, but the expression of a literal fact. With all the language at his command he insists on the reality of the Incarnation, of which he can speak from personal knowledge based on the combined evidence of all the senses. The Docetic heresy of supposing that the Lord's body was unreal, and the Cerinthian heresy of supposing that He who 'was from the beginning' was different from Him whom they heard and saw and handled, is authoritatively condemned by implication at the outset. In the Introduction to the Gospel there is a similar assertion; 'The Word became flesh and dwelt among us—and we beheld His glory' (John i. 14). Comp. 2 Pet. i. 16.

upon, and our hands have handled, of the Word of life;
(for the life was manifested, and we have seen *it*, and bear

which we have looked upon &c.] Rather, **that** *which we* **beheld** *and our hands* **handled**: we have first an imperfect, then a pair of perfects, then a pair of aorists. 'Beheld' implies deliberate and perhaps pleasurable sight (John i. 14, 34; Acts i. 11). We can hear and see without intending to do so; but we can scarcely behold and handle unintentionally. The aorists probably refer to definite occasions on which the beholding and handling took place. 'Handled' seems to be a direct reference to the test demanded by S. Thomas (John xx. 27) and offered to the other disciples (Luke xxiv. 39, where the same verb is used as here). "The clear reference to the Risen Christ in '*handled*' makes it probable that the special manifestation indicated by the two aorists is that given to the Apostles by the Lord after the Resurrection, which is in fact the revelation of Himself as He remains with His Church...The tacit reference is the more worthy of notice because S. John does not mention the fact of the Resurrection in his Epistle" (Westcott). Tertullian is very fond of insisting on the fact that the Lord was 'handled': *Adv. Prax.* xv. twice; *De Animâ* xvii.; *De Pat.* iii.; comp. *Ad Uxorem* iv. So also Ignatius (*Smyr.* iii.); "I know and believe that He was in the flesh even after the resurrection: and when He came to Peter and his company, He said to them, Take, *handle* Me, and see that I am not a bodiless demon." Bede points out that the argument has special force as coming from the disciple who had lain on the Lord's breast. No greater proof of the reality of His Body before and after the Resurrection could be given.

of the word of life] Better, **concerning** *the Word of life;* it is not the single genitive, but the genitive with a preposition. The preposition is strongly in favour of 'Word', i.e. the personal Logos, rather than 'word', i.e. doctrine. For this preposition used of testimony concerning *persons* comp. v. 9, 10; John i. 15, 22, 30, 48, ii. 25, v. 31, 32, 36, 37, 39, 46, &c. We can hardly doubt, moreover, that 'Word' or 'Logos' in this Introduction has the same meaning as in the Introduction to the Gospel; especially as the Epistle was written as a companion to the Gospel. 'The Word', therefore, means the Son of God, in whom had been hidden from eternity all that God had to say to man, and who was the living expression of the Nature and Will of God. See on John i. 1 for the history of the term, which is peculiar to the phraseology of S. John. But of the two terms, Word and Life, the latter is here the emphatic one as is shewn by *v*. 2 and by the fact that 'the Life' is one of the main topics of the Epistle (ii. 25, iii. 14, v. 11, 12, 20), whereas 'the Word' is not mentioned again. 'The Word of life' may be analogous to 'the tree of life', 'the water of life', 'the bread of life', where 'of life' means 'life-giving'; but more probably to 'the temple of His body', 'the sign of healing', where the genitive is one of apposition. 'The Word *which is* the Life' is the meaning. Christ is at once the Word of God and the Life of man.

2. *For the life was manifested*] Better, **And** *the life* &c. It is

witness, and shew unto you *that* eternal life, which was with

S. John's characteristic use of the simple conjunction. 'Manifest' (φανεροῦν) also is one of S. John's characteristic words, frequent in Gospel and Epistle and occurring twice in Revelation. Words and phrases which connect the Epistle with the Gospel, or either of these with the Apocalypse, should be carefully noted. 'Was manifested' means became such that He could be known by man. Note that the sentence does not begin with a relative, 'which was manifested', but that the noun is repeated. This repetition, carrying on a part of one sentence into the next for further elucidation and development, is quite in S. John's style.

have seen] This is the result of the manifestation: the Divine Life has become perceptible by the senses. In what way this took place is told us in iv. 2 and John i. 14.

and bear witness] The simple connexion of these sentences by 'and' is also in S. John's style; and 'bear witness' (μαρτυρεῖν) is another of his favourite words, occurring frequently in Gospel, Epistle, and Apocalypse. Testimony to the truth, with a view to producing belief in the Truth, on which eternal life depends, is one of his frequent thoughts. But the frequency of 'bear witness' in his writings is much obscured in A.V., where the same verb is sometimes rendered 'bear record' (v. 7), 'give record' (v. 10), and 'testify' (iv. 14, v. 9), and so also in the Gospel and the Revelation. Similarly the substantive 'witness' (μαρτυρία) is sometimes translated 'record' (v. 10, 11) and sometimes 'testimony'. The R.V. in this respect has made great improvements. Comp. 'This Jesus did God raise up, whereof (or, of whom) *we all are witnesses*' (Acts ii. 32).

and shew unto you] Better, *and* **declare** *unto you*: it is the same verb as occurs in the next verse; rare in S. John (xvi. 25, but not iv. 51 or xx. 18) but frequent in S. Luke. In this parenthetical verse, as in the main sentence of vv. 1 and 3, the Apostle emphatically reiterates that what he has to communicate is the result of his own personal experience. 'He that hath seen hath borne witness, and his witness is true: and he knoweth that he saith true, that ye also may believe' (John xix. 35: comp. xx. 30, 31, xxi. 24).

that eternal life] Rather, **the** *life,* **the** *eternal (life).* "The repetition of the article brings forward separately and distinctly the two notions of life and eternity" (Jelf). It is well known that the translators of 1611 did not perfectly understand the Greek article. Sometimes they ignore it, sometimes they insert it unwarrantably, sometimes (as here and v. 18) they exaggerate it by turning it into a demonstrative pronoun. Comp. '*that* Prophet', '*that* Christ', '*that* bread' (John i. 21, 25, vi. 14, 48, 69, vii. 40). For 'the Life' as a name for Christ comp. 'I am the Resurrection and the Life': 'I am the Way, and the Truth, and the Life' (John xi. 25, xiv. 6). 'Eternal life' is another of S. John's characteristic phrases, a fact somewhat obliterated in A.V. by the Greek phrase being often rendered 'everlasting life' or 'life everlasting'. 'Eternal' is better than 'everlasting', although in popular

the Father, and was manifested unto us;) *that* which we 3
have seen and heard declare we unto you, that ye also may

language the two words are synonymous. S. John's 'eternal life' has
nothing to do with time, but depends on our relation to Jesus Christ.
S. John tells us over and over again that eternal life can be possessed
in this world (v. 11, 13, 20, iii. 15: see on John iii. 36, v. 24, vi. 47).
He never applies 'eternal' (αἰώνιος) to anything but life, excepting
in Rev. xiv. 6, where he speaks of an 'eternal gospel'.

which was with the Father] Or, *which indeed was with the Father*:
it is not the simple but compound relative, denoting that what follows
is a special attribute; 'which was *such as to be* with the Father'. For
the 'was' see on v. 1. 'With the Father' is exactly parallel to 'with
God' in John i. 1. It is anticipated in the passage on the Divine
Wisdom; 'Then I was by Him as one brought up with Him' (Prov.
viii. 30). It indicates the distinct Personality of 'the Life'. Had
the Apostle written 'which was *in* God', we might have thought
that he meant a mere attribute of God. 'With the Father' is *apud
Patrem*, 'face to face' or 'at home with the Father'. Comp. 'to
tarry a while *with* you' (1 Cor. xvi. 7); 'when we were *with* you'
(1 Thess. iii. 4); 'whom I would fain have kept *with* me' (Philem. 13).

was manifested unto us] Repeated from the beginning of the verse.
In both cases we have a change from the imperfect tense (of the con-
tinuous preexistence of Christ) to the aorist (of the comparatively
momentary manifestation). But S. John's repetitions generally carry
us a step further. The manifestation would be little to us, if we had no
share in it. But that Being who was from all eternity with the Father,
has been made known, and made known *to us*.

3. *That which we have seen and heard*] In returning to the main
sentence he repeats a portion of it. The ideas of the first half and of
the second half of the main sentence are not the same. In *v.* 1 he is
thinking mainly of *what* he has to declare, viz. One existing from all
eternity and intimately known to himself: in *v.* 3 he is thinking mainly
of *why* he declares this, viz. to promote mutual fellowship.

declare we unto you] Add, **also**; 'you as well as we', or possibly,
'you as well as others, who have already been told', must have a share
in the good tidings. Comp. 'We cannot but speak the things which
we saw and heard' (Acts iv. 20). *Where* does S. John declare Him
who was from the beginning and was so well known to him and to
others? Not in this Epistle, for no such declaration is found in it; but
in the Gospel, which consists of such a declaration. We shall miss the
purport of the Epistle if we do not bear constantly in mind that it was
written as a companion to the Gospel. Parallels between the two
abound: in what follows we have a striking one. Note the sequence of
ideas: 1. the *evidence* on which their conviction was based, 'have seen';
2. their declaration of these convictions as *Apostles*, 'bear witness';
3. their declaration of them as *Evangelists*, 'declare'.

that ye also may have fellowship with us] Comp. 'that they may be
one, even as We are' (John xvii. 11). Christ's prayer and S. John's

have fellowship with us: and truly our fellowship *is* with
4 the Father, and with his Son Jesus Christ. And these
5 *things* write we unto you, that your joy may be full. This

purpose are one and the same. See on *v*. 4. 'Ye also', who have *not* heard, or seen, or handled.

fellowship] Or, *communion;* almost always used of fellowship with *persons* (1 Cor. i. 9) or with things personified (2 Cor. vi. 14). The word is rare in N. T. outside S. Paul's writings. It "generally denotes the fellowship of persons with persons in one and the same object, always common to all and sometimes whole to each" (Canon Evans on 1 Cor. x. 16). This is S. John's conception of the Church: each member of it possesses the Son, and through Him the Father; and this common possession gives communion with all other members as well as with the Divine Persons.

and truly our fellowship] Or, *yea, and our fellowship:* there is a double conjunction in the Greek, as in John vi. 51. The Apostle will tell them what 'fellowship with us' really means: 'but *our* fellowship is not merely fellowship with us; it is fellowship with the Father and the Son' (John xiv. 23). The 'our', like 'eternal' in *v*. 2 is very emphatic: 'the fellowship that is ours, that we enjoy'.

His Son Jesus Christ] This full description is given for solemnity; and also perhaps to bring out the idea of which the Epistle is so full, that Christians are all one family, and in their relation to God share in the Sonship of Christ. Comp. 'God is faithful, through whom ye were called into the *fellowship of His Son* Jesus Christ our Lord' (1 Cor. i. 9).

The fulness of the expression (comp. iii. 23) is not so apparent in the English as in the Greek, which literally rendered runs thus; *is with the Father and with the Son of Him, Jesus Christ*. Both the preposition and the definite article are repeated, marking emphatically the distinction and equality between the Son and the Father. Thus two fundamental truths, which the philosophical heresies of the age were apt to obscure or deny, are here clearly laid down at the outset; (1) the distinctness of personality and equality of dignity between the Father and the Son; (2) the identity of the eternal Son of God with the historical person Jesus Christ.

4. *these things write we*] These words apply to the whole Epistle, of which he here states the purpose, just as in John xx. 31 he states the purpose of the Gospel. Both 'write' and 'we' are emphatic: it is a permanent message that is sent, and it is sent by apostolic authority.

that your joy may be full] According to the better reading and rendering, *that* **our** *joy may be* **fulfilled**. Tyndale in his first edition (1525) has 'your', in his second (1534) and third (1535) 'our'. In the Greek we have a passive participle, not an adjective: that our joy may be made full and may remain so. Moreover the expression that joy is made full or fulfilled is one of S. John's characteristic phrases, and this should be brought out in translation. The active 'fulfil my joy' occurs Phil. ii. 2; but the passive only here, John iii. 29, xv. 11, xvi. 24, xvii. 13; 2 John 12. Comp. 'These things have I spoken unto you, that My joy may be in you, and that your joy may be fulfilled', and 'These things I speak in the world, that they may have My joy fulfilled in themselves' (John xv. 11, xvii. 13). Once more Christ's prayer and S. John's purpose are one and the same. See on *v.* 3. '*Our* joy' may mean either the *Apostolic* joy at the good results of Apostolic teaching; or the joy in which the *recipients* of the teaching share—'yours as well as ours'. In either case the joy is that serene happiness, which is the result of conscious union with God and good men, of conscious possession of eternal life (see on v. 13), and which raises us above pain and sorrow and remorse. The first person plural used throughout this Introduction is the plural of authority, indicating primarily S. John, but S. John as the representative of the Apostles. In the body of the Epistle he uses the first person *singular* (ii. 1, 7, 8, 12, 13, 14, 21, 26, v. 13). The concluding words of the Introduction to the Epistle of Barnabas are striking both in their resemblance and difference: "Now I, not as a teacher, but as one of you, will set forth a few things, by means of which in your present case ye may be gladdened." Bede remarks, doubtless as the result of personal experience, that the joy of teachers is made full when by their preaching many are brought to the communion of the Church and of Him through whom the Church is strengthened and increased.

The following profound thoughts struggle for expression in these four opening verses. There is a Being who has existed with God the Father from all eternity: He is the Father's Son: He is also the expression of the Father's Nature and Will. He has been manifested in space and time; and of that manifestation I and others have had personal knowledge: by the united evidence of our senses we have been convinced of its reality. In revealing to us the Divine Nature He becomes to us life, eternal life. With the declaration of all this in our hands as the Gospel, we come to you in this Epistle, that you may unite with us in our great possession, and that our joy in the Lord may be made complete.

We now enter upon the first main division of the Epistle; which extends to ii. 28, the chief subject of which (with much digression) is the theme GOD IS LIGHT, and that in two parts: i. the Positive Side— WHAT WALKING IN THE LIGHT INVOLVES; THE CONDITION AND CONDUCT OF THE BELIEVER (i. 5—ii. 11): ii. the Negative Side— WHAT WALKING IN THE LIGHT EXCLUDES; THE THINGS AND PERSONS TO BE AVOIDED (ii. 12—28). These parts will be subdivided as we reach them.

i. 5—ii. 28. GOD IS LIGHT.

i. 5—ii. 11. WHAT WALKING IN THE LIGHT INVOLVES.

This section is largely directed against the Gnostic doctrine that to the man of enlightenment all conduct is morally indifferent. Against every form of this doctrine, which sapped the very foundations of Christian Ethics, the Apostle never wearies of inveighing. So far from its being true that all conduct is alike to the enlightened man, it is the character of his conduct that will shew whether he is enlightened or not. If he is walking in the light his condition and conduct will exhibit these things; 1. *Fellowship with God and with the Brethren*

then is the message which we have heard of him, and declare unto you, that God is light, and in him is no

(5—7); 2. *Consciousness and Confession of Sin* (8—10); 3. *Obedience to God by Imitation of Christ* (ii. 1—6); 4. *Love of the Brethren* (ii. 7—11).

5—7. FELLOWSHIP WITH GOD AND WITH THE BRETHREN.

5. *This then is the message which we have heard of Him*] Better, **And** *the message which we have heard* **from** *Him* **is this**. 'This' is the predicate, as so often in S. John: 'But the judgment is this' (John iii. 19); 'The commandment is this' (xv. 12); 'The eternal life is this' (xvii. 3): comp. 1 John iii. 11, 23, v. 3, 11, 14; 2 John 6. In all these cases 'is this' means 'This is what it consists in, This is the sum and substance of it'. The conjunction does not introduce an inference: here, as in the Gospel, the main portion of the writing is joined on to the Introduction by a simple 'and'. Tyndale, Cranmer, and the Rhemish all have 'and': 'then' comes from Geneva, apparently under the influence of Beza's *igitur*. The connexion of thought seems to be this. S. John is writing that we may have fellowship with God (*v.* 3): and in order to have this we must know 1. what God is (*v.* 5), and 2. what we consequently are bound to be (6—10). The word for 'message' (ἀγγελία) occurs only in this Epistle (iii. 11) in N.T., but is more frequent in LXX.

Once more we have a striking parallel between Gospel and Epistle: the Gospel opens with a sentence very similar in form; 'And the witness of John is this' (i. 19). All these similarities strengthen the belief that the two were written about the same time, and were intended to accompany one another.

from Him] From Christ. The pronoun used (αὐτός) is not the one (ἐκεῖνος) commonly used for Christ in this Epistle. But here the context decides: 'Him' refers back to 'His Son Jesus Christ' (*v.* 3), the subject of the opening verses (1—3). Moreover, it was from Christ, and not immediately from the Father, that the Apostles received their message.

and declare unto you] Better, *and* **announce** *unto you:* not precisely the same verb as was rendered 'declare' in *vv.* 2, 3. Both are compounds of the same verb; but while the former has merely the notion of proclaiming and making known, this has the notion of proclaiming *again* what has been received elsewhere. The one is *annuntiare*, the other *renuntiare*. S. John *hands on the message* received from Christ: it is no invention of his own. It is a message, and not a discovery. So also the Spirit makes known or reveals to us truths which proceed from the Father (John xvi. 13, 14, 15): comp. John iv. 25; 2 Cor. vii. 7; 1 Pet. i. 12, where the same verb is used in all cases.

God is light] This is the theme of the first main division of the Epistle, as 'God is Love' of the second: so that this verse stands in the same relation to the first great division as *vv.* 1—4 to the whole Epistle. No one tells us so much about the Nature of God as S. John: other

darkness at all. If we say that we have fellowship with 6

writers tell us what God *does*, and what attributes He *possesses*; S. John tells us what He *is*. There are three statements in the Bible which stand alone as revelations of the Nature of God, and they are all in the writings of S. John: 'God is spirit' (John iv. 24); 'God is light', and 'God is love' (1 John iv. 8). In all these momentous statements the predicate has no article, either definite or indefinite. We are not told that God is *the* Spirit, or *the* Light, or *the* Love: nor (in all probability) that He is *a* Spirit, or *a* light. But 'God is spirit, is light, is love': spirit, light, love are His very Nature. They are not mere attributes, like mercy and justice: they are Himself. They are probably the nearest approach to a definition of God that the human mind could frame or comprehend: and in the history of thought and religion they are unique. The more we consider them, the more they satisfy us. The simplest intellect can understand their meaning; the subtlest cannot exhaust it. No philosophy, no religion, not even the Jewish, had risen to the truth that God is light. 'The Lord shall be *to thee* an everlasting light' (Is. lx. 19, 20) is far short of it. But S. John knows it: and lest the great message which he conveys to us in his Gospel, 'God is spirit', should seem somewhat bare and empty in its indefiniteness, he adds this other message in his Epistle, 'God is light, God is love'. No figure borrowed from the material world could give the idea of perfection so clearly and fully as *light*. It suggests ubiquity, brightness, happiness, intelligence, truth, purity, holiness. It suggests excellence without limit and without taint; an excellence whose nature it is to communicate itself and to pervade everything from which it is not of set purpose shut out. 'Let there be light' was the first fiat of the Creator; and on it all the rest depends. Light is the condition of beauty, and life, and growth, and activity: and this is as true in the intellectual, moral, and spiritual spheres as in the material universe.

Of the many beautiful and true ideas which the utterance 'God is light' suggests to us, two are specially prominent in this Epistle; *intelligence* and *holiness*. The Christian, anointed with the Holy Spirit, and in communion with God in Christ, possesses (1) knowledge, (2) righteousness. (1) 'Ye know Him which is from the beginning' (ii. 13, 14); 'I have not written unto you because ye know not the truth, but because ye know it' (ii. 21); 'Ye need not that anyone teach you' (ii. 27); &c. &c. (2) 'Every one that hath this hope on him purifieth himself, even as He is pure' (iii. 3); 'Whosoever is begotten of God doeth no sin, because his seed abideth in him: and he cannot sin, because he is begotten of God'; &c. &c.

and in Him is no darkness at all] Or, retaining the telling order of the Greek, *and darkness in Him there is none at all*. This antithetic parallelism is characteristic of S. John's style. He frequently emphasizes a statement by following it up with a denial of its opposite. Thus, in the next verse, 'We lie, and do not the truth'. Comp. 'We lead ourselves astray, and the truth is not in us' (*v.* 8); 'Abideth in the light, and there is none occasion of stumbling in him' (ii. 10); 'Is

him, and walk in darkness, we lie, and do not the truth:

true, and is no lie' (ii. 27) : comp. ii. 4. So also in the Gospel: see on John i. 3. The denial here is very strong, the negative being doubled in the Greek; 'none whatever, *none at all*'.

Another parallel between the Gospel and the Epistle must here be pointed out. In the Prologue to the former we have these ideas in succession; the Word, life, light, darkness. The same four follow in the same order here; 'the *Word* of life', 'the *life* was manifested', 'God is *light*, and *darkness* in Him there is none'. Must we not suppose that the sequence of thought here has been influenced by the sequence in the corresponding portion of the Gospel?

The figurative use of 'darkness' for moral darkness, i.e. error and sin, is very frequent in S. John (ii. 8, 9, 11; see on John i. 5, viii. 12). These passages shew that the meaning of this verse cannot be, ' God has now been revealed, and no part of His Nature remains unknown'; which, moreover, could never be stated of Him who is incomprehensible. S. John is laying the foundation of Christian Ethics, of which the very first principle is that there is a God who intellectually, morally, and spiritually is *light*.

"In speaking of 'light' and 'darkness' it is probable that S. John had before him the Zoroastrian speculations on the two opposing spiritual powers which influenced Christian thought at a very early date" (Westcott).

6. An inference from the first principle just laid down. God is light, utterly removed from all darkness: therefore to be in darkness is to be cut off from Him.

If we say] With great gentleness he puts the case hypothetically, and with great delicacy he includes himself in the hypothesis. This 'if we' continues in almost every verse until ii. 3, after which it is changed into the equivalent 'he that', which continues down to ii. 11; after that neither form is used. This is one of several indications that from i. 6 to ii. 11 is a definite division of the Epistle, based upon the introductory verse, i. 5. With ii. 12 there is a new departure.

walk in darkness] This 'walk' (περιπατεῖν) is the Latin *versari* and signifies the ordinary course of life. The word in this sense is frequent in S. Paul and in S. John. Comp. ii. 6, 11; 2 John iv. 6; 3 John 3, 4; Rev. xxi. 24; John viii. 12. It expresses not merely action, but habitual action. A life in moral darkness can no more have communion with God, than a life in a coal-pit can have communion with the sun. For 'what communion hath light with darkness?' (2 Cor. vi. 4). Light can be shut out, but it cannot be shut in. Some Gnostics taught, not merely that to the illuminated all conduct was alike, but that to reach the highest form of illumination men must experience every kind of action, however abominable, in order to work themselves free from the powers that rule the world (Eus. *H. E.* IV. vii. 9). 'In darkness' should probably be *in* **the** *darkness:* in *vv.* 6, 7, as in ii. 8, 9, 11, both light and darkness have the article in the Greek, which is not merely generic but emphatic; that which is light indeed is opposed to that

but if we walk in the light, as he is in the light, we have
fellowship one with another, and the blood of Jesus Christ

which is darkness indeed. In 2 Cor. vi. 14, 'What communion hath light with darkness?', neither word has the article.

we lie, and do not the truth] Antithetic parallelism, as in *v.* 5. The negative statement here carries us further than the positive one: it includes conduct as well as speech. See on John iii. 21, where 'doing the truth' is opposed to 'practising evil'. It is also the opposite of '*doing* a lie' (Rev. xxi. 27, xxii. 15). In LXX. 'to *do* mercy and *truth*' is found several times. So also S. Paul opposes truth to *iniquity* (1 Cor. xiii. 6); shewing that neither does he confine truth to truthfulness in words. In this Epistle we find many striking harmonies in thought and language between S. John and S. Paul, quite fatal to the view that there is a fundamental difference in teaching between the two Apostles.

7. A further inference from the first principle laid down in *v.* 5: walking in the light involves not only fellowship with God but fellowship with the brethren. This verse takes the opposite hypothesis to that just considered and expands it. We often find (comp. *v.* 9) that S. John while seeming to go back or repeat, really progresses and gives us something fresh. It would have enforced *v.* 6, but it would have told us nothing fresh, to say 'if we walk in the light, and say that we have fellowship with Him, we speak the truth, and do not lie'. And it is interesting to find that the craving to make this verse the exact antithesis of the preceding one has generated another reading, 'we have fellowship with *Him*', instead of 'with *one another*'. This reading is as old as the second century, for Tertullian (*De Pud.* XIX.) quotes, '*si vero*', *inquit*, '*in lumine incedamus, communionem* cum eo *habebimus, et sanguis &c.*' Clement of Alexandria also seems to have known of this reading. This is evidence of the early date of our Epistle; for by the end of the second century important differences of reading had already arisen and become widely diffused.

as He is in the light] We *walk*, God *is:* we move through space and time; He is in eternity. Of Him who is everywhere, and knows no change, we can only say, 'He is'. Comp. the similar thought of S. Paul; 'Who only hath immortality, *dwelling in light*' unapproachable' (1 Tim. vi. 16). That which *is* light must ever be *in* light. We then must make our spiritual atmosphere similar to His, that our thoughts and conduct may reflect Him.

fellowship one with another] This certainly refers to the mutual fellowship of Christians *among themselves*, as is clear from iii. 23, iv. 7, 12; 2 John 5. It does *not* refer to fellowship *between God and man*, as S. Augustine and others, desiring to make this verse parallel to *v.* 6, have interpreted. S. John would scarcely express the relation between God and man by such a phrase as 'we have fellowship with one another' (μετ' ἀλλήλων). Contrast 'I ascend unto My Father and your Father, and My God and your God' (John xx. 17). In that 'thick darkness', which prevailed 'in all the land of Egypt three days, *they saw not one another, neither rose any from his place* for three days' (Ex.

8 his Son cleanseth us from all sin. If we say that we have

xi. 22, 23): i.e. there was an absolute cessation of fellowship. Society could not continue in the dark: but when the light returned, society was restored. So also in the spiritual world: when the light comes, individuals have that communion one with another which in darkness is impossible. In a similar spirit Cicero declares that real friendship is impossible without virtue (*De Amic.* vi. 20).

and the blood of Jesus Christ] Omit 'Christ' with all the oldest authorities: so also Wiclif and Tyndale's first edition. The 'and' shews that this is a further consequence of walking in the light. "For this is the virtue of the Lord's blood, that such as it has already purified from sin, and thenceforward has set in the light, it renders thenceforward pure, if they continue steadfastly walking in the light" (Tertull. *De Mod.* XIX.). One who walks in spiritual darkness cannot appropriate that cleansing from sin, which is wrought by the blood of Jesus, shed on the cross as a propitiation for sin.

His Son] Not redundant: (1) it is a passing contradiction of Cerinthus, who taught that Jesus was a mere man when His blood was shed, for the Divine element in His nature left Him when He was arrested in the garden; and of the Ebionites, who taught that He was a mere man from His birth to His death; (2) it explains how this blood can have such virtue: it is the blood of One who is the Son of God.

cleanseth] Note the present tense of what goes on continually; that constant cleansing which even the holiest Christians need (see on John xiii. 10). One who lives in the light knows his own frailty and is continually availing himself of the purifying power of Christ's sacrificial death. "This passage shews that the gratuitous pardon of sins is given us not once only, but that it is a benefit perpetually residing in the Church, and daily offered to the faithful" (Calvin). Note also the 'all'; there is no limit to its cleansing power: even grievous sinners can be restored to the likeness of God, in whom is no darkness at all. This refutes by anticipation the error of the Novatians, who denied pardon to mortal sins after baptism. Comp. 'How much more shall the blood of Christ... cleanse your conscience' (Heb. ix. 14), and 'These are they which come out of the great tribulation, and *they washed their robes and made them white in the blood of the Lamb*' (Rev. vii. 14).

8—10. CONSCIOUSNESS AND CONFESSION OF SIN.

8—10. Walking in the light involves the great blessings just stated, —fellowship with God and with our brethren, and a share in the purifying blood of Jesus. But it also involves something on our part. It intensifies our consciousness of sin, and therefore our desire to get rid of it by confessing it. No one can live in the light without being abundantly convinced that he himself is not light.

8. *If we say*] See on *v.* 6. Doubtless there were some who said so, and more perhaps who thought so; 'say' need not mean more than 'say in our hearts'. S. John's own teaching might easily be misunderstood as encouraging such an error, if one portion of it (iii. 9, 10) were taken without the rest.

no sin, we deceive ourselves, and the truth is not in us.
If we confess our sins, he is faithful and just to forgive us 9

we have no sin] 'To have sin' is a phrase peculiar to S. John in
N. T. There is no need to inquire whether original or actual sin is
meant: the expression is quite general, covering sin of every kind.
Only One human being has been able to say 'The things pleasing to
God I always do'; 'Which of you convicteth Me of sin?'; 'The ruler
of the world hath nothing in Me' (John viii. 29, 46, xiv. 30). The
more a man knows of the meaning of 'God is light', i.e. the more he
realises the absolute purity and holiness of God, the more conscious
he will become of his own impurity and sinfulness: comp. Job ix. 2,
xiv. 4, xv. 14, xxv. 4; Prov. xx. 9; Eccles. vii. 20.

we deceive ourselves] Not merely we are mistaken, or are misled,
but *we* **lead ourselves astray**. In the Greek it is neither the middle,
nor the passive, but the active with the reflexive pronoun: the erring is
all our own doing. See on v. 21. We do for ourselves what Satan, the
arch-deceiver (Rev. xii. 9, xx. 10) endeavours to do for us. The active
(πλανᾷν) is frequent in S. John, especially in the Apocalypse (ii. 26,
iii. 7; Rev. ii. 20, xii. 9, xiii. 14, xix. 20, xx. 3, 8, 10). An examination of these passages will shew that the word is a strong one and
implies serious departure from the truth: comp. John vii. 12.

the truth is not in us] Because we are in an atmosphere of self-made
darkness which shuts the truth out. The truth may be all round us,
but we are not in contact with it: it is not *in* us. One who shuts himself in a dark room has no light, though the sun may be shining
brightly. All words about truth, 'the truth, true, truly', are characteristic of S. John. Note the antithetic parallelism, and see on *v*. 5.

9. *If we confess our sins*] The opposite hypothesis is now taken and
expanded, as in *v*. 7; see note there. But there is no conjunction, no
'but', as in *v*. 7; and the asyndeton is telling. Greek has such a
wealth of connecting particles, that in that language asyndeton is
specially remarkable. Here there is expansion and progress, not only
in the second half of the verse where '*He* is faithful and righteous'
takes the place of '*we* are true'; but in the first half also; where 'confess *our sins*' takes the place of 'say *we have sin*'. The latter ad-
mission costs us little: the confession of the particular sins which we
have committed costs a good deal, and is a guarantee of sincerity. He
who refuses to confess, may perhaps desire, but certainly does not *seek*
forgiveness. 'He that covereth his sins shall not prosper: but whoso
confesseth and forsaketh them shall have mercy' (Prov. xxviii. 13).
Obviously confession to Him who is 'faithful and righteous', and to
those 'selves' whom we should otherwise 'lead astray', is all that is
meant. The passage has nothing to do with the question of confession to our fellow-men.

faithful and just] Better, *faithful and* **righteous**, to bring out the
contrast with 'unrighteousness' and the connexion with 'Jesus Christ
the righteous' (ii. 1), where the same word (δίκαιος) is used. The Greek
'and' (καί) sometimes means 'and yet', and frequently does so in

10 *our* sins, and to cleanse us from all unrighteousness. If we say that we have not sinned, we make him a liar, and his word is not in us.

S. John: see on John i. 10. It is possible that it has this meaning here. 'God is faithful (to His promises to us) *and yet* righteous (in hating and punishing sin)'. He keeps His promise of mercy to the penitent without losing His character for righteousness and justice. In any case beware of making 'righteous' a vague equivalent for 'kind, gentle, merciful'. It means 'just' (which is to some extent the opposite of 'merciful'), and affirms that God in keeping His word *gives to each his due*. The distinction which refers 'faithful' to mortal sins and 'righteous' to venial ones is frivolous. For 'faithful' in the sense of keeping promises comp. 'He is faithful that promised' (Heb. x. 23); 'She counted Him faithful who had promised' (Heb. xi. 11): and for 'righteous' in the sense of giving just awards comp. 'Righteous art Thou...because Thou didst thus judge...True and righteous are Thy judgments' (Rev. xvi. 5—7).

to forgive us our sins] In spite of what some eminent scholars have said to the contrary, it is perhaps true that the Greek for these words includes to some extent the idea of *intention* and *aim*. Thus the Vulgate, *fidelis est et justus, ut remittat nobis peccata nostra*; and Wiclif, 'He is feithful and just *that* He forgeve to us oure synnes'; and the Rhemish, 'He is faithful and just, *for to* forgive us our sinnes'. In S. John we find the conviction deeply rooted that all things happen in accordance with the decrees of God: events are the results of His purposes. And this conviction influences his language: so that constructions (ἵνα) which originally indicated a *purpose*, and which even in late Greek do not lose this meaning entirely, are specially frequent in his writings: see on John v. 36. It is God's decree and aim that His faithfulness and righteousness should appear in His forgiving us and cleansing us. Comp. 'Against Thee, Thee only, have I sinned...that Thou mightest be justified when Thou speakest, and be clear when Thou judgest' (Ps. li. 4).

our sins] Those particular acts of sin which we have confessed, and from the punishment due for which we are thus set free. 'I said, I will confess my transgressions unto the Lord; and Thou forgavest the iniquity of my sin' (Ps. xxxii. 5). 'He that covereth his sins shall not prosper: but whoso confesseth and forsaketh them shall have mercy' (Prov. xxviii. 13).

and to cleanse us] This is not a repetition in different words; it is a second and distinct result of our confession: 1. We are absolved from sin's punishment; 2. We are freed from sin's pollution. The forgiveness is the averting of God's wrath; the cleansing is the beginning of holiness.

10. *that we have not sinned*] This is not the same as 'that we have no sin' (v. 8), and therefore we have once more not repetition, but expansion and strengthening of what precedes. 'Have no sin' refers to a sinful state; 'have not sinned' refers to the actual commission of par-

My little children, these *things* write I unto you, that ye 2

ticular acts of sin: the one is the inward principle, the other is its result. But the whole context shews that neither expression refers to sins committed before baptism: no Christian would have denied these: moreover S. John does not write to the recently converted, but to those who have had time to grow lukewarm and indifferent. Both expressions refer to sin after baptism, and the perfect (ἡμαρτήκαμεν) has the common meaning of the Greek perfect, present result of past action; 'we are in the condition of not having sinned'. This use of the perfect is specially frequent in S. John.

we make Him a liar] Worse than 'we lead ourselves astray' (*v*. 8), as that is worse than 'we lie' (*v*. 6). This use of the verb 'make' in the sense of 'assert that one is' is frequent in the Gospel: 'He *made* Himself the Son of God'; 'Every one that *maketh* himself a king' (John xix. 7, 12; comp. v. 18, viii. 53, x. 33). God's promise to forgive sin to the penitent would be a lie if there were no sin to be repented of. And more than this; God's whole scheme of salvation assumes that all men are sinful and need to be redeemed: therefore those who deny their sinfulness charge God with deliberately framing a vast libel on human nature. Whereas S. Paul says, 'Let God be found true, but every man a liar' (Rom. iii. 3).

His word is not in us] God's revelation of Himself has no home in our hearts: it remains outside us, as the light remains outside and separated from him who shuts himself up in darkness. The expressions, 'to be in' and 'to abide in', to express intimate relationship, are characteristic of S. John: and either of the things related can be said to be in the other. Thus, either 'His word is not in us' (comp. ii. 14), or 'If ye abide in My word' (John viii. 31): either 'The truth is not in us' (*v*. 8), or 'He standeth not in the truth' (John xiii. 44). Sometimes the two modes of expression are combined; 'Abide in Me, and I in you' (John xv. 4). 'His word' means especially the Gospel: as it is the sins of *Christians* which are being considered, the O.T., though not excluded, cannot be specially meant. 'Word' is more personal than 'the truth' (*v*. 8), which does not necessarily imply a speaker.

CH. II. 1—6. OBEDIENCE TO GOD BY IMITATION OF CHRIST.

1—6. The Apostle is still treating of the condition and conduct of the believer as determined by his walking in the light; there is no break between the two chapters. Having shewn us that even Christians constantly sin, he goes on (1) to point out the remedy for sin, (2) to exhort us not to sin. The paragraph begins and ends with the latter point, but the former constitutes the chief link with the preceding paragraph: comp. i. 7. He who craves to grow in sanctification, and yet is conscious of his own frailty must constantly have recourse to the Advocate and His cleansing blood: thus he will be enabled to obey God more and more perfectly.

1. *My little children*] The diminutive form (τεκνία) does not at all imply that he is addressing persons of tender age: it is a term of en-

sin not. And if any *man* sin, we have an advocate with the

dearment. Wiclif has 'litil sones' as a rendering of the *filioli* of the Vulgate; Tyndale, Cranmer, and the Genevan Version all waver between 'babes' (which is far too strong) and 'little children'. Setting aside Gal. iv. 19, where the reading is uncertain, the word occurs only in this Epistle (*vv.* 12, 28, iii. 7, 18, iv. 4, v. 21) and once in the Gospel (xiii. 33). Possibly it is a reminiscence of Christ's farewell address in John xiii. S. John's conception of the Church is that of a family, in which all are children of God and brethren one of another, but in which also some who are elders stand in a parental relation to the younger brethren. Thus there were families within the family, each with its own father. And who had a better right to consider himself a father than the last surviving Apostle? "The Apostles loved and cherished that name, and all that it implied, and all that illustrated it. They much preferred it to any title which merely indicated an office. It was more spiritual; it was more personal; it asserted better the divine order; it did more to preserve the dignity and sacredness of all domestic relations" (Maurice). Comp. the story of 'S. John and the Robber' (p. 24).

These things] Probably refers to the preceding paragraph (i. 5—10) rather than to what follows. On the one hand they must beware of the spiritual pride which is one of the worst forms of sin: on the other they must not think that he is bidding them acquiesce in a state of sin.

I write] Henceforward the Apostle uses the more personal and direct first person singular. Only in the Introduction (i. 4) does he use the apostolic 'write *we*': contrast ii. 1, 7, 8, 12, 13, 14, 21, 26, v. 13.

that ye sin not] The Apostle is not giving a command, but stating his reason for writing thus; *in order* **that ye may not sin**. Tyndale's first edition has 'that ye should not sin'. That is his aim; to lead them onward to perfect holiness, to perfect likeness to God. Those who are on the one hand warned of their liability to sin, and on the other are told of what cleanses them from sin, are put in the way towards this high ideal.

And if any man sin] Or, *have sinned* (*peccaverit*): S. John is not telling the intending sinner that sin is a light matter; but the penitent sinner that sin is not irremediable. In both sentences 'sin' is in the aorist, and implies a definite act, not an habitual state, of sin. We are to avoid not merely a life of sin, but any sin whatever. And not merely the habitual sinner, but he who falls into a single sin, needs and has an Advocate. Sin and its remedy are stated in immediate proximity, just as they are found in life.

we have an Advocate] Just as we always have sin (i. 8), so we always have One ready to plead for pardon. S. John does not say '*he* hath an Advocate', but '*we* have' one: he breaks the logical flow of the sentence rather than seem not to include himself in the need and possession of an Advocate. On Advocate or Paraclete ($παράκλητος$) see on John xiv. 16. It means one who is *summoned to the side of* another, especially to serve as his helper, spokesman (*causae patronus*), or inter-

Father, Jesus Christ *the* righteous: and he is the propitiation 2

cessor. The word occurs in N.T. only in S. John; here in the Epistle and four times in the Gospel (xiv. 16, 26, xv. 26, xvi. 7). It is unlikely that S. John would use the word in totally different senses in the two writings, especially if the Epistle was written to accompany the Gospel. We must therefore find some meaning which will suit all five passages. Two renderings compete for acceptation, 'Comforter' and 'Advocate'. Both make good sense in the Gospel, and (though there is by no means agreement on the point) 'Advocate' makes the best sense. 'Advocate' is the only rendering which is at all probable here: it exactly suits the context. 'We have a *Comforter* with the Father' would be intolerable. The older English Versions (excepting Taverner, who has 'spokesman') all have 'Advocate' here; and (excepting the Rhemish, which has 'Paraclete') all have 'Comforter' in the Gospel: and of course this unanimity influenced the translators of 1611. But 'Advocate' as the one rendering which suits all five passages should be adopted throughout. Then we see the full meaning of Christ's promise (John xiv. 16), 'I will pray the Father, and He shall give you *another* Advocate'. Jesus Christ is one Advocate; the Holy Spirit is another. As S. Paul says, 'the Spirit Himself *maketh intercession for* us with groanings which cannot be uttered': and it is worthy of remark that he uses precisely the same language to express the intercession of the Spirit and the intercession of Christ (Rom. viii. 26, 27, 34). Comp. Heb. vii. 25, ix. 24; 1 Tim. ii. 5. Philo's use of the word 'Paraclete' throws considerable light upon its meaning. He often uses it of the high-priest with his breastplate of judgment (Ex. xxviii. 29) interceding on earth for Israel, and also of the Divine Word or Logos giving efficacy in heaven to the intercession of the priest upon earth: 'It was necessary that the priest who is consecrated to the Father of the world should employ an *Advocate* most perfect in efficacy, even the Son, for the blotting-out of sins and the obtaining of abundant blessings' (*De Vita Mosis*, III. xiv. 155). It is evident that the whole passage—'the blood of Jesus cleanseth us', 'to cleanse us from all unrighteousness', 'Advocate', 'propitiation'—points back to the Mosaic purifications by the blood of victims, and especially to the intercession of the high-priest with the blood of the bullock and the goat on the Day of Atonement. That great type, S. John affirms, has been fulfilled in Jesus Christ. Comp. Heb. ix. 24.

with the Father] Literally, *towards the Father*. The idea is either that of *turning towards* in order to *plead* with Him; or, as in i. 2 and John i. 1, *at home* with Him, ever before His face. 'The Father' rather than 'God', to bring out the point that our Advocate is His Son; and that through Him we also are made sons. It is not a stern judge but a loving Father before whom He has to plead.

Jesus Christ the righteous] Or, *a righteous one:* there is no article in the Greek. But in English 'the righteous' comes nearer to the Greek than the apparently more exact 'a righteous one'. It is as being righteous Himself that He can so well plead with the 'righteous Father' for our sins: and not for ours only, but also for *the sins of*

(John xvii. 25; 1 John 9) for those who are not righteous. And, as Bede remarks, "a righteous advocate does not undertake unrighteous causes." It is the Sinless Man, the perfected and glorified Jesus, who pleads for sinners before the Throne of God. Note that neither in the body of the Epistle, any more than in the body of the Gospel, does S. John speak of Christ as 'the Word'. In both cases that title is used in the Introduction only. When he speaks of the historic person Jesus Christ, S. John uses the name by which He is known in history. Of the perfect righteousness of this Man S. John has personal knowledge, and he alludes to it repeatedly in this Epistle.

2. *And He is the propitiation*] Or, *And He* **Himself** *is a propitiation:* there is no article in the Greek. Note the present tense throughout; 'we_have an Advocate, He *is* a propitiation': this condition of things is perpetual, it is not something which took place once for all long ago. In His glorified Body the Son is ever acting thus. Contrast 'He laid down His life for us' (iii. 16). Beware of the unsatisfactory explanation that 'propitiation' is the abstract for the concrete, 'propitiation' (ἱλασμός) for 'propitiator' (ἱλαστήρ). Had S. John written 'propitiator' we should have lost half the truth; viz. that our Advocate propitiates by offering *Himself*. He is both High Priest and Victim, both Propitiator and Propitiation. It is quite obvious that He is the former; the office of Advocate includes it. It is not at all obvious that He is the latter: very rarely does an advocate offer himself as a propitiation.

The word for 'propitiation' occurs nowhere in N. T. but here and in iv. 10; in both places without the article and followed by 'for our sins'. It signifies any action which has *expiation* as its object, whether prayer, compensation, or sacrifice. Thus 'the ram of the atonement' (Num. v. 8) is 'the ram of the propitiation' or 'expiation', where the same Greek word as is used here is used in the LXX. Comp. Ezek. xliv. 27; Num. xxix. 11; Lev. xxv. 9. The LXX. of 'there is forgiveness with Thee' (Ps. cxxx. 4) is remarkable: literally rendered it is 'before Thee is the propitiation' (ὁ ἱλασμός). So also the Vulgate, *apud Te propitiatio est*. And this is the idea that we have here: Jesus Christ, as being righteous, is ever present before the Lord as the propitiation. With this we should compare the use of the cognate verb in Heb. ii. 17 and cognate substantive Rom. iii. 25 and Heb. ix. 5. From these passages it is clear that in N. T. the word is closely connected with that special form of expiation which takes place by means of an *offering* or *sacrifice*, although this idea is not of necessity included in the radical signification of the word itself. See notes in all three places.

for our sins] Literally, *concerning* (περί) *our sins:* our sins are the matter *respecting which* the propitiation goes on. This is the common form of expression in LXX. Comp. Num. xxix. 11; Exod. xxx. 15, 16, xxxii. 30; Lev. iv. 20, 26, 31, 35, &c. &c. Similarly, in John viii. 46, 'Which of you convicteth Me of sin?' is literally, 'Which of you convicteth Me *concerning* sin?' Comp. John xvi. 8, x. 33. Notice that it

the whole world. **And hereby we do know that we know** 3 is 'our sins', not 'our sin': the sins which we are daily committing, and not merely the sinfulness of our nature, are the subject of the propitiation.

and not for ours only, but also for the sins of the whole world] More literally, *but also* **for the whole world**: 'the sins of' is not repeated in the Greek and is not needed in English. Once more we have a parallel with the Gospel, and especially with chap. xvii. 'Neither for these only do I pray, but for them also that shall believe on Me through their word...that *the world* may believe that Thou didst send Me...that *the world* may know that Thou didst send Me, and lovedst them, even as Thou lovedst Me' (xvii. 20—23): 'Behold, the Lamb of God, which *taketh away the sin of the world*' (John i. 29): 'We know that this is indeed *the Saviour of the world*' (iv. 24). Comp. 1 John iv. 14. S. John's writings are so full of the fundamental opposition between Christ or believers and the world, that there was danger lest he should seem to give his sanction to a Christian exclusiveness as fatal as the Jewish exclusiveness out of which he and other converts from Judaism had been delivered. Therefore by this (note especially 'the *whole* world') and other plain statements both in Gospel (see xi. 51 in particular) and Epistle he insists that believers have no exclusive right to the merits of Christ. The expiatory offering was made for the whole world without limitation. All who will may profit by it: *quam late peccatum, tam late propitiatio* (Bengel). The disabilities under which the whole human race had laboured were removed. It remained to be seen who would avail themselves of the restored privileges. 'The world' (ὁ κόσμος) is another of S. John's characteristic expressions. In his writings it generally means those who are *alienated from God*, outside the pale of the Church. But we should fall into grievous error if we assigned this meaning to the word indiscriminately. Thus, in 'the world was made by Him' (John i. 10) it means 'the universe'; in 'This is of a truth the Prophet that cometh into the world' (John vi. 14) it means 'the earth'; in 'God so loved the world' (John iii. 16) it means, as here, 'the inhabitants of the earth, the human race'. But still the prevalent meaning in both Gospel and Epistle is a *bad* one; 'those who have not accepted the Christ, unbelievers.' In the Apocalypse it occurs only thrice, once in the usual sense, 'The kingdom of the world is become the kingdom of our Lord' (xi. 15), and twice in the sense of 'the universe' (xiii. 8, xvii. 8).

3. *hereby we do know that we know Him*] Or, **herein we come to know** *that we know Him:* in the Greek we have the present and perfect of the verb which means 'to come to know, perceive, recognise' (γινώσκειν); the perfect of which, 'I have come to know'='I know.' Comp. the Collect for the First Sunday after Epiphany; 'that they may both *perceive and know* what things they ought to do.' Progressive knowledge gained by experience is implied. 'Herein' followed by 'if', or 'that', or 'because', or 'when', is a frequent construction in S. John: ii. 5, iii. 16, 19, iv. 9, 10, 13, 17, v. 2; John xiii. 35, xv. 8. Excepting Luke x. 20, it occurs nowhere else in N. T.

4 him, if we keep his commandments. He that saith, I know him, and keepeth not his commandments, is a liar, and the 5 truth is not in him. But whoso keepeth his word, in him

if we keep His commandments] This is equivalent to 'not sinning' in v. 1, and to 'walking in the light' in i. 6. There is no real knowledge of God, no fellowship with Him, without practical conformity to His will. *Nam quisquis eum non amat, profecto ostendit, quia quam sit amabilis, non novit* (Bede). S. John is again condemning that Gnostic doctrine which made excellence to consist in mere intellectual enlightenment. Divorced from holiness of life, says S. John, no enlightenment can be a knowledge of God. In his system of Christian Ethics the Apostle insists no less than Aristotle, that in morals knowledge without practice is worthless: 'not speculation but conduct' is the aim of both the Christian and the heathen philosopher. Mere knowledge will not do: nor will knowledge 'touched by emotion' do. It is possible to know, and admire, and in a sort of way love, and yet act as if we had not known. But S. John gives no encouragement to devotion without a moral *life* (comp. i. 6). There is only one way of proving to ourselves that we know God, and that is by loving obedience to His will. Compare the very high standard of virtue set by Aristotle: he only is a virtuous man who does virtuous acts, "first, knowingly; secondly, from deliberate preference, and deliberate preference for the sake of the acts (and not any advantages resulting from them); and thirdly, with firm and unvarying purpose" (*Nic. Eth.* II. iv. 3).

The phrase 'to keep (His) commandments' or 'keep (His) word' is of frequent occurrence in S. John's writings, Gospel (xiv. 15, 21, xv. 10; viii. 51, 52, 55, xiv. 23, xv. 20, xvii. 6), Epistle (ii. 4, iii. 22, 24, v. [2,] 3; ii. 5) and Revelation (xii. 17, xiv. 12; iii. 8, 10). Comp. John xiv. 24; Rev. xxii. 7, 9. The word 'to keep' (τηρεῖν) means to be on the watch to obey and fulfil; it covers both outward and inward observance.

4. The previous statement is enforced by denying the opposite of it. The construction, 'he that saith,' 'he that loveth,' &c. now takes the place of 'if we say,' 'if we walk,' &c., but without change of meaning; and this continues down to v. 11, after which both constructions cease and a new division begins. Comp. i. 6, which is exactly parallel to this: 'to know Him' = 'to have fellowship with Him,' and 'not to keep His commandments' = 'to walk in darkness.'

and keepeth not] By the negative which he uses (μή) S. John states the case as gently as possible, without asserting that any such person exists (see on v. 10).

5. The statement in v. 3 is still further emphasized by taking the opposite of v. 4; but with this we do not return to v. 3, but have an expansion of it.

His word] A wider expression than 'His commandments', covering the sum total of the revelation of God's will: comp. v. 14. Thus Christ says, 'He that hath My commandments, and keepeth them, he it is that loveth Me' (John xiv. 21).

vv. 6, 7.] I. JOHN, II. 91

verily is the love of God perfected: hereby know we that
we are in him. He that saith *he* abideth in him ought 6
himself also so to walk, even as he walked. Brethren, I 7

verily] Or, *truly*, or, *of a truth*. S. John uses this word (ἀληθῶς)
about 8 times; and in the rest of N. T. it occurs about 8 times:
see on i. 6. It must not be confounded with the 'verily' (ἀμήν) in our
Lord's discourses. Here it stands first for emphasis; *verily in him:*
comp. John viii. 31.

is the love of God perfected] Or, *the love of God hath been perfected*.
We need both renderings in order to bring out the full force of the
Greek, which means 'has been made perfect and remains so'. Obedi‑
ence, not feeling, is the test of perfect love. This declaration shews
that it is quite wrong to make 'we know Him' in v. 3 and 'I know
Him' in v. 4 a Hebraism for '*love* Him'. Even if 'know' is ever used in
the sense of 'love', which may be doubted, S. John would hardly in the
same sentence use 'know' in two totally different senses (v. 3). S. John's
mention of love here shews that when he means 'love' he writes 'love'
and not 'know'. He declares that true knowledge involves love, but
they are not identical, any more than convex and concave. 'The love
of God' here means 'the love of man to God': this is the common usage
in this Epistle (ii. 15, iii. 17, iv. 12, v. 3). Only once is the genitive
subjective and means 'the love of God for man'; and there the context
makes this quite clear (iv. 9). 'Love,' both verb and substantive, is one
of S. John's favourite words. His Gospel is the Gospel of Love and his
Epistle the Epistle of Love. 'To perfect' is also much more common
in his writings than elsewhere in N. T., excepting the Epistle to the
Hebrews, especially in the passive voice (iv. 12, 17, 18; John xvii. 23,
xix. 28). S. John is here speaking, as often in this Epistle, of an *ideal*
state of things. No Christian's love to God is perfect: but the more ·
perfect his knowledge, the more perfect his obedience and his love.

hereby we know] Or, *Herein we come to know:* it is the same phrase
as in v. 3, and should probably, as there, be taken with what follows,
rather than with what precedes. It belongs to v. 6 more than to v. 5,
and is parallel to i. 6.

6. *He that saith*] He who declares his position is morally bound to
act up to the declaration which he has made. To profess to abide in God
involves an obligation to imitate the Son, who is the concrete expression
of God's will. 'To abide' is another of the Apostle's very favourite
expressions, a fact greatly obscured in A. V. by capricious changes of
rendering: see on v. 24. 'To abide in' implies *habitual* fellowship.
Note the climax; to know Him (v. 3), to abide in Him (v. 5), to abide in
Him (v. 6): *cognitio, communio, constantia* (Bengel).

ought] It is a debt which he owes (ὀφείλει, *debet*). S. John does not
say 'must' (δεῖ, *oportet*) which might seem to imply constraint. The
obligation is internal and personal. 'Must' (δεῖ), frequent in the
Gospel, does not occur in these Epistles.

even as He walked] Not simply 'as' (ὡς) but 'even as' (καθώς): the
imitation must be exact. The 'He' is a different pronoun (ἐκεῖνος) from

write no new commandment unto you, but an old commandment which ye had from the beginning. The old commandment is the word which ye have heard from the

the preceding 'Him' (αὐτῷ), and this with the context makes it almost certain that while 'in Him' means 'in God', 'even as He walked' refers to Christ. Comp. iii. 3, 5, 7, 16, iv. 17. For 'even as' comp. *vv.* 18, 27, iii. 2, 12, 23; Luke vi. 36, &c. &c. and for 'even as He' comp. iii. 3, 7, iv. 17. S. Peter declares that Christ has 'left us an example, that we should follow His steps' (1 Pet. ii. 21).

7—11. LOVE OF THE BRETHREN.

7—11. Walking in the light involves not only fellowship with God and with the brethren (i. 5—7), consciousness and confession of sin (i. 8—10), obedience by imitation of Christ (ii. 1—6), but also *love of the brethren*. In nothing did Christ more express the Father's Nature and Will than by His love: therefore in obeying the Father by imitating Christ we also must love. "This whole Epistle which we have undertaken to expound to you, see whether it commendeth aught else than this one thing, charity. Nor need we fear lest by much speaking thereof it come to be hateful. For what is there to love, if charity come to be hateful?" (S. Augustine). Comp. iii. 10, iv. 7.

7. *Brethren*] The true reading is **Beloved**. This form of address is specially suitable to this section (*vv.* 7—11), in which the subject of *love* appears. In the second part of the Epistle, in which love is the main topic, this form of address becomes the prevailing one (iii. 2, 21, iv. 1, 7, 11).

I write no new commandment] The order of the Greek is worth keeping: *not a new commandment do I write*. What commandment is meant? To imitate Christ (*v.* 6)? Or, to practise brotherly love (*vv.* 9—11)? Practically it makes little matter which answer we give, for at bottom these are one and the same. They are different aspects of *walking in the light*. But a definite command of some kind is meant, not vaguely the whole Gospel: had he meant the latter, S. John would rather have said 'the word' or 'the truth'. See on *v.* 11.

from the beginning] As already noticed on i. 1, the meaning of 'beginning' must always depend upon the context. Several interpretations have been suggested here, and all make good sense. (1) From the beginning *of the human race:* brotherly love is an original human instinct. Christian Ethics are here as old as humanity. (2) From the beginning *of the Law:* 'Thou shalt love thy neighbour as thyself' (Lev. xix. 18) was commanded by Moses. Christian Ethics are in this only a repetition of Judaism. (3) From the beginning *of your life as Christians:* this was one of the first things ye were taught. On the whole this seems best, especially as we have the aorist, *which* **ye heard**, not the perfect, as A. V., *ye have heard* (see on *v.* 18): comp. *v.* 24 and especially iii. 11; 2 John 5, 6. The second 'from the beginning' is not genuine.

beginning. Again, a new commandment I write unto you, 3
which *thing* is true in him and in you: because the darkness
is past, and the true light now shineth. He that saith *he* 9

8. *Again, a new commandment I write unto you, which thing is true*]
Or, *Again*, as *a new commandment I write unto you* **a thing which** *is
true*. Or, *Again, a new commandment write I unto you*, **namely that
which** *is true*. It is difficult to decide between these three renderings;
but the third is simpler than the first. Both Tyndale and the Genevan
Version have 'a thing that is true'. If we adopt the rendering of A. V.
and R. V., the meaning seems to be, that *the newness of the commandment is* true, both in the case of Christ, who promulgated it afresh,
and in the case of you, who received it afresh. If we prefer the simpler
rendering, the meaning will be, that what has already been shewn to be
true by the pattern life of Christ and by the efforts of Christians to
imitate it, is now given by S. John as a new commandment. The
'Again' introduces a new view: that which from one point of view was
an old commandment, from another was a new one. It was old, but
not obsolete, ancient but not antiquated : it had been renewed in a fuller
sense; it had received a fresh sanction. Thus both those who feared
innovations and those who disliked what was stale might feel satisfied.

in Him and in you] Note the double preposition, implying that it is
true in the case of Christ in a different sense from that in which it is
true in the case of Christians. He reissued the commandment and was
the living embodiment and example of it; they accepted it and
endeavoured to follow it : both illustrated its truth and soundness.
See on i. 3, where 'with' is repeated, and on John xx. 2, where 'to' is
repeated. The reading 'in us' is certainly to be rejected.

because the darkness is past] Rather, *is* **passing away** (*v*. 17):
present tense of a process still going on (*v*. 17). All earlier English
Versions are wrong here, from Wiclif onwards, misled by *transierunt
tenebrae* in the Vulgate. On 'darkness' see on i. 5. The 'because'
introduces the reason why he writes as a new commandment what has
been proved true by the example of Christ and their own experience.
The ideal state of things, to which the perfect fulfilment of this commandment belongs, has already begun : 'The darkness is on the wane,
the true light is shewing its power; *therefore* I bid you to walk as
children of light'. Comp. 1 Thess. v. 5.

the true light now shineth] Or, **the light, the true (light), is already
shining** or, *giving light:* the article is repeated, as in the case of 'the
life, the eternal (life)' in i. 2, and 'the commandment, the old (commandment)' in *v*. 7 ; and if we have 'is passing' rather than 'passeth', we should have 'is shining' rather than 'shineth'. Here we have
not precisely the same word for 'true' as in the previous sentence.
In 'a thing which is true' (ἀληθές) 'true' is opposed to 'lying': here
'true' (ἀληθινόν) is opposed to 'spurious', and is just the old English
'very'. In 'Very God of very God' in the Nicene Creed, 'very'
represents the word here rendered 'true'. 'True' in this sense means
'genuine', or 'that which realises the idea formed of it', and hence

is in the light, and hateth his brother, is in darkness *even* 10 until now. He that loveth his brother abideth in the light,

'perfect'. Christ and the Gospel are 'the perfect light' in opposition to the imperfect light of the Law and the Prophets and the false light of Gnostic philosophy. This form of the word 'true,' is almost peculiar to S. John: it occurs 4 times in this Epistle, 9 times in the Gospel and 10 times in the Apocalypse: elsewhere in the N.T. only 5 times. Christ in the Gospel is called 'the perfect Vine' (xv. 1), 'the perfect Bread' (vi. 32) and 'the perfect Light' (i. 9). It is comparatively unimportant whether we interpret 'the perfect light' here to mean Christ, or the light of the truth, or the kingdom of heaven: but John i. 5, 9 will certainly incline us to the first of these interpretations. The contrast with the impersonal darkness does not disprove this here any more than in John i. 5. Darkness is never personal; it is not an effluence from Satan as light is from God or from Christ. It is the result, not of the presence of the evil one, but of the absence of God. Comp. 'Ye were once darkness, but now light in the Lord: walk as children of light' (Eph. v. 8).

9—11. The form of these three verses is similar to that of *vv*. 3—5, and still more so to i. 8—10. In each of these three triplets a case is placed between two statements of the opposite to it; confession of sin, obedience, and love, between two statements of denial of sin, disobedience, and hate. But in none of the triplets do we go from one opposite to the other and back again: in each case the side from which we start is restated in such a way as to constitute a distinct advance upon the original position. There is no weak tautology or barren see-saw. The emphasis grows and is marked by the increase in the predicates. In *v*. 9 we have *one;* 'is in darkness even until now'; in *v*. 10, *two;* 'abideth in the light, and there is none, &c.'; in *v*. 11, *three;* 'is in the darkness, and walketh &c., and knoweth not &c.'.

9. For the fifth time the Apostle indicates a possible inconsistency of a very gross kind between profession and conduct (i. 6, 8, 10, ii. 4). We shall have a sixth in iv. 20. In most of these passages he is aiming at some of the Gnostic teaching already prevalent. And this introduces a fresh pair of contrasts. We have had light and darkness, truth and falsehood; we now have love and hate.

his brother] Does this mean 'his fellow-Christian' or 'his fellow-man', whether Christian or not? The common meaning in N.T. is the former; and though there are passages where 'brother' seems to have the wider signification, e.g. Matt. v. 22; Luke vi. 41; Jas. iv. 11, yet even here the spiritual bond of brotherhood is perhaps in the background. In S. John's writings, where it does not mean actual relationship, it seems generally if not universally to mean 'Christians': not that other members of the human race are excluded, but they are not under consideration. Just as in the allegories of the Fold and of the Good Shepherd, nothing is said about goats, and in that of the Vine nothing is said about the branches of other trees; so here in the great family of the Father nothing is said about those who do not know Him.

I. JOHN, II.

and there is none occasion of stumbling in him. But he 11

They are not shut out, but they are not definitely included. In *this Epistle* this passage, iii. 10, 14—17 and iv. 20, 21, are somewhat open to doubt: but v. 1, 2 seems very distinctly in favour of the more limited meaning; and in v. 16 the sinning 'brother' is certainly a fellow-Christian. In 2 John the word does not occur: 3 John 3, 5, 10 confirm the view here taken. In the *Gospel* the word is generally used of actual relationship: but in the two passages where it is used otherwise it means Christians: in xx. 17, Christ speaks of the disciples as 'My brethren', and in xxi. 23, Christians are called 'the brethren'. In the *Apocalypse*, omitting xxii. 9 as doubtful, all the passages where the word occurs require the meaning 'Christian' (i. 9, vi. 11, xii. 10, xix. 10). Note that throughout this Epistle the singular is used; 'his *brother*', not 'his *brethren*'.

is in darkness even until now] Or, as in i. 6, in order to bring out the full contrast with the light, *is in* **the** *darkness*. 'Even until now', i.e. in spite of the light which 'is *already* shining', and of which he has so little real experience that he believes light and hatred to be compatible. Years before this S. Paul had declared (1 Cor. xiii. 2), 'If I have the gift of prophecy, and know all mysteries and all knowledge,... but have not love, I am nothing.' The light in a man is darkness until it is warmed by love. The convert from heathendom who professes Christianity and hates his brother, says S. Augustine, is in darkness even until now. "There is no need to expound; but to rejoice if it be not so, to bewail, if it be." The word for 'now' (ἄρτι) is specially frequent in S. John's Gospel: it indicates the present moment not absolutely, but in relation to the past or the future. The peculiar combination, 'even until now' (ἕως ἄρτι) occurs John ii. 10, v. 17, xvi. 24; Matt. xi. 12; 1 Cor. iv. 13, viii. 7, xv. 6, a fact much obscured in A.V. by the variety of renderings; 'until now', 'hitherto', 'unto this day', 'unto this hour', 'unto this present'.

10. *abideth in the light*] Not only has entered into it but has made it his *abode*: see on *v.* 24.

there is none occasion of stumbling in him] There are several ways of taking this. 1. He has *in him* nothing likely to ensnare *him* or cause *him* to stumble. 2. He has *in him* nothing likely to cause *others* to stumble. 3. There is *in his case* nothing likely to cause stumbling. 4. *In the light* there is nothing likely to cause stumbling;—the Greek for 'in him' being either masculine or neuter, and therefore capable of meaning 'in it'. All make good sense, and the last makes a good antithesis to 'knoweth not whither he goeth' in *v.* 11: but the first is to be preferred on account of *v.* 11. Yet in favour of the second it is worth noting that σκάνδαλον is commonly, if not always, used of offence caused to *others*. The parallel expressions 'the truth is not in him' (*v.* 4), 'His word is not in us' (i. 10; comp. i. 8), make 'in him' more probable than 'in his case'. And nothing here suggests the notion that the brother-hater leads *others* astray: it is his own dark condition that is contemplated. Moreover, there is the very close parallel in John xi. 9, 10;

that hateth his brother is in darkness, and walketh in darkness, and knoweth not whither he goeth, because that darkness hath blinded his eyes.

'If a man walk in the day, he stumbleth not, because he seeth the light of this world. But if a man walk in the night, he stumbleth, because the light is not in him.' Comp. Ps. cxix. 165, 'Great peace have they which love Thy law: and nothing shall offend them'; i.e. there is no stumbling-block before them. Where the LXX. is very similar to this passage, omitting the preposition 'in'.

11. *is in darkness and walketh in darkness*] The *darkness* is his home and the scene of his activity. 'The way of the wicked is as darkness: they know not at what they stumble' (Prov. iv. 19).

knoweth not whither he goeth] Literally, *where he is going*: the adverb (ποῦ) is properly one of rest, 'where', and not of motion, 'whither'. But in S. John this adverb is often joined with verbs of motion, and in particular with the verb used here (ὑπάγειν): John iii. 8, viii. 14, xii. 35, 36, xiv. 5, xvi. 5; vii. 35. Elsewhere in the N.T. the construction occurs only Heb. xi. 8. Perhaps both rest and motion are included; 'knoweth not where he is and whither he is going': i.e. neither knows his sin nor the direction in which his sin leads him. It is perhaps a little too definite to explain with S. Cyprian (*On Jealousy and Envy*, XI.), "for he is going without knowing it to Gehenna; in ignorance and blindness he is hurrying to punishment." Comp. John xii. 35, which is almost word for word the same as this, forming another point of contact between Gospel and Epistle.

because that darkness hath blinded] Or, *because* **the** *darkness hath blinded*. It is literally 'blinded', not 'hath blinded', of what took place once for all some time ago: but this is just one of those cases where it is the Greek idiom to use the aorist, but the English idiom to use the perfect; and therefore the Greek aorist should be rendered by the English perfect. 'Blinded' must not be weakened into 'dimmed': the verb means definitely 'to make blind' (John xii. 40; 2 Cor. iv. 4). Animals kept in the dark, e.g. ponies in coal-mines, become blind: the organ that is never exercised loses its power. So also the conscience that is constantly ignored at last ceases to act. The source of the metaphor is perhaps Is. vi. 10: comp. Rom. xi. 10.

Before proceeding further let us briefly sum up the Apostle's line of argument thus far. 'God is light. Christ is that light revealed. The life of Christ was a life of obedience and a life of love. In order, therefore, to have fellowship through Him with God believers must obey and love. The state of things in which this is possible has already begun. Therefore I write to you a command which is both old and new; walk in the light by imitating the love of Christ.' In this manner he lays the foundations of Christian Ethics. The last three verses (9—11) shew that the special aspect of walking in light which is referred to in the commandment which is at once old and new is *love*: and if this be so, we can hardly doubt that in calling it 'a new commandment' he has in his mind Christ's farewell words, John xiii. 34;

'A new commandment I give unto you, that ye love one another; even as I have loved you, that ye also love one another.' The latter half of the verse is, therefore, the special interpretation of 'ought himself also to walk even as He walked'.

It is not easy to determine whether the division which follows (*vv.* 12—28) is best regarded as a subdivision of the first main portion of the Epistle, or as a co-ordinate portion. In favour of the latter view are these facts: 1. The idea of *light* which runs through the whole of the division just concluded (i. 5—ii. 11), and which is mentioned six times in it, now disappears altogether. 2. The Epistle now takes a distinctly hortatory turn. The first part lays down principles: this part gives warnings and exhortations. 3. The Apostle seems to make a fresh start: *vv.* 12—14 read like a new Introduction. In favour of making this part a subdivision of the first main division it may be urged:—1. Though the idea of light is no longer mentioned, yet other ideas to which it directly led, love, the truth, abiding in God, still continue: the parts evidently overlap. 2. The hortatory turn is only a partial change of form occurring merely in *vv.* 15 and 28. In the intermediate verses the aphoristic mode of expression continues. 3. The quasi-Introduction in *vv.* 12—14 no more constitutes a fresh division than the similar addresses in *vv.* 1 and 7.

On the whole it seems best to consider what follows as a subordinate part of the first main division of the Epistle. Thus far we have had THE CONDITION AND CONDUCT OF THE BELIEVER considered on its *positive side*. We now have the *negative side*—WHAT WALKING IN THE LIGHT EXCLUDES.

12—28. THE THINGS AND PERSONS TO BE AVOIDED.

These are summed up under two heads: i. *The World and the Things in the World* (15—17); ii. *Antichrists* (18—26). The section begins with a *threefold statement* of the happy experiences which those addressed have had in the Gospel, and gives these as a reason for their being addressed (12—14), and ends with an *exhortation to abide in Christ* as the best safeguard from the dangers against which the Apostle has been warning them (27, 28).

12—14. THREEFOLD STATEMENT OF REASONS FOR WRITING.

" Hitherto St John has stated briefly the main scope of his Epistle. He has shewn what is the great problem of life, and how the Gospel meets it with an answer and a law complete and progressive, old and new. He now pauses, as it were to contemplate those whom he is addressing more distinctly and directly, and to gather up in a more definite form the charge which is at once the foundation and the end of all he writes" (Westcott).

These verses have given rise to much discussion (1) as to the different classes addressed, (2) as to the meaning of the change of tense, from 'I write' to 'I wrote' or 'have written'.

(1) It will be observed that we have two triplets, each consisting of little children, fathers and young men. There is a slight change of

wording in the Greek not apparent in the English, the word for 'little children' in the first triplet (τεκνία) being not the same as in the second (παιδία). But this need not make us give a different interpretation in each case. 'Little children' throughout the Epistle, whether expressed as in vv. 14 and 18 (παιδία), or as in vv. 1, 12, 28, iii. 7, 18, iv. 4, v. 21 (τεκνία), probably means the Apostle's readers generally, and has nothing to do with age or with standing in the Christian community. It indicates neither those who are of tender years, nor those who are young in the faith. It is a term of affection for all the Apostle's 'dear children'. But this is not the case with either 'fathers' or 'young men'. These terms are probably in each triplet to be understood of the older and younger men among the Christians addressed. This fully accounts for the order in each triplet; first the whole community, then the old, then the young. If 'little children' had reference to age, we should have had either 'children, youths, fathers', or 'fathers, youths, children'. There is, however, something to be said for the view that *all* S. John's readers are addressed *in all three cases*, the Christian life of all having analogies with youth, manhood, and age; with the innocence of childhood, the strength of prime, and the experience of full maturity.

(2) The change of tense cannot be explained with so much confidence. But an important correction of reading must first be noticed. We ought not to read with A.V. 'I write' four times and then 'I have written' twice: but with R.V. 'I write' thrice and then 'I have written' or 'I wrote' thrice. This correction confirms the explanation given above of the different classes addressed. The following interpretations of the change from the present to the aorist have been suggested. 1. 'I write' refers to the Epistle, 'I wrote' to the Gospel which it accompanies. The Apostle first gives reasons why he *is writing* this letter to the Church and to particular portions of it; and then gives reasons, partly the same and partly not, why *he wrote* the Gospel to which it makes such frequent allusions. On the whole this seems most satisfactory. It gives a thoroughly intelligible meaning to each tense and accounts for the abrupt change. 2. 'I write' refers to this Epistle; 'I wrote' to a former Epistle. But of any former Epistle we have no evidence whatever. 3. 'I write' refers to the whole Epistle; 'I wrote' to the first part down to ii. 11. But would S. John have *first* said that he wrote the *whole* letter for certain reasons, and *then* said that he wrote a *portion* of it for much the same reasons? Had 'I wrote' preceded 'I write', and had the reasons in each triplet been more different, this explanation would have been more satisfactory. 4. 'I write' refers to what follows, 'I wrote' to what precedes. This is a *construction louche* indeed! The objection urged against the preceding explanation applies still more strongly. 5. 'I write' is written from the writer's point of view, 'I wrote' from the reader's point of view: the latter is the epistolary aorist, like *scripsi* or *scribebam* in Latin (comp. Phil. ii. 25, 28; Philem. 12, and especially 19 and 21). But is it likely that S. John would make three statements from his own stand-point, and then repeat them from his readers' stand-point? And if so, why make any change in them? 6. The repetition is made for emphasis. This explains the repetition, but not the change of tense. Hence 'What

I write unto you, little children, because *your* sins are 12
forgiven you for his name's sake. I write unto you, fathers, 13
because ye have known him that is from the beginning.

I have written, I have written' (John xix. 22), and 'Rejoice...and again I will say, rejoice' (Phil. iv. 4) are not analogous; for there the same *tense* is repeated. 7. S. John may have left off writing at the end of *v*. 13, and then on resuming may have partly repeated himself from the new point of time, saying 'I wrote' where he had previously said 'I write'. This is conceivable, but is a little fine-drawn.—Without, therefore, confidently affirming that it is the right explanation, we fall back upon the one first stated, as intelligible in itself and more satisfactory than the others.

little children] All his readers; as in *vv*. 1, 28, iii. 7, 18, &c.

because your sins are forgiven you] Some would render '*that* your sins are forgiven you'; and so in each of these sentences substituting 'that' for 'because'. This is grammatically quite possible, but is otherwise highly improbable: comp. *v*. 21. S. John is not telling them *what* he is writing, but *why* he writes it. The forgiveness of sins is the very first condition of Christian morals (i. 7); therefore he reminds them all of this first.

for His name's sake] Of course Jesus Christ's. It was by believing on *His Name* that they acquired the right to become children of God (John i. 12). 'The Name of Jesus Christ' is not a mere periphrasis for Jesus Christ. Names in Scripture are constantly given as marks of character possessed or of functions to be performed. This is the case with all the Divine Names. The Name of Jesus Christ indicates His attributes and His relations to man and to God. It is through these that the sins of S. John's dear children have been forgiven.

13. *fathers*] The older men among his readers: comp. Jud. xvii. 10, xviii. 19; 2 Kings ii. 12, vi. 21, xiii. 14. The address stands alone in N. T. The nearest approaches to it are Eph. vi. 4 and Col. iii. 21, where the actual fathers of children are addressed. S. Augustine thinks that *all* the readers are included throughout. Christians from one point of view are children, from another young men, and from another old men. This is possible, but it ignores the order in which the three groups are ranged. Comp. Tit. ii. 1—8, where S. Paul in like manner gives directions as to the exhortations suitable for Christians of different ages.

ye have known] Rather, **ye know**: 'ye have come to know and therefore know', as in *v*. 3. The word expresses the result of progressive experience, and is therefore very suitable to the knowledge possessed by the old.

Him which is from the beginning] Christ, not the Father, as is plain from the opening words of the Epistle. Moreover, S. John never speaks of the First Person of the Godhead under any designation but 'God' or 'the Father'. By the knowledge which these older Christians had come to possess of Christ is certainly not meant having seen Him in the flesh. Very few of S. John's readers could have done that; and if they

I write unto you, young men, because you have overcome the wicked one. I write unto you, little children, because
14 ye have known the Father. I have written unto you, fathers, because ye have known him that is from the beginning. I have written unto you, young men, because ye are strong, and the word of God abideth in you, and ye

had, S. John would not have attached any moral or spiritual value to the fact. Besides which to express this we should expect 'ye have seen Jesus Christ', rather than 'ye have come to know Him that was from the beginning'.

young men] The younger among his readers, men in the prime of life.

ye have overcome] Comp. John xvi. 33. Throughout both Gospel and Epistle S. John regards eternal life as a prize already won by the believer (John iii. 36, v. 24, vi. 47, 54, xvii. 3): the contest is not to gain, but to retain. We have perfects in each case ('have been forgiven', 'have come to know', 'have overcome'), expressing, as so frequently in S. John, the abiding result of past action. He bases his appeals to the young on the victory which their strength has gained, just as he bases his appeals to the old on the knowledge which their experience has gained.

the wicked one] It is important to have a uniform rendering for the word here used ($\pi o \nu \eta \rho \acute{o}s$), respecting which there has been so much controversy with regard to the last petition in the Lord's Prayer. The A. V., following earlier Versions, wavers between 'wicked' and 'evil', even in the same verse (iii. 12). 'Evil' is to be preferred throughout. Almost all are agreed that *the evil one* here means the devil, although the Genevan Version has 'the evil *man*', as in Matt. xii. 35. Wiclif, Tyndale, and Cranmer supply neither 'man' nor 'one', but write 'the wicked' or 'that wicked.' 'The wicked' in English would inevitably be understood as plural. For this name for Satan comp. v. 18; Matt. xiii. 19 and also 1 John iii. 12, v. 19; John xvii. 15; Eph. vi. 16. In these last four passages the gender, though probably masculine, may, as in Matt. vi. 13, possibly be neuter.

I write unto you, little children] The true reading, as determined by both internal and external evidence, certainly gives **I have written** or **I wrote.** The second triplet begins here, 'little ones' ($\pi\alpha\iota\delta\acute{\iota}\alpha$, which occurs as a form of address nowhere else in N. T. except *v.* 18 and John xxi. 5), meaning, as before, *all* his readers.

ye have known the Father] Or, as in *vv.* 3 and 13, *ye* **know**. In *v.* 12 the Apostle attributes to them the possession of spiritual *peace* through the remission of sins: here he attributes to them the possession of spiritual *truth* through knowledge of the Father.

14. *because ye are strong*] Strong in the spiritual warfare in which they have already won the victory: comp. Heb. xi. 34, where, however, 'strong in war' probably refers to actual warfare between the Jews and other nations.

have overcome the wicked one. Love not the world, neither 15

the word of God abideth in you] An echo of John xv. 7. This is the secret of their strength and the source of their victory. They conquer because they are strong, and they are strong because God's word is ever in their hearts. They have God's will, especially as revealed in Scripture, and in particular in the Gospel, as a *permanent* power within them: hence the permanence of their victory. So long as they trust in this and not in themselves, and remember that their victory is not yet final, they may rejoice in the confidence which the consciousness of strength and of victory gives them.

It is plain from the context and from John v. 38, x. 35, xvii. 6, 14; Rev. i. 9, vi. 9, that 'the word of God' here does not mean the Word, the Son of God. S. John never uses the term 'Word' in this sense in the body either of his Gospel or of his Epistle, but only in the theological Introductions to each.

15—17. THE THINGS TO BE AVOIDED;—THE WORLD AND ITS WAYS.

Having reminded them solemnly of the blessedness of their condition as members of the Christian family, whether old or young, and having declared that this blessedness of peace, knowledge, and strength is his reason for writing to them, he goes on to exhort them to live in a manner that shall be worthy of this high estate, and to avoid all that is inconsistent with it.

15. *Love not the world*] The asyndeton is remarkable. S. John has just stated his premises, his readers' happiness as Christians. He now abruptly states the practical conclusion, without any introductory 'therefore'. As was said above on *v.* 2, we must distinguish between the various meanings of the Apostle's favourite word, 'world'. In John iii. 16 he tells us that 'God loved the world', and here he tells us that *we* must *not* do so. "S. John is never afraid of an apparent contradiction when it saves his readers from a real contradiction......The opposition which is on the surface of his language may be the best way of leading us to the harmony which lies below it" (Maurice). The world which the Father loves is the whole human race. The world which we are not to love is all that is alienated from Him, all that prevents men from loving Him in return. The world which God loves is His creature and His child: the world which we are not to love is His rival. The best safeguard against the selfish love of what is sinful in the world is to remember God's unselfish love of the world. 'The world' here is that from which S. James says the truly religious man keeps himself 'unspotted', friendship with which is 'enmity with God' (Jas. i. 27, iv. 4). It is not enough to say that 'the world' here means 'earthly things, so far as they tempt to sin', or 'sinful lusts', or 'worldly and impious men'. It means all of these together: all that acts as a rival to God; all that is alienated from God and opposed to Him, especially sinful men with their sinful lusts. 'The world' and 'the

the *things* that are in the world. If any *man* love the world,
15 the love of the Father is not in him. For all that is in the
world, the lust of the flesh, and the lust of the eyes, and the

darkness' are almost synonymous; to love the one is to love the other (John iii. 19): to be in the darkness is to be of the world.
neither the things that are in the world] Or, *nor yet the things, &c.*, i.e. 'Love not the world; no, nor anything in that sphere.' Comp. 'Not to consort with...no, nor eat with' (1 Cor. v. 11). 'The things in the world', as is plain from *v.* 16, are not material objects, which can be desired and possessed quite innocently, although they may also be occasions of sin. Rather, they are those elements in the world which are necessarily evil, its lusts and ambitions and jealousies, which stamp it as the kingdom of 'the ruler of this world' (John xii. 31) and not the kingdom of God.
If any man love the world] Once more, as in *v.* 1, the statement is made quite general by the hypothetical form: everyone who does so is in this case. The Lord had proclaimed the same principle; 'No man *can* serve two masters......Ye *cannot* serve God and mammon' (Matt. vi. 24). So also S. James; 'Whosoever would be a friend of the world maketh himself an enemy of God' (iv. 4). Comp. Gal. i. 10. Thus we arrive at another pair of those opposites of which S. John is so fond. We have had light and darkness, truth and falsehood, love and hate; we now have love of the Father and love of the world. The world which is coextensive with darkness must exclude the God who is light. By writing 'the love of the Father' rather than 'the love of God' (which some authorities read here) the Apostle points to the duty of Christians as *children* of God. 'The love of the Father' (a phrase which occurs nowhere else) means man's love to Him, not His to man: see on *v.* 5. A fragment of Philo declares that 'it is impossible for love to the world to coexist with love to God'.
16. Proof of the preceding statement by shewing the fundamental opposition in detail.
all that is in the world] Neuter singular: in *v.* 15 we had the neuter plural. The *material* contents of the universe cannot be meant. To say that these did not originate from God would be to contradict the Apostle himself (John i. 3, 10) and to affirm those Gnostic doctrines against which he is contending. The Gnostics, believing everything material to be radically evil, maintained that the universe was created, not by God, but by the evil one, or at least by an inferior deity. By 'all that is in the world' is meant the spirit which animates it, its tendencies and tone. These, which are utterly opposed to God, did not originate in Him, but in the free and rebellious wills of His creatures, seduced by 'the ruler of this world'.
the lust of the flesh] This does not mean the lust *for* the flesh, any more than 'the lust of the eyes' means the lust *for* the eyes. In both cases the genitive is not objective but subjective, as is generally the case with genitives after 'lust' ($\dot{\epsilon}\pi\iota\theta\nu\mu\iota\alpha$) in N. T. Comp. Rom. i. 24, Gal.

pride of life, is not of the Father, but is of the world. And 17
v. 16, Eph. ii. 3. The meaning is the lusts which have their seats in the flesh and in the eyes respectively.

"Tell me where is fancy bred.
* * * * *
It is *engendered in the eyes."*
Merchant of Venice, III. ii.

The former, therefore, will mean the desire for *unlawful pleasures of sense;* for enjoyments which are sinful either in themselves or as being excessive.

Note that S. John does not say 'the lust of the *body*'. 'The body' in N.T. is perhaps never used to denote the innately corrupt portion of man's nature: for that the common term is 'the flesh.' 'The body' is that neutral portion which may become either good or bad. It may be sanctified as the abode and instrument of the Spirit, or degraded under the tyranny of the flesh.

the lust of the eyes] The desire of seeing unlawful sights for the sake of the sinful pleasure to be derived from the sight; idle and prurient curiosity. Familiar as S. John's readers must have been with the foul and cruel exhibitions of the circus and amphitheatre, this statement would at once meet with their assent. Tertullian, though he does not quote this passage in his treatise *De Spectaculis*, is full of its spirit: " The source from which all circus games are taken pollutes them...... What is tainted taints us" (VII., VIII.). Similarly S. Augustine on this passage; "This it is that works in spectacles, in theatres, in sacraments of the devil, in magical arts, in witchcraft; none other than curiosity." See also *Confessions* VI. vii., viii., X. xxxv. 55.

the pride of life] Or, as R. V., *the* **vainglory** *of life.* Latin writers vary much in their renderings: *superbia vitae; ambitio saeculi; jactantia hujus vitae; jactantia vitae humanae.* The word (ἀλαζονεία) occurs elsewhere only Jas. iv. 16, and there in the plural; where A. V. has 'boastings' and R. V. 'vauntings'. The cognate adjective (ἀλαζών) occurs Rom. i. 30 and 2 Tim. iii. 2, where A.V. has 'boasters' and R.V. 'boastful'. Pretentious ostentation, as of a wandering mountebank, is the radical signification of the word. In classical Greek the pretentiousness is the predominant notion; in Hellenistic Greek, the ostentation. Compare the account of this vice in Aristotle (*Nic. Eth.* IV. vii.) with Wisd. v. 8, 2 Macc. ix. 8, xv. 6. Ostentatious pride in the things which one possesses is the signification of the term here; 'life' meaning 'means of life, goods, possessions'. The word for 'life' (βίος) is altogether different from that used in i. 1, 2 and elsewhere in the Epistle (ζωή). This word (βίος) occurs again iii. 17, and elsewhere in N.T. only 8 times, chiefly in S. Luke. The other word occurs 13 times in this Epistle, and elsewhere in N. T. over 100 times. This is what we might expect. The word used here means (1) *period of human life*, as 1 Tim. ii. 2; 2 Tim. ii. 4; (2) *means of life*, as here, iii. 17, Mark xii. 44; Luke viii. 14, 43, xv. 12, 30, xxi. 4 (in 1 Pet. iv. 3 the word is not

the world passeth away, and the lust thereof: but he that
18 doeth the will of God abideth for ever. Little children, it

genuine). With the duration of mortal life and the means of prolonging it the Gospel has comparatively little to do. It is concerned rather with that spiritual life which is not measured by time (i. 2), and which is independent of material wealth and food. For this the other word (ζωή) is invariably used. By 'the vainglory of life' then is meant *ostentatious pride in the possession of worldly resources*.
These three evil elements or tendencies 'in the world' are co-ordinate: no one of them includes the other two. The first two are wrongful desires of what is not possessed; the third is a wrongful behaviour with regard to what is possessed. The first two may be the vices of a solitary; the third requires society. We can have sinful desires when we are alone, but we cannot be ostentatious without company. See Appendix A.
is not of the Father] Does not derive its origin from (ἐκ) Him, and therefore has no natural likeness to Him or connexion with Him. S. John says 'the Father' rather than 'God' to emphasize the idea of parentage. Its origin is from the world and its ruler, the devil. Comp. 'Ye are of (ἐκ) your father the devil, and the lusts of your father ye will to do' (John viii. 44). The phrase 'to be of' is highly characteristic of S. John.
17. *and the world passeth away*] Or, **is passing away**; as in *v.* 8: the process is now going on. We owe the verb '*pass* away' here to Coverdale: it is a great improvement on Tyndale's '*vanisheth* away.' Comp. 'The fashion of this world *is passing away*' (1 Cor. vii. 31), where the same verb is used, and where the active in a neuter sense is equivalent to the middle here and in *v.* 8.
and the lust thereof] Not the lust *for* the world, but the lust which it exhibits, the sinful tendencies mentioned in *v.* 16. The world is passing away with all its evil ways. How foolish, therefore, to fix one's affections on what not only cannot endure but is already in process of dissolution! 'The lust thereof' = 'all that is in the world'.
the will of God] This is the exact opposite of 'all that is in the world'. The one sums up all the tendencies to good in the universe, the other all the tendencies to evil. We see once more how S. John in giving us the antithesis of a previous idea expands it and makes it fructify. He says that the world and all its will and ways are on the wane: but as the opposite of this he says, not merely that God and His will and ways abide, but that 'he that doeth the will of God abideth for ever'. This implies that he who follows the ways of the world will not abide for ever. Again he speaks of the love of the world and the love of the Father; but as the opposite of the man who loves the world he says not 'he that loveth the Father', but 'he that doeth the will of the Father'. This implies that true love involves obedience. Thus we have a double antithesis. On the one hand we have the world and the man who loves it and follows its ways: they both pass away. On the other hand we have God and the man who loves Him

is the last time: and as ye have heard that antichrist shall

and does His will: they both abide for ever. Instead of the goods of this life (βίος) in which the world would allow him to vaunt for a moment, he who doeth the will of God has that eternal life (ζωή) in which the true Christian has fellowship with God. 'For ever' is literally 'unto the age', i.e. 'unto the age to come', the kingdom of heaven; the word for 'age' (αἰών) being the substantive from which the word for 'eternal' (αἰώνιος) is derived. He who does God's will shall abide until the kingdom of God comes *and be a member of it*. The latter fact, though not stated, is obviously implied. It would be a punishment and not a blessing to be allowed, like Moses, to see the kingdom but not enter it. The followers of the world share the death of the world: the children of God share His eternal life.

Here probably we should make a pause in reading the Epistle. What follows is closely connected with what precedes and is suggested by it: but there is, nevertheless, a new departure, which is made with much solemnity.

18—26. THE PERSONS TO BE AVOIDED;—ANTICHRISTS.

18. *Little children*] Or, *Little ones*. It is difficult to see anything in this section specially suitable to children: indeed the very reverse is rather the case. The same word (παιδία) is used here as in *v.* 14 and John xxi. 5. S. John's readers in general are addressed, irrespective of age. Both his Epistle and Gospel are written for adults and for well-instructed Christians.

it is the last time] More literally, *it is the last* **hour**; possibly, but not probably, *it is a last hour*. The omission of the definite article is quite intelligible and not unusual: the idea is sufficiently definite without it, for there can be only one last hour. Similarly (Jude 18) we have '*in* (*the*) *last time* there shall be mockers walking after their own ungodly lusts': and (Acts i. 8, xiii. 47) '*unto* (*the*) *uttermost part* of the earth'. A great deal has been written upon this text in order to avoid a very plain but unwelcome conclusion, that by the 'last hour' S. John means the time immediately preceding the return of Christ to judge the world. Hundreds of years have passed away since S. John wrote these words, and the Lord is not yet come. Rather, therefore, than admit an interpretation which seemed to charge the Apostle with a serious error, commentators have suggested all kinds of explanations as substitutes for the obvious one. The following considerations place S. John's meaning beyond all reasonable doubt.
1. He has just been stating that the world is on the wane and that its dissolution has already begun. 2. He has just declared that the obedient Christian shall abide 'unto the age' of Christ's kingdom of glory. 3. He goes on to give as a proof that it is the 'last hour', that many Antichrists have already arisen; it being the common belief of Christians that Antichrist would immediately precede the return of Christ. 4. 'The last day' is a phrase peculiar to S. John (John vi. 39, 40, 44, 54, xi. 24, xii. 48), and invariably means the end of the world,

not the Christian dispensation. 5. Analogous phrases in other parts of N.T. point in the same direction: 'In the last days grievous times shall come' (2 Tim. iii. 1); 'Ye are guarded through faith unto a salvation ready to be revealed in the last time' (1 Pet. i. 5); 'In the last days mockers shall come with mockery' (2 Pet. iii. 3). These and other passages shew that by 'the last days', 'last time', 'last hour', and the like, Christian writers did not mean the whole time between the first and second coming of Christ, but only the concluding portion of it. 6. We find similar language with similar meaning in the sub-apostolic age. Thus Ignatius (*Eph.* XI.) writes; "These are the last times. Henceforth let us be reverent; let us fear the longsuffering of God, lest it turn into a judgment against us. For either let us fear the wrath which is to come, or let us love the grace which now is."

Of other interpretations of 'the last hour' the most noteworthy are these. (1) *The Christian dispensation*, which we have every reason to believe is the last. This is the sense in which S. John's words are *true ;* but this is plainly not his *meaning*. The appearance of Christ, not of Antichrist, proves that the Christian dispensation is come. (2) *A very grievous time, tempora periculosa pessima et abjectissima*. This is quite against usage whether in classical or N.T. Greek: comp. 2 Tim. iii. 1. The classical phrase, 'to suffer the last things', i.e. 'to suffer extremities' (τὰ ἔσχατα παθεῖν), supplies no analogy: here the notion of 'grievous' comes from the verb. (3) *The eve of the destruction of Jerusalem*. How could the appearance of Antichrist prove that this had arrived? And Jerusalem had perished at least a dozen years before the probable date of this Epistle. (4) *The eve of S. John's own death*. Antichrists could be no sign of that.

It is admitted even by some of those who reject the obvious interpretation that "the Apostles expected a speedy appearing or manifestation of Jesus as the Judge of their nation and of all nations" (Maurice): which is to admit the whole difficulty of the rejected explanation. Only gradually was the vision of the Apostles cleared to see the true nature of the spiritual kingdom which Christ had founded on earth and left in their charge. Even Pentecost did not at once give them perfect insight. Being under the guidance of the Holy Spirit they could not teach what was untrue: but, like the Prophets before them, they sometimes uttered words which were true in a sense far higher than that which was present to their own minds. In this higher sense S. John's words here are true. Like others, he was wrong in supposing 'that the kingdom of God was immediately to appear' (Luke xix. 11), for 'it was not for them to know times or seasons which the Father hath set within His own authority' (Acts i. 7). He was right in declaring that, the Messiah having come, it was the 'last hour'. No event in the world's history can ever equal the coming of Christ until He comes again. The epoch of Christianity, therefore, is rightly called the 'last hour', although it has lasted nearly two thousand years. What is that compared with the many thousands of years since the creation of man, and the limitless geological periods which preceded the creation of man? What again in the eyes of Him in whose sight 'a thousand years are but yesterday?'

come, even now are there many antichrists; whereby we

"It may be remarked that the only point on which we can certainly say that the Apostles were in error, and led others into error, is in their expectation of the immediate coming of Christ; and this is the very point which our Saviour says (Mark xiii. 32) is known only to the Father" (Jelf).

as ye have heard that Antichrist shall come] Better, **even** *as ye* **heard** *that Antichrist* **cometh**: the first verb is aorist, not perfect; the second present, not future; and the conjunction is of the same strong form as in *v*. 6. This seems to be a case in which the aorist should be retained in English (see on *v*. 11). As in *v*. 7, the reference is probably to a definite point in their instruction in the faith: and 'cometh' should be retained in order to bring out the analogy between the Christ and the Antichrist. The one was hoped for, and the other dreaded, with equal certainty; and hence each might be spoken of as 'He that cometh'. 'Art Thou *He that cometh?*' (Matt. xi. 3; Luke xix. 20). Comp. Mark viii. 38, xi. 9; John iv. 25, vi. 14, xi. 27, &c. &c. And as to the coming of Antichrists the N. T. seems to be as explicit as the O. T. with regard to the coming of Christ. 'Many shall come in My name, saying I am the Christ; and shall lead many astray... There shall arise false Christs, and false prophets, and shall shew great signs and wonders; so as to lead astray, if possible even the elect' (Matt. xxiv. 5, 24). Comp. Mark xiii. 22—23; Acts xx. 29; 2 Tim. iii. 1; 2 Pet. ii. 1; and especially 2 Thess. ii. 3, which like the passage before us seems to point to one distinct person or power as the one Antichrist, whose spirit animates all antichristian teachers.

The term 'Antichrist' in Scripture occurs only in the First and Second Epistles of S. John (ii. 18, 22, iv. 3; 2 John 7). The earliest instance of its use outside Scripture is in S. Polycarp (*Ep. ad Phil.* VII.), in a passage which shews that this disciple of S. John (A.D. 140—155) knew our Epistle: see on iv. 3. The term does not mean merely a *mock Christ* or *false Christ*, for which the N.T. term is 'pseudo-Christ' (Matt. xxiv. 24; Mark xiii. 22). Nor does it mean simply *an opponent of Christ*, for which we should probably have 'enemy of Christ', like 'enemy of the Cross of Christ' (Phil. iii. 18) and 'enemy of God' (Jas. iv. 4). But it includes *both* these ideas of counterfeiting and opposing; it means an *opposition Christ* or *rival Christ;* just as we call a rival Pope an 'antipope'. The Antichrist is, therefore, a *usurper*, who under false pretences assumes a position which does not belong to him, and who *opposes* the rightful owner. The idea of opposition is the predominant one.

It is not easy to determine whether the Antichrist of S. John is personal or not. But the discussion of this question is too long for a note: see Appendix B.

even now are there many Antichrists] Better, as R.V., even now **have there arisen** *many Antichrists*: the Christ *was* from all eternity (i. 1), the Antichrist and his company *arose* in time; they *are come into being*. We have a similar contrast in the Gospel: 'In the begin-

19 know that it is the last time. They went out from us, but

ning *was* the Word'; but 'There *arose* a man, sent from God, whose name was John' (John i. 1, 6). These 'many Antichrists' are probably to be regarded as at once forerunners of the Antichrist and evidence that his spirit is already at work in the world: the one fact shews that he is not far distant, the other that in a sense he is already here. In either case we have proof that the return of Christ, which is to be heralded by the appearance of Antichrist, is near.

whereby we know that it is the last time] Or, **whence we come to know** *that it is the last* **hour**: as in *vv.* 3 and 5 the verb indicates acquisition of and progress in knowledge. 'Whence' in the sense of 'from which data, from which premises' hardly occurs elsewhere in N.T. except perhaps in the Epistle to the Hebrews (ii. 17, vii. 25, viii. 3), where the same Greek word (ὅθεν) is uniformly rendered 'wherefore' in both A.V. and R.V.

It is difficult to see what S. John could have meant by this, if by the 'last hour' he understood the Christian dispensation as a whole and not the concluding portion of it (comp. 2 Tim. iii. 1). The multitude of false teachers who were spreading the great lie (*v.* 22) that Jesus is not the Christ, were evidence, not of the existence of Christianity, but of antichristianity. Nor could evidence of the former be needed by S. John's readers. They did not need to be convinced either that the Gospel dispensation had begun, or that it was the last in the history of the Divine Revelation. The Montanist theory that a further dispensation of the Spirit, distinct from that of the Son, was to follow and supersede the Gospel, as the Gospel had superseded Judaism, the dispensation of the Father, was a belief of later growth. (For an account of this theory as elaborated by Joachim of Flora [fl. A.D. 1180—90] see Döllinger's *Prophecies and the Prophetic Spirit in the Christian Era*, pp. 114—119.) In the Apostolic age the tendency was all the other way;—to believe that the period since the coming of Christ was not only the last in the world's history, but would be very brief. It was thought that some of the generation then existing might live to see the end (1 Thess. iv. 15, 16; 1 Cor. xv. 51, 52).

19. The relation of these antichristian teachers to the Church of Christ. They were formerly nominal members, but never real members of it. They are now not members in any sense. Note the repetition, so characteristic of S. John, of the key-word 'us', which means the Christian Church. It occurs 5 times in this one verse.

They went out from us] It was their own doing, a distinct secession from our communion: in the Greek, 'from us' comes first for emphasis. It is incredible that the words can mean 'they proceeded from us *Jews*'. What point would there be in that? Moreover, S. John never writes as a Jew, but always as a Christian to Christians. 'Us' includes all true Christians, whether of Gentile or Jewish origin. Comp. S. Paul's warning to the *Ephesian* presbyters; '*From among your own selves* shall men arise, speaking perverse things, to draw away the disciples after them' (Acts xx. 30); where the Greek is similar to what we have

they were not of us; for if they had been of us, they would *no doubt* have continued with us: but *they went out*, that they might be made manifest that they were not all of us.

here: and 'Certain men, the children of Belial', *are gone out from among you*, and have withdrawn the inhabitants of their city, saying, Let us go and serve other gods, which ye have not known' (Deut. xiii. 13); where the Greek of LXX. is still closer to this passage.

but they were not of us] They have a foreign origin. The single act of departure (aorist) is contrasted with the lasting condition of being 'of us' (imperfect). 'Of us' here is exactly analogous to 'of the Father' and 'of the world' in *v.* 16. It is difficult to bring out in English the full force of the antithesis which is so easily expressed in the Greek. 'From out of us they went forth, but they were not from out of us'; where 'from out of us' (ἐξ ἡμῶν) is of course used in two different senses, 'out from our midst' and 'originating with us.'

they would no doubt have continued with us] Better, *they* **would have abided** *with us*: there is nothing in the Greek to represent 'no doubt,' and the verb is S. John's favourite word 'abide' (see on *v.* 24). Almost all the earlier English Versions go wrong as to 'no doubt'. Tyndale and Cranmer have 'no dout', the Genevan has 'douteles', and the Rhemish 'surely'. Probably these are attempts to translate the *utique* of the Vulgate, *permansissent utique nobiscum:* and the *utique*, which is as old as Tertullian (*De Praescr. Haer.* III.) is a mistaken endeavour to give a separate word to represent the Greek particle ἄν. Oddly enough, Wiclif, who worked from the Vulgate, has nothing to represent *utique;* 'they hadden dwelte with us'. Luther inserts 'ja'; 'so wären sie *ja* bei uns geblieben'; which looks as if he also were under the influence of the *utique*. There is a similar instance John viii. 42, where Wiclif has '*sothli* ye schulden love Me', Cranmer, '*truly* ye wolde love Me', and the Rhemish, '*verely* ye would love Me', because the Vulgate (not Tertullian) gives *diligeretis utique Me* for ἠγαπᾶτε ἄν ἐμέ. The meaning here is that seccssion proves a want of fundamental union from the first. As Tertullian says: *Nemo Christianus, nisi qui ad finem perseveraverit.* Note that S. John does not say 'they would have abided *among* us (ἐν ἡμῖν)', but '*with* us (μεθ' ἡμῶν)'. This brings out more clearly the idea of *fellowship:* 'these antichrists had no real sympathy with us'.

but they went out that they might be made manifest] As the italics in A.V. shew, there is no Greek to represent 'they went out'. 'But that' or 'but in order that' (ἀλλ' ἵνα) is an elliptical expression very frequent in S. John's Gospel (i. 8, ix. 3, xiii. 18, xiv. 31, xv. 25). We may often fill up the ellipse in some such way as 'but this *took place*', or 'this *came to pass*, in order that'. S. John's favourite construction 'in order that' (see on i. 9) again points to the Divine government of events. It was in accordance with God's will that these spurious members should be made known as such. The process which all through his Gospel the Apostle depicts as a necessary result of Christ's coming, still continues after His departure; the separation of light from darkness,

20 But ye have an unction from the Holy One, and ye know

of the Church from the world, of real from unreal Christians (see introductory note to John v.). S. John assures his readers that the appearance of error and unbelief in the Church need not shake their faith in it: it is all in accordance with the Divine plan. Revelation of the truth necessarily causes a separation between those who accept and those who reject it, and is designed to do so. God does not will that any should reject the truth; but He wills that those who reject should be made manifest. S. Paul states this truth the other way; that the *faithful* need to be distinguished. 'For there *must* be also heresies among you, *that* (ἵνα) *they which are approved may be made manifest* among you' (1 Cor. xi. 19).

that they were not all of us] Or, *that* **not all are** *of us*, as in the margin of R.V. But this is doubtful; the Greek being οὐκ εἰσὶν πάντες, not οὐ πάντες εἰσιν. The Greek is somewhat ambiguous, but certainly we must have 'are' and not 'were'. Two ideas seem to be in the Apostle's mind, and his words may be the expression partly of the one, and partly of the other: 1. that these antichrists may be made manifest as not really of us; 2. that it may be made manifest that not all professing Christians are really of us.

In this verse S. John does not teach that the Christian cannot fall away; his exhortations to his readers not to love the world, but to abide in Christ, is proof of that. He is only putting in another form the declaration of Christ, 'I give unto them eternal life; and they shall never perish, and no one shall snatch them out of My hand' (John x. 28). Apostasy is possible, but only for those who have never really made Christ their own, never fully given themselves to Him.

20. *But ye have an unction from the holy One*] Better, as R.V., **And** *ye have an* **anointing** (as in *v.* 27) *from the Holy One*. S. John, in his manner, puts two contrasted parties side by side, the Antichrist with his antichrists, and the Christ with His christs; but the fact of there being a contrast does not warrant us in turning S. John's simple 'and' (καί) into 'but'. Tyndale holds fast to 'and', in spite of Wiclif's 'but' and the Vulgate's *sed*. Just as the Antichrist has his representatives, so the Anointed One, the Christ, has His. All Christians in a secondary sense are what Christ is in a unique and primary sense, the Lord's anointed. 'These anointed', says the Apostle to his readers, '*ye* are'. The 'ye' is not only expressed in the Greek, but stands first after the conjunction for emphasis: 'ye' in contrast to these apostates. The word for 'anointing' or 'unction' (χρίσμα) strictly means the 'completed act of anointing:' but in LXX. it is used of the unguent or anointing oil (Deut. xxx. 25); and Tyndale, Cranmer and the Genevan have 'oyntment' here. In N.T. it occurs only here and *v.* 27. Kings, priests, and sometimes prophets were anointed, in token of their receiving Divine grace. Hence oil both in O. and N.T. is a figure of the Holy Spirit (Ps. xlv. 6, 7, cv. 15; Is. lxi. 1; Acts x. 38; Heb. i. 9; 2 Cor. i. 21). It is confusing cause and effect to suppose that this passage was influenced by the custom of anointing candidates

all *things*. I have not written unto you because ye know 21

at baptism: the custom though ancient (for it is mentioned by S. Cyril of Jerusalem, c. A.D. 350, *Catech. Lect.* XXI. 3, 4), is later than this Epistle. More probably the custom was suggested by this passage. The opening of S. Cyril's 21st Lecture throws much light on this passage. "Having been baptized into Christ and...being made partakers of Christ, *ye are properly called christs*, and of you God said, Touch not My christs, or anointed. Now ye were made christs *by receiving the emblem of the Holy Spirit*; and all things were in a figure wrought in you, because ye are figures of Christ. He also bathed Himself in the river Jordan, and...came up from them; and the Holy Spirit in substance lighted on Him, like resting upon like. In the same manner to you also, after you had come up from the pool of the sacred streams, was given the unction, the emblem of that wherewith Christ was anointed; and this is the Holy Spirit". Similarly S. Augustine; "In the unction we have a sacramental sign (*sacramentum*); the virtue itself is invisible. The invisible unction is the Holy Spirit" (*Hom.* III. 12).

It may be doubted whether S. John in this verse makes any allusion to the anointing which was a feature in some Gnostic systems.

from the holy One] This almost certainly means *Christ*, in accordance with other passages both in S. John and elsewhere (John vi. 69; Rev. iii. 7; Mark i. 24; Acts iii. 14; Ps. xx. 10), and in harmony with Christ being called 'righteous' in *vv.* 1, 29, and 'pure' in iii. 3. Moreover in John xiv. 26, xv. 26, xvi. 7, 14 Christ promises to give the Holy Spirit. It may possibly mean God the Father (Hab. iii. 3; Hos. xi. 9; 1 Cor. vi. 19). It cannot well mean the Holy Spirit, unless some other meaning be found for 'anointing'.

and ye know all things] There is very high authority for reading *and* **ye all know** (*this*), or, omitting the conjunction and placing a colon after 'Holy One', *ye all know* (*this*). If the reading followed in A.V. and R.V. be right, the meaning is, 'It is you (and not these antichristian Gnostics who claim it) that are, in virtue of the anointing of the Spirit of truth, in the possession of the true knowledge'. Christians are in possession of *the truth* in a far higher sense than any unchristian philosopher. All the unbeliever's knowledge is out of balance and proportion. The assertion here is strictly in harmony with the promise of Christ; 'When He, the Spirit of truth is come, He shall guide you into *all the truth*' (John xvi. 13). In the same spirit S. Ignatius writes, "*None of these things is hidden from you*, if ye be perfect in your faith and love towards Jesus Christ" (*Eph.* xiv. 1); and similarly S. Polycarp, "*Nothing is hidden from you*" (*Phil.* xii. 1). Comp. 'They that seek the Lord understand all things' (Prov. xxviii. 5).

21. *I have not written*] Literally, as in *vv.* 13, 14, 26, *I wrote not*, or, *did not write:* it is the aorist in the Greek. But (whatever may be true of *vv.* 13, 14) what we have here is almost certainly the *epistolary aorist*, which may be represented in English either by the present or by the perfect. 'I have written' probably does not refer to the whole letter, but only to this section about the antichrists; this seems clear from *v.* 26.

not the truth, but because ye know it, and that no lie is of
22 the truth. Who is a liar but he that denieth that Jesus is

'Do not think from my warning you against lying teachers that I suspect
you of being ignorant of the truth: you who have been anointed with the
Spirit of truth cannot be ignorant of the truth. I write as unto men
who will appreciate what I say. I write, not to teach, but to confirm'.
"S. John does not treat Christianity as a religion containing elements of
truth, or even more truth than any religion which had preceded it. S.
John presents Christianity to the soul as a religion which must be everything to it, if it is not really to be worse than nothing" (Liddon).

because ye know not the truth; but because ye know it, and that, &c.]
There are no less than three ways of taking this, depending upon the
meaning given to the thrice-repeated conjunction (ὅτι), which in each
place may mean either 'because' or 'that'. 1. As A.V.; *because*,...but
because...and *that*. The A.V. follows the earlier Versions in putting
'that' in the last clause: so Wiclif, Tyndale, Cranmer, &c. 2. As
R.V.; 'because' in each clause. 3. 'That' in each clause: 'I have not
written *that* ye know not the truth, but *that* ye know it, and *that* &c.'
This last is almost certainly wrong. As in *vv.* 13, 14 the verb 'write'
introduces the reason for writing and not the subject-matter or contents
of the Epistle. And if the first conjunction is 'because', it is the simplest and most natural to take the second and third in the same way.
The Apostle warns them against antichristian lies, not because they are
ignorant, but (1) because they possess the truth, and (2) because every
kind of lie is utterly alien to the truth they possess. "There is the
modesty and the sound philosophy of an Apostle! Many of us think
that we can put the truth *into* people, by screaming it into their ears.
We do not suppose that they have any truth *in* them to which we can
make appeal. S. John had no notion that he could be of use to his
dear children at Ephesus unless there was a truth in them, a capacity
of distinguishing truth from lies, a sense that one must be the eternal
opposition of the other" (Maurice).

no lie is of the truth] Literally, *every lie is not-of-the-truth*: the negative belongs to the predicate (comp. iii. 15). 'Of the truth' here is
exactly analogous to 'of the Father' and 'of the world' in *v.* 16 and to
'of us' in *v.* 19. Every lie is *in origin* utterly removed from the truth:
the truth springs from God; lying from the devil, 'for he is a liar and
the father thereof' (John viii. 44). See on *v.* 16.

22. *Who is a liar*] More accurately, as R.V., *Who is the liar:* the
A.V. here again follows the earlier English Versions. But we must
beware of exaggerating the article in *interpretation*, although it is right
to *translate* it. It merely marks the passage from the abstract to the
concrete: 'Every lie is absolutely alien from the truth. Who then is
the one who speaks lies? There are no liars if he who denies that Jesus
is the Christ is not one'. The exactly parallel construction in *v.* 4, 5
shews that 'the liar' here does not mean 'the greatest liar possible'.
Moreover, this would not be true. Is denying that Jesus is the Christ
a greater lie than denying the existence of the Son, or of God?

the Christ? He is antichrist, that denieth the Father and
the Son. Whosoever denieth the Son, the same hath not 23
the Father: [*but*] *he that acknowledgeth the Son hath the*

The abruptness of the question is startling. Throughout these verses
(22—24) "clause stands by clause in stern solemnity without any connecting particles."

but he that denieth] These Gnostic teachers, who profess to be in
possession of the higher truth, are really possessed by one of the worst
of lies.—For the way in which the Gnostics denied the fundamental
Christian truth of the Incarnation see the Introduction, p. 19.

He is Antichrist] Better, as R.V., **This** *is* **the** *antichrist*, or *The
antichrist is this man:* 'this', as in v. 25 and i. 5, may be the predicate. The article before 'antichrist', almost certainly spurious in v.
18, is certainly genuine here, iv. 3, and 2 John 7. But 'the antichrist'
here probably does not mean the great personal rival of Christ, but the
antichristian teacher who is like him and in this matter acts as his mouthpiece.

that denieth the Father and the Son] This clause is substituted for
'that denieth that Jesus is the Christ'. By this substitution, which
is quite in S. John's manner, he leads us on to see that to deny the one
is to deny the other. Jesus is the Christ, and the Christ is the Son of
God; therefore to deny that Jesus is the Christ is to deny the Son.
And to deny the Son is to deny the Father; not merely because Son
and Father are correlatives and mutually imply one another, but
because the Son is the revelation of the Father, without whom the
Father cannot be known. 'Neither doth any know the Father, save
the Son, and *he to whomsoever the Son willeth to reveal Him*' (Matt.
xi. 27). 'No one cometh unto the Father *but by Me*' (John xiv. 6).
Comp. John v. 23, xv. 23. Some would put a full stop at 'antichrist,'
and connect what follows with v. 23, thus; *This is the antichrist. He
that denieth the Father* (*denieth*) *the Son also: every one that denieth the
Son hath not the Father either.*

23. The previous statement is emphasized by an expansion of it
stated both negatively and positively. The expansion consists in
declaring that to deny the Son is not merely to do that, and indeed
not merely to deny the Father, but also (οὐδέ) to debar oneself from
communion with the Father. So that we now have a third consequence
of denying that Jesus is the Christ. To deny this is (1) to deny the
Son, which is (2) to deny the Father, which is (3) to be cut off from the
Father. 'To have the Father' must not be weakened to mean 'to
hold as an article of faith that He is the Father'; still less, 'to know
the Father's will '. It means, quite literally, 'to have Him as his own
Father'. Those who deny the Son cancel their own right to be called
'sons of God': they *ipso facto* excommunicate themselves from the great
Christian family in which Christ is the Brother, and God is the Father,
of all believers. 'To as many as received Him, to them gave He the
right to become children of God' (John i. 12).

but he that acknowledgeth the Son] Better, as R. V., **he that con-**

24 *Father also.* Let *that* therefore abide in you, which ye have heard from the beginning. If *that* which ye have heard from the beginning shall remain in you, ye also shall 25 continue in the Son, and in the Father. And this is the 26 promise that he hath promised us, *even* eternal life. These

fesseth *the Son:* it is the same verb (ὁμολογεῖν) as is used i. 9, iv. 2, 3, 15; 2 John 7. It is surprising that A. V., while admitting the passage about the three Heavenly Witnesses (v. 7) without any mark of doubtfulness, prints the second half of this verse in italics, as if there were nothing to represent it in the Greek. Excepting the 'but', the sentence is undoubtedly genuine, being found in all the best MSS. (אABC) and many other authorities. A few authorities omit it accidentally, owing to the two halves of the verse ending in the Greek with the same three words (τὸν πατέρα ἔχει). Tyndale and the Genevan omit the sentence: Cranmer and the Rhemish retain it; Cranmer marking it as wanting authority, and both omitting 'but', which Wiclif inserts, although there is no conjunction in the Vulgate. The asyndeton is impressive and continues through three verses, 22, 23, 24. "The sentences fall on the reader's soul like notes of a trumpet. Without cement, and therefore all the more ruggedly clasping each other, they are like a Cyclopean wall" (Haupt). It would be possible to translate, 'He that confesseth, hath the Son and the Father' (comp. 2 John 9): but this is not probable.

24. *Let that therefore abide in you*] The 'therefore' is undoubtedly to be omitted: it is a mistaken insertion in many of those inferior MSS. which omit the second half of *v.* 23. This verse begins with a very emphatic pronoun; **As for you** (in contrast to these antichristian liars), *let that abide in you which* **ye heard** *from the beginning.* The pronoun in the Greek is a *nominativus pendens:* comp. John vi. 39, vii. 38, xiv. 12, xv. 2, xvii. 2; Rev. ii. 26, iii. 12, 21. The verb is an aorist and should be retained as such, as in *v.* 7: it points to the definite period when they were first instructed in the faith. 'Hold fast the Gospel which ye first heard, and reject the innovations of these false teachers'.

If that which ye have heard...shall remain in you, ye also shall continue] Better, as R. V., *if that which* **ye heard**...**abide** *in you, ye also shall* **abide.** Here the arbitrary distinctions introduced by the translators of 1611 reach a climax: the same Greek word (μένειν) is rendered in three different ways in the same verse. Elsewhere it is rendered in four other ways, making seven English words to one Greek: 'dwell' (John i. 39, vi. 56, xiv. 10, 17), 'tarry' (iv. 40, xxi. 22, 23), 'endure' (vi. 27), 'be present' (xiv. 25). The translators in their *Address to the Reader* tell us that these changes were often made knowingly and sometimes of set purpose. They are generally regrettable, and here are doubly so: (1) an expression characteristic of S. John and of deep meaning is blurred, (2) the emphasis gained by iteration, which is also characteristic of S. John, is entirely lost. 'Let the truths which were first taught you have a home in your hearts: if these have a home in you, ye also shall have a home in the Son and in the Father'.

25. *And this is the promise that he hath promised us*] Or, *and the*

things have I written unto you concerning them that seduce you. But the anointing which ye have received of him 27 abideth in you, and ye need not that any *man* teach you:

promise which He promised us is this: the aorist had better be retained, and 'this' is probably the predicate, referring to what follows (comp. *v.* 22, i. 5, v. 14) and not the subject, referring to what precedes. This view is confirmed by iii. 23 and v. 11. The connexion with what precedes is close, 'eternal life' being only another view of 'abiding in the Father and the Son'. The 'He' is emphatic, and perhaps 'He Himself' would not be too strong as a rendering. Of course Christ is meant, "who in this whole passage forms the centre round which all the statements of the Apostle move" (Huther). For the promise see John iii. 15, iv. 14, vi. 40, &c. &c. The best MS. (B) reads 'promised *you*', for 'promised *us*'.

26. *These things have I written unto you*] 'These things' probably mean the warnings about the antichrists, not the whole Epistle. 'I have written', or 'I wrote', is the epistolary aorist as in *v.* 21.

that seduce you] Better, **that lead you astray**, i.e. that are endeavouring to do so. It is the active of the verb which is used in 1. 8 (see note there); and the present participle, which indicates the tendency and habit, but not the success, of the antichristian teachers.

27, 28. THE PLACE OF SAFETY;—CHRIST.

27. *But the anointing which ye have received*] As in *v.* 2, we have the false and the true Christians put side by side in contrast; but this does not justify us in turning S. John's simple 'and' (καί) into 'but'. As in *v.* 24, we have the pronoun put first with great emphasis, and as a *nominativus pendens*. Moreover, the reception of the chrism refers to the definite occasion when Christ poured out His Spirit upon them, viz. their baptism; and therefore the aorist should be retained. Wherefore, as R. V., **And as for you**, *the anointing which* **ye received**.

abideth in you] We often, in order to convey a command or a rebuke gently, state as a fact what ought to be a fact. This is perhaps S. John's meaning here. If not, it is an expression of strong confidence in those whom he adresses.

ye need not that any man teach you] This seems to confirm the reading 'ye know all things' in *v.* 20. The believer who has once been anointed with the Spirit of truth has no need even of an Apostle's teaching. This seems to be quite conclusive against 'little children' anywhere in this Epistle meaning children in years or children in knowledge of the Gospel. S. John writes throughout for adult and well-instructed Christians, to whom he writes not to give information, but to confirm and enforce and perhaps develope what they have all along known. Of course S. John does not mean that the anointing with the Spirit supersedes all necessity for instruction. The whole Epistle, and in this chapter *vv.* 6, 7, 24, are conclusive against such a view. S. John assumes that his readers have been thoroughly instructed in 'the word' and 'the truth', before receiving the outpouring of the Spirit which

but as the same anointing teacheth you of all *things*, and is truth, and is no lie, and even as it hath taught you, ye shall 23 abide in him. And now, little children, abide in him; that,

shews them the full meaning of 'the word' and confirms them in 'the truth'. If S. John has no sympathy with a knowledge which professed to rise higher than Christian teaching, still less has he sympathy with a fanaticism which would dispense with Christian teaching. While he condemns the Gnosticism of his own age, he gives no encouragement to the Montanism of a century later.

but as the same anointing...ye shall abide in him] We have here to settle, first the question of readings, and then the question of construction. 'But as *His* anointing' (אBC, Vulgate, Syriac) is certainly superior to 'But as the *same* anointing' (AKL, Coptic), and still more is '*ye abide*' or '*abide ye*' (אABC, Versions) superior to 'ye *shall* abide' (KL). The A. V. deserts Wiclif, Tyndale, Cranmer, and the Rhemish, to follow the Genevan in adopting the future. The construction is not so easily determined, but does not seriously affect the sense. We may render, (1) *But as His anointing teacheth you concerning all things, and is* true, *and is no lie, and even as* it taught *you,—*do ye abide *in Him;* making only one sentence with a long protasis. Or (2) we may break it into two sentences, each with a protasis and apodosis; *But as His anointing teacheth you concerning all things, it is* true *and is no lie; and even as* it taught *you,* do ye abide *in Him*. The majority of English Versions, including R. V., are for the former: so also the Vulgate. Commentators are much divided; but Huther claims to have most on his side for the latter. He has against him Alford, Braune, De Wette, Düsterdieck, Ewald, Lücke, Neander, Westcott. The sentence seems to be a recapitulation of the section. 'As His anointing teaches you concerning all things' recalls *v.* 20; 'is true and is no lie' recalls *vv.* 21—23; 'do ye abide in Him' recalls *vv.* 24, 25. Probably we ought to supply a new nominative for 'taught', viz. 'He', i.e. Christ understood from 'in Him'. This explains the difference of tense: 'taught' refers to the gift of the Spirit of truth made once for all by Christ; 'teacheth' to the continual illumination which is the result of the gift. It is comparatively unimportant whether we consider 'do ye abide' ($\mu\acute{\epsilon}\nu\epsilon\tau\epsilon$) as indicative, like 'abideth' just before, or as imperative, like 'abide' in the next verse. See on *v.* 29.

28. *And now*] Introducing the practical conclusion: comp. John xvii. 5, where Jesus, 'having accomplished the work given Him to do', prays, '*And now*, O Father, glorify Thou Me'. So also in Acts vii. 34, x. 5. See on 2 John 5. Haupt thinks that 'And now' introduces the new division of the Epistle, which almost all agree begins near this point. The truth seems to be that these two verses (28, 29) are at once the conclusion of one division and the beginning of another.

little children] Recalling the beginning of this section, *v.* 18: it is the same word ($\tau\epsilon\kappa\nu\iota\alpha$) as is used in *vv.* 1, 12, and means all S. John's readers.

when he shall appear, we may have confidence, and not be
ashamed before him at his coming. If ye know that he is 29

that, when he shall appear] Better, as R.V., *that,* **if** *He shall* **be
manifested.** The 'when' (ὅταν) of A.V. (KL) must certainly give
place to '**if**' (ἐάν), which is more difficult and has overwhelming support (אABC). 'If' *seems* to imply a doubt as to Christ's return, and
the change to 'when' has probably been made to avoid this. But 'if'
implies no doubt as to the *fact*, it merely implies indifference as to the
time: 'if He should return in our day' (see on John vi. 62, xii. 32, xiv.
3). **Be manifested** is greatly superior to 'appear' (as Augustine's *manifestatus fuerit* is superior to the Vulgate's *apparuerit*) because (1) the
Greek verb is passive; (2) it is a favourite word (φανεροῦν) with S. John
and should be translated uniformly in order to mark this fact (i. 2, ii.
19, iii. 2, 5, 8, iv. 9; Rev. iii. 18, xv. 4; John i. 31, iii. 21, &c. &c.).
As applied to Christ it is used of His being manifested in His Incarnation (i. 2, iii. 5, 8), in His words and works (John ii. 11, xvii. 6), in His
appearances after the Resurrection (John xxi. 1, 14), in His return to
judgment (here and iii. 2). S. John alone uses the word in this last
sense, for which other N.T. writers have 'to be revealed' (ἀποκαλύπτεσθαι), a verb never used by S. John excepting once (John xii. 38)
in a quotation from O.T. (Is. lxiii. 1), where he is under the influence
of the LXX.

we may have confidence] The R.V. has *we may have* **boldness.** At
first sight this looks like one of those small changes which have been
somewhat hastily condemned as 'vexatious, teasing, and irritating'.
The A.V. wavers between 'boldness' (iv. 17; Acts iv. 13, 29, 31, &c.)
and 'confidence', with occasionally 'boldly' (Heb. iv. 16) instead of
'with boldness'. The R.V. consistently has 'boldness' in all these
places. The Greek word (παρρησία) means literally 'freedom in *speaking,*
readiness to *say anything*, frankness, intrepidity'. In this Epistle and
that to the Hebrews it means especially the fearless trust with which
the faithful soul meets God: iii. 21, iv. 17, v. 14. Comp. 1 Thess.
ii. 19.

not be ashamed before him] This cannot well be improved, but it is
very inadequate: the Greek is 'be ashamed *from* Him', or 'be shamed
away from Him'; strikingly indicating the averted face and shrinking
form which are the results of the shame. 'Turn with shame' or 'shrink
with shame from Him' have been suggested as renderings. Similarly,
in Matt. x. 28, 'Be not afraid of them' is literally 'Do not shrink away
in fear *from* them'. The interpretation 'receive shame from Him' is
probably not right. Comp. the LXX. of Is. i. 29; Jer. ii. 36, xii. 13.

at his coming] The Greek word (παρουσία = presence) occurs nowhere else in S. John's writings. In N.T. it amounts almost to a
technical term to express Christ's return to judgment (Matt. xxiv. 3, 27,
37, 39; 1 Cor. xv. 23; 1 Thess. ii. 19, iii. 13, iv. 15, v. 23; Jas. v. 7. 8;
2 Pet. i. 16, &c.). S. John uses it, as he uses 'the Word' and 'the
evil one', without explanation, confident that his readers understand
it. This is one of many small indications that he writes to wellinstructed believers, not to children or the recently converted.

righteous, ye know that every one which doeth righteousness is born of him.

S. John's divisions are seldom made with a broad line across the text (see on iii. 10 and 24). The parts dovetail into one another and intermingle in a way that at times looks like confusion. Wherever we may place the dividing line we find similar thoughts on each side of it. Such is the case here. If we place the line between *vv.* 27, 28 we have the idea of *abiding in Christ* (*vv.* 24, 27, 28) on both sides of it. If we place it between *vv.* 28, 29, we have the idea of Divine *righteousness and holiness* (i. 9, ii. 1, 12, 20, 29) prominent in both divisions. If we make the division coincide with the chapters, we have the leading ideas of *boldness towards Christ and God* (*v.* 28, iii. 2, 21, iv. 17, v. 14), of *Christ's return to judgment* (*v.* 28, iii. 2, iv. 17), of *doing righteousness* (*v.* 29, iii. 7—10), and of *Divine sonship* (*v.* 29, iii. 1, 2, &c.), on both sides of the division. It seems quite clear therefore that both these verses (28, 29) belong to both portions of the Epistle, and that *v.* 29 at any rate is more closely connected with what follows than with what precedes.

The close connexion between the parts must not lead us to suppose that there is no division here at all. The transition is gentle and gradual, but when it is over we find ourselves on new ground. The antithesis between light and darkness is replaced by that between love and hate. The opposition between the world and God becomes the opposition between the world and God's children. The idea of having fellowship with God is transformed into that of being sons of God. Walking in the light is spoken of as doing righteousness. And not only do previous thoughts, if they reappear, assume a new form, but new thoughts also are introduced: the Second Advent, the boldness of the faithful Christian, the filial relation between believers and God. Although there may be uncertainty to where the new division should begin, there is none as to fact of there being one.

ii. 29—v. 12. GOD IS LOVE.

There seems to be no serious break in the Epistle from this point onwards until we reach the concluding verses which form a sort of summary (v. 13—21). The key-word 'love' is distributed, and not very unevenly, over the whole, from iii. 1 to v. 3. Subdivisions, however, exist and will be pointed out as they occur. The next two subdivisions may be marked thus; *The Children of God and the Children of the Devil* (ii. 29—iii. 12); *Love and Hate* (iii. 13—24). The two, as we shall find, are closely linked together, and might be placed under one heading, thus; *The Righteousness of the Children of God in their relation to the Hate of the World*.

ii. 29—iii. 12. THE CHILDREN OF GOD AND THE CHILDREN OF THE DEVIL.

29. *If ye know that he is righteous*] This probably does not mean Christ, although the preceding verse refers entirely to Him. 'To be born of Christ', though containing "nothing abhorrent from our Christian ideas", is not a Scriptural expression; whereas 'to be born of God' is not only a common thought in Scripture, but is specially common in this Epistle and occurs in the very next verse. And clearly 'He' and 'Him' must be interpreted alike: it destroys the argument (*justus justum gignit*, as Bengel puts it) to interpret 'He is righteous' of Christ and 'born of Him' of God. Moreover, this explanation gets rid of one abrupt change by substituting another still more abrupt. That 'He, Him, His' in *v*. 28 means Christ, and 'He, Him' in *v*. 29 means God, is some confirmation of the view that a new division of the letter begins with *v*. 29. That 'God is righteous' see i. 9 and John xvii. 25. But S. John is so full of the truth that Christ and the Father are one, and that Christ is God revealed to man, that he makes the transition from one to the other almost imperceptibly. Had his readers asked him of one of these ambiguous passages, 'Are you speaking of Christ or of God'? he would perhaps have replied, 'Does it matter'?

ye know] Or, *know ye*; but this is less probable, though the Vulgate has *scitote*, and Wiclif, Tyndale, Cranmer, and the Rhemish, all take it as imperative. 'Ye know' is more in harmony with *vv*. 20, 21. It is remarkable how frequently in S. John's writings we are in doubt as to whether a verb is imperative or indicative (*v*. 27, John v. 39, xii. 19, xiv. 1, xv. 18). Even in *v*. 28, though there is scarcely a doubt, it is possible to take 'abide' as an indicative. After, 'ye know that every one' we must supply 'also'; *ye know that every one* also.

There is a change of verb from 'if ye know' (ἐὰν εἰδῆτε) to 'ye know that' (γινώσκετε ὅτι). The former means 'to have intuitive knowledge' or simply 'to be aware of the fact' (*vv*. 11, 20, 21): the latter means 'to come to know, learn by experience, recognise, perceive' (*vv*. 3, 4, 5, 13, 14, 18). 'If ye *are aware* that God is righteous, ye cannot fail to *perceive* that &c.' Comp. 'What I do thou *knowest* not now, but thou shalt *understand* (get to know) hereafter' (John xiii. 7); 'Lord, Thou *knowest* all things; Thou *perceivest* that I love Thee' (xxi. 17): and the converse change: 'If ye had *learned to know* Me, ye would *know* My Father also' (xiv. 7; comp. viii. 55).

which doeth righteousness] Perhaps we should translate, *that doeth His righteousness*. It is literally, *that doeth the righteousness;* but in Greek the definite article is often equivalent to our possessive pronoun. Or 'the righteousness' may mean 'the righteousness which is truly such': comp. 'to do the truth' (i. 6). The present tense expresses habitual action.

is born of him] Literally, *hath been begotten from Him*. Only he who habitually does righteousness is a true son of the God who is righteous; just as only he who habitually walks in the light has true fellowship with the God who is light (i. 6, 7). In a similar spirit S. Paul says, 'Let every one that nameth the name of the Lord depart from unrighteousness' (2 Tim. ii. 19). Other signs of Divine birth are *love* of the brethren (iv. 7) and *faith* in Jesus as the Christ (v. 1).

3 Behold, what manner of love the Father hath bestowed upon us, that we should be called the sons of God: therefore the world knoweth us not, because it knew him not.

CHAP. III.

1. *what manner of*] The same word (ποταπός) occurs Matt. viii. 27; Mark xiii. 1; Luke i. 29, vii. 39; 2 Pet. iii. 11: it always implies astonishment, and generally admiration. The radical signification is 'of what country', the Latin *cujas*; which, however, is never used as its equivalent in the Vulgate, because in N. T. the word has entirely lost the notion of place. It has become *qualis* rather than *cujas*: 'what amazing love'. In LXX. the word does not occur.

love] This is the key-word of this whole division of the Epistle (ii. 29—v. 12), in which it occurs 16 times as a substantive, 25 as a verb, and 5 times in the verbal adjective 'beloved'. The phrase 'to bestow love' occurs nowhere else in N. T.

the Father...upon us] In the Greek these words are in striking juxtaposition: to *us* miserable sinners *the Father* hath given this priceless right. 'The Father' rather than 'God', because of what follows: He who is *the* Father is *our* Father.

that we should be called] Literally, *in order that we should be called*: it is S. John's characteristic construction (ἵνα), as in i. 9. "The final particle has its full force" (Westcott): comp. *vv.* 11, 23, iv. 21; John, xiii. 34, xv. 12, 17. This was the purpose of His love, its tendency and direction. 'That we should be' must not be understood as future: we already have the title.

the sons of God] So the earlier English Versions: better, as R. V., **children** *of God*. There is no article in the Greek; and we must not confuse S. Paul's expression, 'sons of God' (υἱοί) with S. John's (τέκνα). The confusion has arisen in English Versions through the *filii Dei* of the Vulgate. Both Apostles tell us that the fundamental relation of believers to God is a *filial* one: but while S. Paul gives us the legal side (adoption), S. John gives us the natural side (generation). The latter is the closer relationship of the two. But we must remember that in the Roman Law, under which S. Paul lived, adoption was considered as absolutely equivalent to actual parentage. In this 'unique apostrophe' in the centre of the Epistle two of its central leading ideas meet, Divine love and Divine sonship; a love which has as its end and aim that men should be called children of God. After 'children of God' we must insert on overwhelming authority (אABC and Versions), **and we are**: God has allowed us to be *called* children, and we *are* children. The *simus* of the Vulgate and S. Augustine and the 'and *be*' of the Rhemish are probably wrong. The present indicative after ἵνα is not impossible: but would S. John have put 'called' in the subjunctive, and 'are' in the indicative, if the two verbs were co-ordinate?

therefore] Better, as R. V., **for this cause** (διὰ τοῦτο), reserving 'therefore' for a particle (οὖν) which is very frequent in the narrative

Beloved, now are we the sons of God, and it doth not yet **2** appear what we shall be: but we know that, when he shall

portions of the Gospel, but does not occur in this Epistle (it is not genuine in ii. 24 or iv. 19). Tyndale, Cranmer, the Genevan and the Rhemish all have 'for this cause': the A.V., as not unfrequently, has altered for the worse. It may be doubted whether the R.V. has not here altered the punctuation for the worse, in putting a full stop at 'we are'. 'For this cause' in S. John does not merely anticipate the 'because' or 'that' which follows; it refers to what precedes. 'We are children of God; and for this cause the world knows us not: because the world knew Him not'. The third sentence explains how the second sentence follows from the first. Comp. John v. 16, 18, vii. 22, viii. 47, x. 17, xii. 18, 27, 39. For 'the world' see on ii. 2. S. Augustine compares the attitude of the world towards God to that of sick men in delirium who would do violence to their physician.

2. *Beloved*] This form of address only occurs once in the first part of the Epistle (ii. 7), just where the subject of love appears for a few verses: it becomes the more common form of address (*vv.* 2, 21, iv. 1, 7, 11) now that the main subject is love. Similarly, in *v.* 13, where *brotherly* love is the special subject, 'brethren' is the form of address.

now are we the sons of God] Rather, as before, *now are we* **children of God.** 'Now' is placed first in emphatic contrast to 'not yet,' which has a similar position. Our privileges in this world are certain; our glories in the world to come still continue veiled. The term 'children' is in harmony with this: 'child' necessarily implies future development; 'son' does not.

it doth not yet appear] Better, as R.V., *it is not yet* **made manifest**; it is the same verb as we have already had i. 2, ii. 19, 28. As it is one of S. John's favourite expressions it is all the more important that it should be rendered in the same way throughout his writings. See on ii. 28.

but we know that, when he shall appear] The 'but' must be omitted on overwhelming evidence (אABC, Vulgate): *We know that* **if it shall be manifested.** Here there is no difference of reading (as there is in ii. 28) between 'when' and 'if'; but earlier English Versions, under the influence of the Vulgate (*cum apparuerit*), have '<u>when</u>' in both cases. 'If' in both cases is right; but it has been either changed in the Greek, or shirked in translation, as appearing to imply a doubt respecting the manifestation. It implies no doubt as to the fact, but shews that the *results* of the fact are more important than the *time:* comp. '*If* I be lifted up from the earth', and '*If* I go and prepare a place for you' (John xii. 32, xiv. 3).

It is less easy to determine between 'if *it* shall be manifested' and 'if *He* shall be manifested; 'it' meaning what we shall be hereafter, and 'He' meaning Christ. No nominative is expressed in the Greek, and it is rather violent to supply a new nominative, differing from that of the very same verb in the previous sentence: therefore 'it' seems preferable. 'We know that if our future state is made manifest we, who are children of God, shall be found like our Father'. On the

appear, we shall be like him; for we shall see him as he is.
3 And every *man* that hath this hope in him purifieth himself,

other hand, ii. 28 favours 'if *He* shall be manifested.' The word for know (οἴδαμεν) is that used in ii. 20, 21, not that used in ii. 3, 13, 14, 18, iii. 1. No *progress* in knowledge is implied, no additional *experience*: our future resemblance to our Father is a fact of which as Christians we are aware: comp. v. 18, 19, 20.

we shall be like him] If we render 'if *He* (i.e. Christ) shall be manifested', this naturally means 'we shall be like *Christ*;' which, however true in itself, is not the point. The point is that children are found to be like their Father. This is an additional reason for preferring 'if *it* shall be manifested'. Tyndale and Cranmer have 'it', Wiclif, Genevan, and Rhemish have 'he'.

for we shall see him as he is] Better, because *we shall see Him* **even as** *He is:* 'because' as in *vv.* 9, 20, 22, ii. 13, 14, &c., and 'even as' as in *vv.* 3, 7, 23, ii. 6, 27, &c. 'Because' or 'for' may give the cause either (1) of our *knowing* that we shall be like Him, or (2) of our *being* like Him. Both make good sense; but, in spite of 'we know' being the principal sentence *grammatically*, the statement which most needs explanation is the subordinate one, that we shall be like God. 'We shall be like Him', says the Apostle, 'because, as you know, we shall see Him'. Comp. 'But we all, with unveiled face *reflecting* as a mirror *the glory of the Lord, are transformed into the same image* from glory to glory' (2 Cor. iii. 18); the sight of God will glorify us. This also is in harmony with the prayer of the great High Priest; 'And the glory which Thou hast given Me, I have given unto them' (John xvii. 22). Comp. 'And they shall see His face' (Rev. xxii. 4). The '*even* as' emphasizes the reality of the sight: no longer 'in a mirror, darkly', but 'face to face'.

3. *that hath this hope in him*] This is certainly wrong: the preposition is 'on', not 'in', and 'Him' is either the Father or Christ; probably the former. It is precisely the man who has the hope, *based upon God*, of one day being like Him, that purifies himself. For the construction 'to have hope *on*' a person comp. '*On* Him shall the Gentiles hope' (Rom. xv. 12; comp. 1 Tim. iv. 10, vi. 17).

purifieth himself] In LXX. this verb (ἁγνίζειν) is used chiefly in a technical sense of ceremonial purifications, e.g. of the priests for divine service: and so also even in N.T. (John xi. 55; Acts xxi. 24, 26, xxiv. 18). But we need not infer that, because the outward cleansing is the dominant idea in these passages, it is therefore the only one. Here, Jas. iv. 8, and 1 Pet. ii. 22, the inward purification and dedication become the dominant idea, though perhaps not to the entire exclusion of the other.

'Purifieth *himself*'. See on i. 8 and v. 21. S. John once more boldly gives us an apparent contradiction, in order to bring out a real truth. In i. 7 it is 'the blood of Jesus' which 'cleanseth us from all sin:' here the Christian 'purifieth himself'. Both are true, and neither cleansing will avail to salvation without the other. Christ cannot save

even as he is pure. Whosoever committeth sin transgresseth 4
also the law: for sin is the transgression of the law. And 5

us if we withhold our efforts: we cannot save ourselves without His merits and grace.

even as he is pure] As in v. 2, the '*even* as' brings out the reality of the comparison: similarly in John xvii. 11, 22 we have 'that they may be one, *even* as we are'. It is not easy to determine with certainty whether 'He' means the Father or Christ. There is a change of pronoun in the Greek from 'on Him' (ἐπ' αὐτῷ) to 'He' (ἐκεῖνος), and this favours, though it does not prove, a change of meaning. Probably throughout this Epistle ἐκεῖνος means Christ (vv. 5, 7, 16, ii. 6, iv. 17). He who, relying on God, hopes to be like God hereafter, purifies himself now after the example of Christ. Christ conformed Himself to the Father, we do the like by conforming ourselves to Christ. This interpretation brings us once more in contact with Christ's great prayer. 'For their sakes I consecrate Myself, that they themselves may be consecrated in truth' (John xvii. 19). Moreover, would S. John speak of God as 'pure'? God is 'holy' (ἅγιος): Christ in His perfect sinlessness as man is 'pure' (ἁγνός). Note that S. John does not say 'even as He purified Himself:' that grace which the Christian has to seek diligently is the inherent attribute of Christ. The consecration of Christ for the work of redemption is very different from the purification of the Christian in order to be like Him and the Father. Comp. Heb. xii. 14.

4. As so often, the Apostle emphasizes his statement by giving the opposite case, and not the simple opposite, but an expansion of it. Instead of saying 'every one that hath not this hope' he says **every one that doeth** *sin*. The A. V. not only obscures this antithesis by changing 'every man' to 'whosoever', but also the contrast between 'doing righteousness' (ii. 29) and 'doing sin' by changing from 'do' to 'commit'. This contrast is all the more marked in the Greek because both words have the article; 'doeth the righteousness', 'doeth the sin'.

transgresseth also the law] This is very unfortunate, destroying the parallelism: *Every man that* **doeth** *sin,* **doeth** *also* **lawlessness.** It is imperative to have the same verb in both clauses and also in ii. 29: to do sin is to do lawlessness, and this is the opposite of to do righteousness. The one marks the children of God, the other the children of the devil. 'Lawlessness' both in English and Greek (ἀνομία) means not the *privation* of law, but the *disregard* of it: not the having no law, but the acting as if one had none. This was precisely the case with some of the Gnostic teachers: they declared that their superior enlightenment placed them above the moral law; they were neither the better for keeping it nor the worse for breaking it. Sin and lawlessness, says the Apostle, are convertible terms: they are merely different aspects of the same state. And it is in its aspect of disregard of God's law that sin is seen to be quite irreconcilable with being a child of God and having fellowship with God. See on v. 17.

ye know that he was manifested to take away our sins; and
6 in him is no sin. Whosoever abideth in him sinneth not:

Note that throughout these verses (3—15) S. John uses the strong
expression, '*Every* man that' and not simply 'He that.' It has been
suggested that "in each case where this characteristic form of language
occurs there is apparently a reference to some who had questioned the
application of a general principle in particular cases" (Westcott):
comp. ii. 23, 29, iv. 7, v. 1, 4, 18; 2 John 9.

5. That sin is incompatible with Divine birth is still further enforced
by two facts respecting the highest instance of Divine birth. The Son
of God (1) entered the world of sense to put away all sin, (2) was
Himself absolutely free from sin.

ye know] The Apostle once more (ii. 21, iii. 2) appeals to the
knowledge which as Christians they must possess.

that he was manifested] See on ii. 28: the rendering here should
govern the rendering there and in *v.* 2. Here, as in *v.* 8 and i. 2, the
manifestation of the Word in becoming visible to human eyes is meant;
the Incarnation. The expression necessarily implies that He existed
previous to being made manifest.

to take away our sins] Literally, *to take away the sins*, i.e. all the
sins that there are. If 'our sins' means 'the sins of us men' and not
'the sins of us Christians', the rendering is admissible, even if the addition
'of us' (NC Thebaic) is not genuine. As already stated, the article is
often used in Greek where in English we use a possessive pronoun. 'To
take away' (αἴρειν) is the safest rendering; for this is all that the Greek
word necessarily means (see on John i. 29). Yet it is not improbable
that the meaning of 'to bear' is included: He took the sins away *by
bearing them Himself* (1 Pet. ii. 24). This, however, is not S. John's
point. His argument is that the Son's having become incarnate in
order to abolish sin shews that sin is inconsistent with sonship: the
way in which He abolished it is not in question.

in him is no sin] This is an independent proposition and must not
be connected with 'ye know that'. The order of the Greek is impressive; *sin in Him does not exist*. Christ not merely was on earth,
but *is* in heaven, the eternally sinless One. He is the perfect pattern
of what a son of God should be. This, therefore, is yet another proof
that sin and sonship are incompatible. Comp. John vii. 18.

6. *Whosoever abideth*] Better, **Every one that** *abideth:* we have
the same Greek form of expression here as in ii. 23, 29, iii. 3, 4, 9, 10,
15, iv. 7, v. 1, 4, 18, and it is better to mark this in translation.

sinneth not] The Christian sometimes sins (i. 8—10). The Christian
abides in Christ (ii. 27). He who abides in Christ does not sin (iii. 6).
By these apparently contradictory statements put forth one after another
S. John expresses that internal contradiction of which every one who is
endeavouring to do right is conscious. What S. John delivers as a
series of aphorisms, which mutually qualify and explain one another,
S. Paul puts forth dialectically as an argument. 'If what I would not,
that I do, it is no more I that do it, but sin which dwelleth in me'

whosoever sinneth hath not seen him, neither known him.
Little children, let no *man* deceive you: he that doeth 7
righteousness is righteous, even as he is righteous. He 8

(Rom. vii. 20). And on the other hand, 'I live; yet not I, but Christ liveth in me' (Gal. ii. 20).

whosoever sinneth, hath not seen him, neither known him] Or, **every one that** *sinneth, hath not seen Him, neither* **knoweth** *Him*. The second verb is the perfect of the commonest verb in Greek for 'to see' (ὁρᾷν), a verb of which S. John uses no tense but the perfect. The third verb, though perfect in form, is present in meaning, 'I have come to know, I know' (see on ii. 3). No one who sins has seen Christ or attained to a knowledge of Him. What does S. John mean by this strong statement? It will be observed that it is the antithesis of the preceding statement; but, as usual, instead of giving us the simple antithesis, 'Every one that sinneth abideth *not* in Him', he expands and strengthens it into 'Every one that sinneth hath not seen Him, neither come to know Him'. S. John does not say this of every one who commits a sin, but of the habitual sinner (present participle). Although the believer sometimes sins, yet not sin, but opposition to sin, is the ruling principle of his life; for whenever he sins he confesses it, and wins forgiveness, and perseveres with his self-purification.

But the habitual sinner does none of these things: sin is his ruling principle. And this could not be the case if he had ever really known Christ. Just as apostates by leaving the Church prove that they have never really belonged to it (ii. 19), so the sinner by continuing in sin proves that he has never really known Christ.—Seeing and knowing are not two names for the same fact: to see Christ is to be spiritually conscious of His presence; to know Him is to recognise His character and His relation to ourselves. For a collection of varying interpretations of this passage see Farrar's *Early Days of Christianity*, II. p. 434, note.

7. *Little children*] From the point of view of the present section, viz. the Divine parentage, the Apostle again warns his readers against the ruinous doctrine that religion and conduct can be separated, that to the spiritual man all conduct is alike. The renewed address, 'Little children', adds solemnity and tenderness to the warning.

let no man deceive you] Better, as R. V., *let no man* **lead you astray**: see on i. 8. The word implies seduction into error of a grave kind.

he that doeth righteousness] As in *v*. 6, we have the present participle; he who *habitually* does righteousness, not merely one who does a righteous act. If faith without works is dead (Jas. ii. 17, 20), much more is knowledge without works dead. There is only one way of proving our enlightenment, of proving our parentage from Him who is Light; and that is by *doing* the righteousness which is characteristic of Him and His Son. This is the sure test, the test which Gnostic self-exaltation pretended to despise. Anyone that committeth sin is of the devil; for the devil sinneth from the beginning. For this purpose the Son of God was

can say that he possesses a superior knowledge of Divine truth; but does he act accordingly? Does he do divine things?

even as he is righteous] As in v. 3, we are in doubt whether 'He' means the Father or Christ. It is the same pronoun (ἐκεῖνος) as in v. 3, but there is not here any abrupt *change* of pronoun. Here also it seems better to interpret 'He' as Christ (ii. 2), rather than God (i. 9).

8. *He that committeth sin*] Better, as in v. 4, in order to bring out the full antithesis, *He that* **doeth** *sin*. 'To do sin' is the exact opposite of 'to do righteousness': as before, both substantives have the article in the Greek: see on v. 4. And, as before, the present participle indicates the *habitual* doer of sin. Such an one has the devil as the source (ἐκ), not of his existence, but of the evil which rules his existence and is the main element in it. "The devil made no man, begat no man, created no man: but whoso imitates the devil, becomes a child of the devil, as if begotten of him. In what sense art thou a child of Abraham? Not that Abraham begat thee. In the same sense as that in which the Jews, the children of Abraham, by not imitating the faith of Abraham, are become children of the devil" (S. Augustine). It is one of the characteristics of these closing words of N. T. that they mark with singular precision the personality of Satan, and his relation to sin, sinners, and redemption from sin.

for the devil sinneth from the beginning] Or, **because from the beginning the devil sinneth.** 'From the beginning' stands first for emphasis. What does it mean? Various explanations have been suggested. (1) From the beginning of *sin*. The devil was the first to sin and has never ceased to sin. (2) From the beginning of the *devil*. This comes very near to asserting the Gnostic and Manichaean error of two co-eternal principles or Creators, one good and one evil. The very notion of sin involves departure from what is good. The good therefore must have existed first. To avoid this, (3) from the beginning of the devil *as such*, i.e. from the time of his becoming the devil, or (4) from the beginning of his *activity;* which is not very different from (3) if one believes that he is a fallen angel, or from (2) if one does not. (5) From the beginning of the *world*. (6) From the beginning of the *human race*. The first or last seems best. "The phrase 'From the beginning' intimates that there has been no period of the existence of human beings in which they have not been liable to the assaults of this Tempter; that accusations against God, reasons for doubting and distrusting Him, have been offered to one man after another, to one generation after another. This is just what the Scripture affirms; just the assumption which goes through the book from Genesis to the Apocalypse." (Maurice.) Note the present tense: not he has sinned, but he is sinning; his whole existence is sin.

the Son of God] In special contrast to those habitual sinners who are morally the children of the devil.

manifested, that he might destroy the works of the devil.
Whosoever is born of God doth not commit sin; for his 9
seed remaineth in him: and he cannot sin, because he is

that he might destroy] Literally, *that he might unloose* or *dissolve* or *undo*. All destruction is dissolution. The metaphor here has probably nothing to do with loosening bonds or snares. It is a favourite one with S. John; '*Destroy* this sanctuary' (John ii. 19). Comp. v. 18, vii. 23, x. 35, where either notion, loosening or dissolving, is appropriate.
the works of the devil] The sins (*v.* 5) which he causes men to commit. Christ came to *undo* the sins of men.
9. This is the opposite of *v.* 8, as *v.* 8 of *v.* 7; but, as usual, not the plain opposite, but something deduced from it, is stated.
Whosoever is born of God] Or, *Every one that* (see on *v.* 6) *is* **begotten** *of God*. Note the perfect tense; 'every one that has been made and that remains a child of God'. The expression is very frequent throughout the Epistle (ii. 29, iv. 7, v. 1, 4, 18) and the rendering should be uniform; all the more so, because the phrase is characteristic. The A. V. wavers between 'born' and 'begotten', even in the same verse (v. 1, 18). The R. V. rightly prefers 'begotten' throughout: 'born' throughout is impossible, for in v. 1 we have the active, 'begat'. The expression 'to be begotten of God' is found only in S. John; once in the Gospel (i. 13) and eight or nine times in the Epistle: comp. John iii. 3, 5, 6, 7, 8.
doth not commit sin] Better, as R. V., **doeth no sin** (see on *v.* 4): the opposition between 'doing sin' and 'doing righteousness' must be carefully marked. This strong statement is exactly parallel to *v.* 6 and is to be understood in a similar sense. It is literally true of the Divine nature imparted to the believer. That does not sin and cannot sin. A child of the God who is Light can have nothing to do with sin which is darkness: the two are morally incompatible.
for his seed remaineth in him] Better, as R. V., **because** *his seed* **abideth** *in him*: see on ii. 24. This may mean either (1) 'His seed', the new birth *given by God*, 'abideth in him'; or (2) 'his seed', the new birth *received by him*, 'abideth in him'; or (3) 'His seed', *God's child*, 'abideth in *Him*'. The first is probably right. The third is possible, but improbable: 'seed' is sometimes used for 'child' or 'descendant'; but would not S. John have written 'child' as in *vv.* 1, 2, 10, v. 2? To resort to the parable of the sower for an explanation, and to interpret 'seed' as 'the word of God' is scarcely legitimate. The whole analogy refers to human generation, not to the germination of plants; but comp. 1 Pet. i. 23. John iii. 5—8 would lead us to interpret seed as meaning the Holy Spirit.
he cannot sin] It is a moral impossibility for a child of God to sin. It is because of the imperfection of our sonship that sin is possible, an imperfection to be remedied and gradually reduced by the blood of Jesus (i. 7) and self-purification (iii. 3). 'Cannot' of what is morally

10 born of God. In this the children of God are manifest, and the children of the devil: whosoever doeth not righteousness is not of God, neither he that loveth not his 11 brother. For this is the message that ye heard from the

impossible is frequent in S. John's Gospel (v. 30, vi. 44, 65, vii. 7, viii. 43, xii. 39, xiv. 17); comp. iv. 20.

10. *In this*] These words, like 'for this cause' (*v.* 1) refer to what precedes rather than to what follows: but here what follows is similar to what precedes, so that in any case 'in this' means 'by doing or not doing righteousness'.

are manifest] A man's principles are invisible, but their results are visible: 'By their fruits ye shall know them' (Matt. vii. 16—20).

the children of the devil] The expression occurs nowhere else in N. T., but we have 'son of the devil,' Acts xiii. 10: comp. 'children of wrath' (Eph. ii. 3), and 'ye are of your father the devil' (John viii. 44). All mankind are God's children by creation: as regards this a creature can have no choice. But a creature endowed with free will can choose his own parent in the moral world. The Father offers him the 'right to become a child of God' (John i. 12); but he can refuse this and become a child of the devil instead. There is no third alternative.

It was for pressing the doctrine that a tree is known by its fruits to an extreme, and maintaining that a world in which evil exists cannot be the work of a good God, that the heretic Marcion was rebuked by S. John's disciple Polycarp, in words which read like an adaptation of this text, "I know thee for the *firstborn of Satan*" (Iren. *Haer.* III. iii. 4). And in his Epistle (VII. 1) Polycarp writes, "Whosoever does not confess the witness of the cross is *of the devil*".

neither he that loveth not his brother] Here again note the way in which S. John's divisions shade off into one another (see on ii. 28, 29). Doing righteousness, the mark of God's children, suggests the thought of brotherly love, for love is *righteousness in relation to others;* 'For the whole law is fulfilled in one word, even in this; Thou shalt love thy neighbour as thyself' (Gal. v. 14). Love suggests its opposite, hate; and these two form the subject of the next paragraph. Some editors would make the new section begin here in the middle of *v.* 10. It is perhaps better to draw the line between *vv.* 12 and 13, considering *vv.* 11 and 12 as transitional.

'He that loveth not his brother is not of God', for a child of God will love all whom God loves. This prepares us for the statements in iv. 7, 20, 21.

11. *For this is the message that ye heard, &c.*] Or, **Because** *the message which ye heard from the beginning* is this: 'this' is probably the predicate (see on i. 5). 'From the beginning' as in ii. 7: it was one of the very first things conveyed to them in their instruction in Christianity and had been ceaselessly repeated, notably by the Apostle himself. Jerome tells us that during S. John's last years 'Little children, love one another' was the one exhortation which, after he had

beginning, that we should love one another. Not as Cain, 12
who was of *that* wicked one, and slew his brother. And
wherefore slew he him? Because his own works were evil,
and his brother's righteous. Marvel not, my brethren, if 13

become too old to preach, he never ceased to give. "It is the Lord's
command," he said; "and if this is done, it is enough." 'Love one
another' addressed to Christians must primarily mean the love of Christians to fellow-Christians; and this shews what 'loving his brother'
must mean. But the love of Christians to non-Christians must certainly
not be excluded: the arguments for enforcing brotherly love cover the
case of love to all mankind.

12. A brother's love suggests its opposite, a brother's hate, and that
in the typical instance of it, the fratricide Cain.

Not as Cain, who was of that wicked one] Better, as R.V., *Not as* Cain
was *of* the evil *one:* there is no 'who' in the Greek, nor any pronoun
before 'the evil one.' Here as in John i. 21, 25, vi. 14, 48, 69, vii. 40,
the definite article has been turned into a demonstrative pronoun in
A. V. See on i. 2. In 'from the beginning' (v. 8) S. John has gone
back to the earliest point in the history of sin. The instance of Cain
shewed how very soon sin took the form of hate, and fratricidal hate.
It is better not to supply any verb with 'not': although the sentence is
grammatically incomplete, it is quite intelligible. 'We are not, and
ought not to be, of the evil one, as Cain was.' Commentators quote
the "strange Rabbinical view" that while Abel was the son of Adam,
Cain was the son of the tempter. Of course S. John is not thinking
of such wild imaginations: Cain is only *morally* 'of the evil one'. Here,
as elsewhere in the Epistle (ii. 13, 14, v. 18, 19), S. John uses 'the evil
one' as a term with which his readers are quite familiar. He gives no
explanation.

and slew his brother] This was evidence of his devilish nature. The
word for 'slay' (σφάζειν) is a link between this Epistle and Revelation
(vi. 4, &c.; see below), occurring nowhere else in N. T. Its original
meaning was 'to cut the throat' (σφαγή), especially of a victim for
sacrifice. In later Greek it means simply to slay, especially with
violence. But perhaps something of the notion of slaying a victim
clings to it here, as in most passages in Revelation (v. 6, 9, 12, vi. 9,
xiii. 3, 8, xviii. 24).

And wherefore slew he him?] S. John puts this question to bring
out still more strongly the diabolical nature of the act and the agent.
Was Abel at all to blame? On the contrary, it was his *righteousness*
which excited the murderous hate of Cain. Cain was jealous of the
acceptance which Abel's righteous offering found, and which his own
evil offering did not find: and 'who is able to stand before envy?'
(Prov. xxvii. 4). Cain's offering was evil, (1) because it 'cost him
nothing' (2 Sam. xxiv. 24); (2) because of the spirit in which it was
offered.

and his brother's righteous] The last mention of the subject of
righteousness with which this section opened (ii. 29; comp. iii. 7, 10).

14 the world hate you. We know that we have passed from

Neither 'righteousness' nor 'righteous' occur again in the Epistle; righteousness being merged in the warmer and more definite aspect of it, love. This is a reason for including from ii. 29 to iii. 12 in one section, treating of the righteousness of the children of God. Comp. 'By faith Abel offered unto God a more excellent sacrifice than Cain, through which he had witness borne to him *that he was righteous*' (Heb. xi. 4).

13—24. LOVE AND HATE: LIFE AND DEATH.

Marvel not, my brethren] Comp. John v. 28, iii. 7. The antagonism between the light and the darkness, between God and the evil one, between righteousness and unrighteousness, has never ceased from the time of the first sin (*v.* 8) and of the first murder (*v.* 12). The moral descendants of Cain and of Abel are still in the world, and the wicked still hate the righteous. Therefore Christians need not be perplexed, if the world (as it does) hates *them*.

Both in Jewish (Philo, *De sacr. Abelis et Caini*) and in early Christian (*Clem. Hom.* III. xxv., xxvi) literature Abel is taken as the prototype of the good and Cain as the prototype of the wicked. For the wild sect of the Cainites, who took *exactly the opposite view*, see Appendix C. It is possible that some germs of this monstrous heresy are aimed at in *v.* 12.

brethren] This form of address, which occurs nowhere else in the Epistle (not genuine in ii. 7), is in harmony with the subject of *brotherly love*.

if the world hate you] Better, as R. V., *if the world* **hateth** *you:* in the Greek we have the indicative, not the subjunctive or optative. The fact is stated gently, but not doubtfully. The verse is another echo of Christ's last discourses as recorded in the Gospel: '*If* the world *hateth* you (same construction as here), ye know that it hath hated Me before it hated you' (John xv. 18). Comp. Mark xv. 44.

14. Love means life and hate means death.

We know] The pronoun is very emphatic: 'the dark world which is full of devilish hate may think and do what it pleases about us; *we know* that we have left the atmosphere of death for one of life.' This knowledge is part of our consciousness (οἴδαμεν) as Christians: comp. ii. 20, 21; iii. 2, 5. Cain hated and slew his brother: the world hates and would slay us. But for all that, it was Cain who passed from life into death, while his brother passed to eternal life, and through his sacrifice 'he being dead yet speaketh' (Heb. xi. 4). The same is the case between the world and Christians. Philo in a similar spirit points out that Cain really slew, not his brother, but himself.

have passed from death unto life] Better, *have passed* **over out of** *death* **into** *life*, have left *an abode in* the one region for *an abode in* the other: another reminiscence of the Gospel (John v. 24). The Greek perfect here has the common meaning of permanent result of past action: 'we have passed into a new home *and abide there*.' The meta-

death unto life, because we love the brethren. He that
loveth not *his* brother abideth in death. Whosoever hateth 15
his brother is a murderer: and ye know that no murderer

phor is perhaps taken from the passage of the Red Sea (Exod. xv. 16),
or of the Jordan.

because we love the brethren] This depends on 'we know,' not on
'we have passed': our love is the infallible sign that we have made the
passage. The natural state of man is selfishness, which involves
enmity to others, whose claims clash with those of self: to love others
is proof that this natural state has been left. Life and love are two
aspects of the same fact in the moral world, as life and growth in the
physical: the one marks the state, the other the activity.

He that loveth not his brother] Omit 'his brother', which, though
correct as an interpretation, is no part of the true text. Wiclif and the
Rhemish, following the Vulgate, omit the addition.

abideth in death] Which implies that death is the original condition
of all. The believer passes out of this by becoming a child of God and
thereby of necessity loving God's other children. He who does not
love them shews that he is still in the old state of death.

15. *Whosoever hateth his brother*] Or, **Every one that** *hateth his
brother:* see on *v.* 4. Quite as a matter of course S. John passes from
not loving to hating. The crisis caused in the world by the coming of
the light leaves no neutral ground: all is either light or darkness, of
God or of the evil one, of the Church or of the world, in love or in
hate. A Christian cannot be neither loving nor hating, any more than
a plant can be neither growing nor dying.

is a murderer] Or, as most of the earlier Versions, *is a manslayer.*
The word (ἀνθρωποκτόνος) occurs only here and John viii. 44. The
mention of Cain just before renders it certain that 'murderer' is not to
be understood figuratively as '*soul*-destroyer'. Human law considers
overt acts; God considers motives. The motives of the hater and of
the murderer are the same: the fact that one is, and the other is not,
deterred by laziness or fear from carrying out his hatred into homicidal
action, makes no difference in the moral character of the men, though
it makes all the difference in the eyes of the law. This is only apply-
ing to the sixth commandment the principle which the Lord Himself
applies to the seventh (Matt. v. 28).

ye know that no murderer] Once more (*v.* 14) the Apostle appeals to
their consciousness as Christians (οἴδατε): it is not a matter of experience
gradually acquired (γινώσκετε), but of knowledge once for all possessed.
He who is a murderer at heart cannot along with the deadly spirit
which he cherishes have eternal life as a sure possession. Comp. 'Ye
have not His word *abiding in* you,' John v. 38. S. John of course does
not mean that hatred or murder is a sin for which there is no forgiveness. But 'the soul that sinneth, it shall *die*'; and the sin of which the
special tendency is destruction of life is absolutely incompatible with
the possession of eternal life. 'But for...murderers...their part shall
be in the lake that burneth with fire and brimstone; which is the

9—2

16 hath eternal life abiding in him. Hereby perceive we the love *of God*, because he laid down his life for us: and we 17 ought to lay down *our* lives for the brethren. But whoso

second death' (Rev. xxi. 8). Here, as elsewhere, S. John speaks of eternal life as something which the Christian already *has*, not which he hopes to *win*: comp. v. 13; John iii. 36, v. 24, vi. 47, 54, &c. Eternal life has nothing to do with time, and is neither lost nor gained by physical death: see on John xi. 25.—The form of expression in this verse is similar to ii. 19, being literally, *every murderer hath not*, instead of 'no murderer hath'.

16. *Hereby perceive we the love of God*] Better, **Herein know we love**: see on ii. 3. The Greek is literally, 'we have perceived,' and therefore **we know**, as R. V., and there is no 'of God'. The A. V. here collects the errors of other Versions: Tyndale and Cranmer have 'perceave', Wiclif and the Rhemish insert 'of God'; the Genevan is right on both points, 'Herby have we perceaved love.' We have obtained the knowledge of what love is, in the concrete example of Christ's vicarious death. Christ is the archetype of self-sacrificing love, as Cain is of brother-sacrificing hate. Love and hate are known by their works.

because he laid down his life] For 'herein' followed by 'because' see on ii. 3. 'To lay down' may mean either 'to *pay* down' in the way of ransom or propitiation, or simply 'to lay *aside*.' Classical usage sanctions the former interpretation: Demosthenes uses the verb (τίθεσθαι) of paying interest, tribute, taxes. And this is supported by 'for us' (ὑπὲρ ἡμῶν), i.e. 'on our behalf'. But 'I lay down My life that I may *take it again*' (John x. 17, 18), and 'layeth *aside* His garments' (xiii. 4; comp. xiii. 12), are in favour of the latter: they are quite against the rendering 'He *pledged* His life'. The phrase 'to lay down one's life' is peculiar to S. John (x. 11, 15, 17, xiii. 37, 38, xv. 13). In Greek the pronoun (ἐκεῖνος as in ii. 6 and iii. 7) marks more plainly than in English *who* laid down His life: but S. John's readers had no need to be told.

and we ought] The 'we' is emphatic: this on *our* side is a Christian's duty; he 'ought himself also to walk *even as* He walked' (ii. 6). The argument seems to shew that though 'the brethren' specially means believers, yet heathen are not to be excluded. Christ laid down His life not for Christians only, 'but also *for the whole world*' (ii. 2). Christians must imitate Him in this: their love must be (1) practical, (2) absolutely self-sacrificing, (3) all-embracing. 'God commendeth His own love toward us, in that, *while we were yet sinners*, Christ died for us' (Rom. v. 8). Tertullian quotes this dictum of the Apostle in urging the duty of martyrdom: "If he teaches that we must die for the brethren, how much more for the Lord" (*Scorp.* xii.). Comp. Prov. xxiv. 11. See on iv. 18.

17. *But whoso hath this world's good*] Better, as R. V., *But whoso hath* **the** *world's* **goods**. The 'But' is full of meaning. 'But not many of us are ever called upon to die for another: smaller sacrifices,

hath *this* world's good, and seeth his brother hath need, and shutteth up his bowels *of compassion* from him, how dwelleth the love of God in him? My little children, let 18 us not love in word, neither in tongue; but in deed and in

however, may be demanded of us; and what if we fail to make them?' The word for 'good' or 'goods' (βίος) is the same as that rendered 'life' in ii. 16, where see note. It signifies there and here 'means of life, subsistence'. 'The world's life', therefore, means that which supports the life of mankind, or life in this world (see on ii. 15) in marked contrast to eternal life (*v.* 15).

and seeth his brother have need] Better, *and* **beholdeth** *his brother* **having** *need*. The verb implies that he not only sees him (ἰδεῖν), but looks at him and considers him (θεωρεῖν). It is a word of which the contemplative Apostle is very fond; and outside the Synoptic Gospels and the Acts it occurs nowhere but in S. John's writings and Heb. vii. 4. It is a pity to spoil the irony of the original by weakening '*having* need' into '*in* need' (R. V.). The one *has* as his possession the world's *wealth*, the other *has* as his possession *need*.

shutteth up his bowels of compassion from him] There is no 'of compassion' in the Greek and we hardly need both substantives. The ancients believed the bowels to be the seat of the affections (Gen. xliii. 30; 1 Kings iii. 26; Jer. xxxi. 20; Phil. i. 8, ii. 1; Philem. 7, 12, 20) as well as the heart, whereas we take the latter only. Coverdale (here, as often, following Luther) alters Tyndale's 'shutteth up his compassion' into 'shutteth up his heart.' And in fact, 'shutteth up his bowels from him' is the same as 'closeth his heart against him.' The phrase occurs nowhere else in N. T., but comp. 2 Cor. vi. 12. The '*from* him' is picturesque, as in ii. 28: it expresses the moving away and turning his back on his brother. In LXX. 'Thou shalt not harden thine heart' (Deut. xv. 7) is 'Thou shalt not *turn away* thine heart'.

how dwelleth the love of God in him?] Better, as R. V., *how doth the love of God* **abide** *in him?* this preserves the order of the Greek better and marks the recurrence of S. John's favourite verb 'abide' (see on ii. 24). 'The love of God', as usual in this Epistle (see on ii. 5), means man's love to God. The question here is equivalent to the statement in iv. 20, that to love God and hate one's brother is impossible.

18. *My little children, let us not love in word*] S. John, as in ii. 28, iii. 13, iv. 1, 7, hastens on to a practical application of what he has been stating as the principles of Christian Ethics; and in each case he prefaces his gentle exhortation with a word of tender address. 'Dear children, do not think that I am giving you a series of philosophical truisms; I am telling of the principles which must govern your conduct and mine, if we are children of the God who is Light and Love.'

let us not love in word, neither in tongue] Or, as R. V., *neither with* **the** *tongue*. This is more accurate, for in the Greek 'word' has no article and 'tongue' has: both are datives of the instrument, and the article marks the tongue as the special instrument of the hypocritical love. Is there any difference between loving in word and loving with

19 truth. And hereby we know that we are of the truth, and
20 shall assure our hearts before him. For if *our* heart condemn

the tongue? And is there any difference between loving in deed and loving in truth? The answer must be the same to both questions. The oppositions between 'word' and 'deed' and between 'tongue' and 'truth' are so exact as to lead us to believe that there *is* a difference. To love in word is to have that affection which is genuine as far as it goes, but which is so weak that it never gets further than affectionate words: such love is opposed, not to truth, but to loving *acts*. To love with the tongue is to profess an affection which one does not feel, which is sheer hypocrisy: it is opposed, not to deeds, but to *truth*. It may shew itself also in hypocritical acts, done (as Bede points out) not with the wish to do good, but to win praise, or to injure others.

in deed and in truth] Omit the second 'in': the preposition is not repeated in the Greek. Tyndale and the Rhemish Version have no second 'in'. Comp. James ii. 15; Rom. xii. 9. What follows, though intimately connected with the first part of the section (see next note), almost amounts to a fresh departure. The subject of love and its opposite is transformed into *the security and serenity of conscience which genuine and active love is able to produce.*

19. *And hereby we know*] Rather, **Herein we shall know**: the 'and', though well supported, is probably not genuine, and the evidence for the future as against the present is overwhelming. 'Herein' (ἐν τούτῳ) sometimes refers to what follows (*v.* 16, iv. 2, 9), sometimes to what precedes (ii. 5). Here the latter is the case: by loving in deed and truth we shall arrive at the knowledge that we are morally the children of the Truth. 'The Truth' here is almost equivalent to 'God'. 'To be of the Truth' is to have the Truth as the source whence the guiding and formative influences of thought and conduct flow: comp. ii. 21; John iii. 31, viii. 47, and especially xviii. 37. The preposition 'of' here = 'out of' (ἐκ), and the notion of *origin* must not be lost sight of any more than in ii. 16, 19, 21, iii. 8, 10, 12, iv. 1, 2, 3, &c.

The construction and punctuation of what follows is doubtful; also the reading in the first and second clauses of *v.* 20. Certainty is not attainable, and to give all possible variations of reading and rendering would take up too much space. The conclusions adopted here are given as good and tenable, but not as demonstrably right.

and shall assure our hearts] Literally, *and shall* **persuade** *our hearts.* Is this clause *coordinate* with 'we shall know', or dependent upon it ('we shall know that we shall assure')? Probably the former. The meaning is, 'Herein we shall know that we are of the truth, and herein we shall persuade our heart.' Authorities are much divided between 'heart' (B, Peschito, Thebaic) and 'hearts' (אCKL); the former seems preferable. S. John elsewhere always uses the singular both in Gospel and Epistle: it "fixes the thought upon the personal trial in each case" (Westcott). In any case it obviously means, not the *affections* (2 Cor. vii. 3; Phil. i. 7), but the *conscience* (Acts ii. 37, vii. 54). It is worth noting that the Greek word (καρδία) is cognate with the English

us, God is greater than our heart, and knoweth all *things*.

'heart.' The substitution of 'assure' for 'persuade' appears to be somewhat violent, for it is a meaning which the verb (πείθειν) does not in itself possess. But if the context justifies the substitution, because the meaning plainly is 'persuade our heart *that it need not condemn us*', then the context may speak for itself in the English, as in the Greek. Comp. 'We will *persuade* him and rid you of care' (Matt. xxviii. 14); and 'having made Blastus their friend', literally 'having *persuaded* Blastus' (Acts xii. 20).

before him] This is placed first for emphasis in the Greek; *and* **before Him** *shall assure our hearts*. The important thing is that we can quiet our consciences *in the sight of God*. The self-deceiver, who is not 'of the Truth', but 'walks in darkness' hating his brother (ii. 1), can quiet his heart, 'because the darkness hath blinded his eyes': but this is not done 'before God'.

20. *For if our heart condemn us*] It is possible to attach this to the preceding verse (reading ὅ τι ἐάν, a construction found Acts iii. 23 and Gal. v. 10, and perhaps Col. iii. 17, for ὅτι ἐάν), and to render with R. V., **whereinsoever** *our heart condemn us:* but see next note. "A Christian's heart burdened with a sense of its own unworthiness forms an unfavourable opinion of the state of the soul, pronounces against its salvation. If we are conscious of practically loving the brethren, we can adduce this as evidence of the contrary, and give the heart ground to change its opinion, and to reassure itself. Anyone who has had experience of the doubts and fears which spring up in a believer's heart from time to time, of whether he is or is not in a state of condemnation, will feel the need and the efficacy of this test of faith and means of assurance" (Jelf).

God is greater than our heart] On overwhelming evidence (ℵBCKL) we must insert 'because' or 'that' (ὅτι) before 'God is greater'. If the reading and rendering of the preceding clause adopted in R. V. is right, '*because* God is greater' will make good sense. Because God is superior to our consciences in being omniscient, we may (when our love is sincere and fruitful), persuade our consciences before Him to acquit us. Our consciences through imperfect knowledge may be either too strict or too easy with us: God cannot be either, for He knows and weighs all.

But it seems almost certain that 'if our heart condemn us' must be right, as the natural correlative of 'if our heart condemn us not', which is indisputably right. This progress by means of opposites stated side by side has been S. John's method all through: 'if we confess our sins' and 'if we say that we have not sinned' (i. 9, 10); 'he that loveth his brother' and 'he that hateth his brother' (ii. 10, 11); 'he that doeth righteousness' and 'he that doeth sin' (iii. 7, 8); 'every spirit that confesseth' and 'every spirit that confesseth not' (iv. 2, 3). But, if this is accepted, what is to be done with the apparently redundant 'because' or 'that'? Two plans are suggested: 1. to supply 'it is' before 'because'; 2. to supply 'it is plain' (δῆλον) before 'that'. The latter

21 Beloved, if our heart condemn us not, *then* have we con-
22 fidence towards God. And whatsoever we ask, we receive

seems preferable: for what can be the meaning of 'if our heart condemn us, (it is) *because* God is greater than our heart'? Whereas, 'if our heart condemn us, (it is plain) that God is greater than our heart' makes excellent sense. There is perhaps a similar ellipse of 'it is plain' (ὅτι= δῆλον ὅτι) 1 Tim. vi. 7; 'We brought nothing into the world, and (it is plain) that we can carry nothing out.' And other instances are quoted from S. Chrysostom (X. p. 38 BD; p. 122 B, where some editors insert δῆλον).

We must not give 'God is greater' a one-sided interpretation, either 'God is more merciful' or 'God is more strict'. It means that He is a more perfect judge than our heart can be. It is the difference between conscience and Omniscience.

and knoweth all things] The 'and' is epexegetic; it explains the special character of God's superiority when the soul stands before the judgment-seat of conscience. He knows all things; on the one hand the light and grace against which we have sinned, on the other the reality of our repentance and our *love*. It was to this infallible omniscience that S. Peter appealed, in humble distrust of his own feeling and judgment; 'Lord, Thou knowest all things; Thou knowest that I love Thee' (John xxi. 17). It is the reality and activity of our love (*vv.* 18, 19) which gives us assurance under the accusations of conscience. Comp. 'If ye forgive men their trespasses', having genuine love for them, 'your heavenly Father will also forgive you', and ye will be able to persuade your hearts before Him (Matt. vi. 14).

The force of *vv.* 19, 20 may be thus summed up: 'By loving our brethren in deed and truth we come to know that we are God's children and have His presence within us, and are enabled to meet the disquieting charges of conscience. For, if conscience condemns us, its verdict is neither infallible nor final. We may still appeal to the omniscient God, whose love implanted within us is a sign that we are not condemned and rejected by Him.'

21. *Beloved*] See on *v.* 2.

if our heart condemn us not] An argument *à fortiori:* if before God we can persuade conscience to acquit us, when it upbraids us, much more may we have assurance before Him, when it does *not* do so. It is not quite evident whether 'condemn us not' means '*ceases* to condemn us', because we have persuaded it, or 'does not condemn us *from the first*', because it has had no misgivings about us. Either makes good sense. The same word for 'condemn' occurs Gal. ii. 11 of S. Peter's dissimulation at Antioch: 'I resisted him to the face, because he stood *condemned*', and in Ecclus. xiv. 2, 'Blessed is he whose conscience hath not condemned him' (οὐ κατέγνω).

then have we confidence towards God] 'Then', which is not in the Greek, may be omitted; *we have* **boldness** (see on ii. 28) *toward God* (v. 14). We approach to Him as children to a Father and not as criminals to a Judge. This is not the same as 'persuading our heart' (*v.* 19),

of him, because we keep his commandments, and do those
things that are pleasing in his sight. And this is his com- 23
mandment, That we should believe on the name of his Son

but may be the result of it. Compare 'to have peace *toward God*'
(Rom. v. 1), i.e. in our relations to Him: both A.V. and R. V. render
'have peace *with* God', but the Greek is the same as here (πρὸς τὸν
Θεόν).

22. This verse is so closely connected with the preceding one, that
not more than a comma or semicolon should be placed between them.
When a good conscience gives us boldness towards God our prayers
are granted, for children in such relations to their heavenly Father
cannot ask anything which He will refuse.

And whatsoever we ask] The 'and' is probably epexegetic, as in
v. 20, and explains the special character of our boldness. See on v. 15.

we receive of him] The present is to be taken quite literally; not
as the present for the future. It may be a long time before we see the
results of our prayer; but it is granted at once. As S. Augustine says,
'He who gave us love cannot close His ears against the groans and
prayers of love'.

because we keep his commandment] This should certainly be plural,
commandments: previous English Versions have the plural, and there
seems to be no trace of a various reading, so that one suspects a
misprint in the edition of 1611. 'Because' depends upon 'receive',
not upon 'have boldness': we receive because we are loyal. This is
in harmony with the Gospel and with Scripture generally: 'We know
that God heareth not sinners: but if any man be a worshipper of God,
and *do His will, him He heareth*' (John ix. 31); 'The Lord is far from
the wicked, but He heareth the prayer of the righteous' (Prov. xv. 29;
comp. Ps. lxvi. 18, 19; Job xxvii. 8, 9; Isai. i. 11—15). For 'keep
His commandments' see on ii. 3.

do those things which are pleasing in his sight] Not the same as
'keeping His commandments': the one is *obedience*, which may be
slavish, the other is *love*. We seem here to have another reminiscence
of the Gospel (viii. 29): 'Because the things pleasing to Him I always
do'. Excepting Acts vi. 2, xii. 3, the word for 'pleasing' occurs
nowhere else in N. T. Comp. Heb. xiii. 21; 1 Tim. ii. 3.

23. *And this is his commandment*] Or, *And His commandment is
this;* see on i. 5. Here the singular is right: the various commandments, especially the two here named, faith and love, are summed up
as one whole. This verse is the answer to those who would argue from
the preceding verses that all that is required of us is to *do* what is right;
it does not much matter what we *believe*. Not so says the Apostle.
In order to do what is right it is necessary to believe: this is the first
step in our obedience to God's commands.

that we should believe] For 'that' (ἵνα) see on i. 9: here perhaps it
merely "gives the nature and contents of the commandment, not the
aim" (Jelf).

Jesus Christ, and love one another, as he gave us command-
24 ment. And he that keepeth his commandments dwelleth
in him, and he in him. And hereby we know that he
abideth in us, by the Spirit which he hath given us.

believe on the name of his son Jesus Christ] More accurately, *believe the Name of &c.* It is not the precise phrase used v. 13, John i. 12, ii. 23, iii. 18 (πιστεύειν εἰς τὸ ὄνομα), a construction of which S. John is very fond, but a phrase which occurs nowhere else in N. T. (πιστεύειν τῷ ὀνόματι), a construction similar to that in iv. 1, v. 10. The former is the stronger expression, marking the more permanent trust and repose; but in such a phrase as this there cannot be much difference between 'believing' and 'believing on'. 'To believe His Name' means to believe all that His Name (here given with solemn fulness) signifies and implies; His Divinity, His Sonship, and His office as Mediator, Advocate and Saviour.

and love one another] 'Faith if it have not works is dead' (James ii. 17): hence the necessity for adding 'and love one another', which of course means love 'in *deed* and truth' (*v.* 18). 'And' here is not epexegetic: it adds something fresh, giving active love as the necessary effect of living faith. 'Love' is in the present tense of what must be continual.

as he gave us commandment] Or **even** *as* (to mark the difference between καθώς and ὡς). 'He gave' refers to Christ, just mentioned; and this limits 'commandment' to 'love one another' (John xiii. 34, xv. 12, 17): moreover love rather than faith is the subject of this portion of the Epistle. 'To give commandment' is a phrase which in N. T. is peculiar to S. John (xi. 57, xii. 49, xiii. 34): it occurs in Demosthenes.

24. *And he that keepeth his commandments*] This looks back to the same phrase in *v.* 22, not to the conclusion of *v.* 23, which is parenthetical. Therefore 'His' means God's, not Christ's.

dwelleth in him] Better, **abideth** *in Him:* it is S. John's favourite word, which occurs twice in this verse (see on ii. 24). "Let God be a home to thee, and be thou a home of God" (Bede). This mutual abiding expresses union of the strongest and closest kind: comp. iv. 13, 16; John vi. 56, xv. 4, 5. S. John once more insists on what may be regarded as the main theme of this exposition of Christian Ethics; that *conduct* is not only not a matter of indifference, but is all-important. We may possess many kinds of enlightenment, intellectual and spiritual; but there is no union with God, and indeed no true knowledge of Him, without *obedience:* comp. i. 6, ii. 4, 6, 29, iii. 6, 7, 9. 'He that *willeth to do His will* shall know' (John vii. 17).

and hereby] Or, *and herein*, as in *vv.* 16, 19, ii. 3, 5, iv. 9, 10, 13, 17, v. 2. This probably refers to what follows; but the change of preposition in the Greek, a change obliterated in both A. V. and R. V., renders this not quite certain. S. John writes, not 'here*by* we know... *by* the Spirit' (which would place the connexion beyond a doubt), but 'here*in* (ἐν) we know... *from* (ἐκ) the Spirit'.

we know] Literally, *we come to know:* it is a matter of Christian experience.

by the Spirit] Better, from *the Spirit:* this is the source from which the knowledge is derived. This is the first mention of the Spirit in the Epistle, although He is alluded to in ii. 20.

which he hath given us] Or, *which He* **gave** *us*. The verb is aorist, not perfect; and though this is a case where the English perfect might represent the Greek aorist, yet as the Apostle probably refers to the definite occasion when the Spirit was given, the aorist seems better. This occasion in S. John's case would be Pentecost, in that of his readers, their baptism. Thus in our Baptismal Service we are exhorted to pray that the child "may be baptized with water and the Holy Ghost"; and in what follows we pray, "wash him and sanctify him with the Holy Ghost"; and again, "give Thy Holy Spirit to this infant, that he may be born again": after which follows the baptism.

It would be possible to translate 'by the Spirit *of* which He has given us', a partitive genitive, meaning '*some* of which' as in *Macbeth*, I. iii. 80,

"The earth hath bubbles as the water has,
And these are *of them*".

And in Bacon's Essays, *Of Atheisme,* "You shall have *of them*, that will suffer for Atheisme, and not recant". But the Greek genitive here is probably not partitive but the result of attraction. S. John commonly inserts a preposition (ἐκ) with the partitive genitive (2 John 4; 1 John i. 24, vii. 40, xvi. 17; Rev. ii. 10, xi. 9; comp. John xxi. 10). Tyndale here translates 'Therby we knowe that ther abydeth in us *of* the sprete which He gave us', making 'of the Spirit' (=a portion of the Spirit) the nominative to 'abideth'; which is grammatically possible, but scarcely in harmony with what precedes. The change from Tyndale's rendering to the one adopted in A. V., and (with change of 'hath given' to 'gave') in R. V. also, is due to Coverdale.

Once more (see note between ii. 28 and 29 and on iii. 10) we are led to a fresh section almost without knowing it. In the last six verses of this chapter (19—24) the transition from verse to verse is perfectly smooth and natural; so also in the previous six verses (13—18). Nor is the transition from *v.* 18 to *v.* 19 at all violent or abrupt. By a very gradual movement we have been brought from the contrast between love and hate to the gift of the Spirit. And this prepares the way for a new subject; or rather for an old subject treated from a new point of view. Like the doublings of the Maeander near which he lived, the progress of the Apostle at times looks more like retrogression than advance: but the progress is unmistakable when the whole field is surveyed. Here we seem to be simply going back to the subject of the antichrists (ii. 18—28); but whereas there the opposition between the Holy Spirit in true believers and the lying spirit in the antichrists is only suggested (ii. 20, 22, 27), here it is the dominant idea.

4 Beloved, believe not every spirit, but try the spirits

CHAP. IV.

The main subject still continues, that **God is Love**; and that from this truth flows the moral obligation on Christians not only to love God but one another. But, as in Chap. iii., there are subdivisions, each of which has a unity in itself as well as intimate and subtle relations to the whole. These subdivisions are mainly two; *The Spirit of Truth and the Spirit of Error* (1—6); *Love is the Mark of the Children of the God who is Love* (7—21). If we are asked as to the relation which this chapter bears to the preceding one, the answer would seem to be something of this kind. Chap. iii. insists upon the necessity of *deeds* in order to prove our relationship to God (iii. 3, 7, 10, 16—18, 22); chap. iv. points out the *certainty* of our relationship to God as attested by our deeds (iv. 4, 6, 7, 12, 13, 15—17). The one gives us the *evidence* of our sonship, viz. deeds of righteousness towards God (iii. 1—10) and deeds of love towards men (iii. 11—21): the other shews us the *source* of our sonship, viz. possession of the Spirit as shewn by confession of the Incarnation (iv. 1—6) and by love of the brethren (iv. 7—21).

1—6. THE SPIRIT OF TRUTH AND THE SPIRIT OF ERROR.

1—6. This section is an amplification of the sentence with which the preceding chapter ends. We certainly have the Holy Spirit as an abiding gift from God, for otherwise we could not believe and confess the truth of the Incarnation. As usual, S. John thinks and teaches in antitheses. The test which proves that we have the Spirit of God proves that the antichrists have not this gift but its very opposite. In chap. ii. the antichrists were introduced as evidence of the transitoriness of the world (ii. 18): here they are introduced as the crucial negative instance which proves that every true believer has the Spirit of God.

Beloved] See on iii. 2.

believe not every spirit] This exhortation does not give us the main subject of the section, any more than 'Marvel not, brethren, if the world hate you' (iii. 13) gave us the main subject of the last section (iii. 12—24). In both cases the exhortation is introductory and momentary. Having spoken of the Spirit by which we know that God abides in us, the Apostle goes on to speak of other spiritual influences which indubitably exist, and of which every one has experience, but which are not necessarily of God because they are spiritual. "He does not discredit the fact that spiritual influences were widely diffused; he does not monopolize such influences for the Christian Church. How could he discredit this fact? How can we? Are there not myriads of influences about us continually, which do not act upon our senses but upon our spirits, which do not proceed from things which may be seen and handled, but from the spirits of men?" (Maurice). But besides ordinary spiritual influences, S. John probably has in his mind those extraordinary and supernatural powers which at various periods of the Church's history persons have claimed to possess. Such claims exhibit themselves in professed revelations, prophecies, miracles, and the like.

whether they are of God: because many false prophets are

About all such things there are two possibilities which must put us on our guard: (1) they may be unreal; either the delusions of fanatical enthusiasts, or the lies of deliberate impostors: (2) even if real, they need not be of God. Miraculous powers are no absolute guarantee of the possession of truth.

try the spirits] Or, as R. V., *prove the spirits*. There are two words in N. T. meaning 'to try, test, prove'; the one which we have here (δοκιμάζειν), and the one which is used where the Jews try or tempt Christ (Mark viii. 11, x. 2, &c.), and of the temptations of Satan (Matt. iv. 1, 3, &c.). The former occurs about 20, the latter about 40 times in N. T. Neither are common in S. John's writings: he nowhere else uses the word which we have here, and the other only 4 times (John vi. 6; Rev. ii. 2, 10, iii. 10). The A. V. is very capricious in its renderings of the former; 'allow' (Rom. xiv. 22), 'approve' (Rom. ii. 18), 'discern' (Luke xii. 56), 'examine' (1 Cor. xi. 28), 'like' (Rom. i. 28), 'prove' (Luke xiv. 19), 'try' (1 Cor. iii. 13); while the latter is rendered 'examine' (2 Cor. xiii. 5), 'prove' (John vi. 6), 'tempt' (Matt. xxii. 18), 'try' (Rev. ii. 2). The Revisers have somewhat reduced this variety. In the one case 'allow' has been changed to 'approve'; 'examine' and 'try' to 'prove': in the other case 'examine' has been changed to 'try'. The difference between the two words (which are found together 2 Cor. xiii. 5 and Ps. xxvi. 2) is on the whole this, that the one here used commonly implies a good, if not a friendly object; to prove or test in the hope that what is tried will stand the test: whereas the other often implies a sinister object; to try in the hope that what is tried will be found wanting. The metaphor here is from testing metals. Comp. '*Prove* all things; hold fast that which is good' (1 Thess. v. 21).

whether they are of God] Whether their origin (ἐκ) is from God: comp. iii. 2, 12.

A verse such as this cuts at the root of such pretensions as the Infallibility of the Pope. What room is left for Christians to 'prove the spirits', if all they have to do is to ask the opinion of an official? The Apostle's charge, 'prove *ye* the spirits', may be addressed to Christians singly or to the Church collectively: it cannot be addressed to an individual. Comp. Rom. xii. 2; Eph. v. 10; 1 Cor. x. 15, xi. 13. The verse also shews us in what spirit to judge of such things as the reported miracles at Lourdes and the so-called 'manifestations' of Spiritualism. When they have been proved to be real, they must still further be proved to see 'whether they are of God'. We are not to judge of doctrine by miracles, but of miracles by doctrine. A miracle enforcing what contradicts the teaching of Christ and His Apostles is not 'of God' and is no authority for Christians. Comp. Gal. i. 8; Deut. xiii. 1—3.

because many false prophets] The caution is against no imaginary or merely possible danger; it already exists. Warnings respecting the coming of such had been given by Christ, S. Paul, S. Peter, and S.

2 gone out into the world. Hereby know ye the Spirit of
God: Every spirit that confesseth that Jesus Christ is come

Jude; and now S. John tells his readers that these prophecies have been
fulfilled. These 'false prophets' include the antichrists of ii. 18, and
what is here said of them seems to indicate that like Mahomet, Sweden-
borg, the Irvingites, and others, they put forth their new doctrine as a
revelation.

are gone out into the world] This probably has no reference to their
'going out from us' (ii. 19). Possibly it means no more than that they
have appeared in public; but it perhaps includes the notion of their
having a *mission* from the power that sent them: comp. John iii. 17, vi.
14, x. 36, xi. 27, xii. 47, 49, and especially xvi. 28. We need not confine these 'many false prophets' to the antichrists who had left the
Christian communion. There would be others who, like Apollonius of
Tyana, had never been Christians at all: and others even more dangerous who still professed to be members of the Church. The difficulties
in the Church of Corinth caused by the unrestrained 'speaking with
tongues' point to dangers of this kind.

2. *Hereby know ye*] Or, *Herein ye know:* the verb may be either
indicative or imperative (comp. ii. 27, 29). The indicative is preferable,
in spite of the imperatives in *v.* 1: comp. iii. 16, 19, 24, which are very
closely parallel to this. 'Ye know' is literally 'ye come to know, perceive, recognise': 'herein' refers to what follows: see on iii. 19.

every spirit that confesseth] This idea of 'confessing' one's belief is
specially frequent in S. John: ii. 23, iv. 15; 2 John 7; John ix. 22, xii.
42; comp. Rom. x. 9.

that Jesus Christ is come in the flesh] See on 2 John 7. This is the
crucial test, and one which would at once expose 'the spirits' of
Cerinthian and Docetic teachers. We are not to suppose that all other
articles of faith are unimportant; or that to deny this truth is the worst
of all denials (see on ii. 22); or that such denial involves every kind of
doctrinal error. But against the errors prevalent in that age this was
the great safeguard. The confession must of course be not with the
tongue only but in truth, and in deed as well as in word (iii. 18): *non
lingua sed factis, non sonando sed amando* (Bede).

The sentence may be taken in more ways than one: (1) as both A.V.
and R.V.; (2) more accurately, and with some difference of meaning;
confesseth **Jesus Christ as come** *in the flesh;* (3) *confesseth* **that Jesus is
the Christ** *come in the flesh.* Remark that S. John does not say 'come
into the flesh', but '*in* the flesh': Christ did not descend (as Cerinthus
said) into an already existing man, but He came in human nature; He
'*became* flesh'. Moreover he does not say that the confession is to be of
a Christ who *came* (ἐλθόντα), but of a Christ who *is come* (ἐληλυθότα).
This 'coming' is not an exhausted fact: He is come and abides in the
flesh.

S. Paul gives almost exactly the same test: 'I give you to understand
that no man speaking in the Spirit of God saith, Jesus is anathema; and
no man can say, Jesus is Lord, but in the Holy Spirit' (1 Cor. xii. 3).

in the flesh is of God: and every spirit that confesseth not 3
that Jesus Christ is come in the flesh is not of God: and

is of God] Proceeds from Him as its source: comp. iii. 10. "To
confess that Jesus the anointed is come in the flesh, is to confess that
there is a medium of spiritual communications between the visible and
the invisible world, between earth and heaven. It is to confess that
there is one Mediator for all men" (Maurice).

3. *confesseth not that Jesus Christ is come in the flesh*] On overwhelming evidence (AB, Coptic, Aethiopic, Vulgate, &c.) we must omit
the words 'that Christ is come in the flesh', retaining only **confesseth
not Jesus**: the additional words are an obvious interpolation by one
who wished to make the two sides of the antithesis exactly equal. But,
as we have repeatedly seen (i. 5, 6, 7, 8, ii. 10, 22, 23, &c.), this is
rarely the case in S. John's oppositions.

There is yet another very ancient and very interesting difference of reading here: *every spirit which* **severeth** *Jesus*, or, *unmaketh Jesus*, or,
destroyeth Jesus, or, as the margin of R. V., which *annulleth Jesus* (ὁ
λύει, *qui solvit*), the verb which in iii. 8 is used for 'to destroy'. This
reading appears to have been known to Tertullian (A. D. 210), who
quotes S. John as speaking of "the forerunners of Antichrist denying
that Christ has come in the flesh and severing (*solventes*) Jesus" (*Adv.
Marcion* V. xvi.), and to Irenaeus (A. D. 180), who quotes the whole
passage, and in this place has "every spirit which severeth (*qui solvit*)
Jesus" (*Haer.* III. xvi. 8). But it can scarcely be genuine, for it is *not
found in a single Greek MS., nor in any version* except the Vulgate.
And we have no certain knowledge that any Greek Father had this
reading. 'Qui solvit' in Irenaeus may be interpretation rather than
literal translation. Socrates the historian (A. D. 440) charges the
Nestorians with tampering with the text and ignoring the reading
'which *severeth* Jesus'; just as Tertullian accuses the Valentinians of
falsifying the text of John i. 13, and S. Ambrose the Arians of mutilat-
ing John i. 6. In all these cases the supposed heretical reading is
the right one.

The passage in S. Polycarp's Epistle already alluded to (see on ii. 18)
is against the reading advocated by Socrates: 'For every one who confesseth not that Jesus Christ has come in the flesh is an Antichrist; and
whosoever confesseth not the witness of the Cross is of the devil' (*Phil.*
VII.). The expressions 'confess', 'come in the flesh', 'Antichrist', 'is
of the devil', place S. Polycarp's knowledge of his master's First Epistle
beyond all reasonable doubt. This is very early testimony (A.D. 140—
155) to the existence of the First Epistle.

The variations as regards reading are testimony to the same effect.
Such things take time to arise and spread. If a corrupt reading is
known to Tertullian in Africa, and (apparently) adopted by Irenaeus in
Gaul, before the end of the second century, then the original document
written in Asia Minor cannot be much later than the end of the first
century, at which time S. John was still living.

is not of God] S. John gives two tests, one for trying human conduct,

this is *that spirit* of antichrist, whereof you have heard that it should come; and *even* now already is it in the world.
4 Ye are of God, little children, and have overcome them: because greater is he that is in you, than he that is in the

and one for trying spiritual claims: 'Every one that doeth not righteousness *is not of God*, neither he that loveth not his brother' (iii. 10); and 'Every spirit which confesseth not Jesus *is not of God*.'
  and this is that spirit of Antichrist] 'That' should rather be 'the', as in R.V. The word 'spirit' is not expressed in the Greek, but is rightly understood from the context. The similar Greek expressions in Matt. xxi. 21; 1 Cor. x. 24; James iv. 14; 2 Pet. ii. 22 are not quite parallel.
  that it should come] Better, with R.V., *that it* cometh. Wiclif and the Rhemish have 'that *he cometh*'. Most English Versions before 1611 have 'he' for 'it'; as also has Luther. This is due to the Vulgate, which has 'Antichrist' for 'the (spirit) of Antichrist'. 'It' is certainly right. Not Antichrist, but the antichristian nature is affirmed to be *now in the world already*. The spirit of antagonism to Christ has passed from "the invisible world of spiritual wickedness" to the visible world of human action. The addition of 'already' hints that something more may be expected to follow. Comp. 'The mystery of lawlessness doth already work' (2 Thess. ii. 7).
  4. *Ye are of God*] As in ii. 20 the Apostle passes abruptly from the false teachers to his true children with an emphatic pronoun, made still more emphatic here by the asyndeton. *Ye*, in marked contrast to them, *are of God*.
  and have overcome them] By withstanding the seducers they have proved their superiority. In the masculine 'them' (αὐτούς) the Apostle passes from the antichristian spirits to the false prophets who are their mouth-pieces. Comp. 'And a stranger will they not follow, but will flee from him; for they know not the voice of strangers' (John x. 5): thus the stranger is defeated.
  because greater is He that is in you] Not in their own strength has the victory been won, but in His whose word abideth in them (ii. 14). It is precisely for this reason that they may have confidence against all spiritual enemies: it is not confidence in themselves (1 Cor. xv. 57 especially Ephes. vi. 10—17).
  he that is in the world] 'The ruler of this world' (John xii. 31), the devil, the father of these lying teachers (iii. 10; John viii. 44), whose works Christ came to destroy (iii. 8). By saying 'in the world' rather than 'in them', the Apostle indicates that they belong to 'the world'. "S. John constantly teaches that the Christian's work in this state of probation is to conquer 'the world'. It is, in other words, to fight successfully against that view of life which ignores God, against that complex system of attractive moral evil and specious intellectual falsehood which is organized and marshalled by the great enemy of God, and which permeates and inspires non-Christianized society" (Liddon).

vv. 5, 6.] I. JOHN, IV. 145

world. They are of the world, therefore speak they of the
world, and the world heareth them. We are of God: he
that knoweth God heareth us; *he that is not of God heareth
not us*. Hereby know we the spirit of truth, and the spirit

5. *They are of the world*] This follows, though it has not yet been stated, from their not being 'of us' (ii. 19): for there is no middle position. The verse is another reminiscence of the Lord's farewell discourses: 'If ye were of the world, the world would love its own' (John xv. 19; comp. xvii. 14).

therefore speak they of the world] Or, *therefore of the world they speak:* as in John iii. 31, the Greek order is impressive and worth preserving. (See on iii. 1; but here διὰ τοῦτο is not followed by ὅτι.) The impressive repetition of 'the world' is very characteristic of S. John's style; e.g. John i. 10, iii. 17, xv. 19, xvii. 14. Comp. 'He that is of the earth, of the earth he is, and of the earth he speaketh' (iii. 31): where, however, 'to speak of the *earth*' or '*earthly things*' is to speak of God's work on earth; whereas 'to speak of the *world*' is to speak what is alien from God's work and opposed to it. 'To speak *of*' (λαλεῖν ἐκ) is not the same as 'to speak *concerning*' (λέγειν περί) v. 16; John i. 22, 47, ii. 21, &c. 'To speak of the world' is to have the world as the *source* of one's words, so that one's inspiration flows from it: and of course the world 'heareth', i.e. loves to hear, the wisdom derived from itself.

6. *We are of God*] 'We' with great emphasis, like 'ye' in *v.* 4, in contrast to the false prophets. 'We' is probably not equivalent to 'ye', viz. all true believers: 'we' means the Apostles. See on *v.* 14 and on i. 4. The opposition here is not between true and false *Christians*, but between true and false *teachers*. Comp. 1 Cor. xiv. 37.

he that knoweth God heareth us] We might render, 'He that *increaseth* in the knowledge of God' (ὁ γινώσκων τὸν Θεόν). Here once more we have that magisterial tone of Apostolic authority which is so conspicuous in the Prologue (i. 1—4). It underlies the whole Epistle, as it does the whole of the Fourth Gospel, but here and there comes to the surface. It is the quiet confidence of conscious strength. Comp. 'He that is of God heareth the words of God; for this cause ye hear them not because ye are not of God'; and, 'Every one that is of the Truth heareth My voice' (John viii. 47, xviii. 37). For ordinary Christians to adopt this language is presumptuous sectarianism.

Note that, as usual, the antithesis is not exact: 'he that *knoweth* God' is balanced by 'he that *is not of* God'; indicating that it is the child of God who comes by experience to know Him.

Hereby know we] Literally, *From this*. A fresh sentence should begin here. It is not certain whether 'from this' refers to the whole section (1—6), or to the latter half (4—6), or only to the first half of *v.* 6. In any case the meaning is, *not* that those who hear the Apostle have the Spirit of truth, while those who refuse to hear have the spirit of error; *but* that the Apostles have the Spirit of truth because God's

7 of error. Beloved, let us love one another: for love is of God; and every one that loveth is born of God, and

children hear them, while the false prophets have the spirit of error because the world hears them.

the spirit of truth] The Holy Spirit; John xiv. 17, xv. 26, xvi. 13: comp. 1 Cor. ii. 12, where the whole passage is very similar to this. It is not easy to determine whether the genitive 'of truth' expresses the *character* of the Spirit, as in 'the Holy Spirit of promise' (Eph. i. 13), 'the Spirit of grace (Heb. x. 29), or the *source*, as in 'the Spirit of God' and 'the Spirit of Christ' (Rom. viii. 9, 11). The Spirit is the Truth (v. 7), proceeds from Him who is the Truth (John xiv. 6, 26), communicates and interprets the Truth (John xvi. 13, 14).

7—21. LOVE IS THE MARK OF THE CHILDREN OF THE GOD WHO IS LOVE.

7. *Beloved, let us love one another*] See on iii. 2. The transition seems abrupt, as if the Apostle had summarily dismissed an unwelcome subject. But the connexions of thought in S. John's writings are often so subtle, that it is rash to assert anywhere that two consecutive verses or sections are entirely without connecting links. Two such links may be found here. 1. The power to love one another, no less than the power to confess the Incarnation, is the gift of the Spirit (*vv.* 2, 12, 13). And faith and love mutually aid one another. This is the case even between man and man. Faith and trust soon pass into love. 2. The antichristian spirit is a selfish one; it makes self, i.e. one's own intellect and one's own interest, the measure of all things. Just as it severs the Divine from the human in Christ, so it severs Divine love from human conduct in man. 'Beloved, let us do far otherwise. Let us love one another'.

For the third and last time in this Epistle the Apostle introduces the subject of brotherly love. First it was introduced as a consequence and sign of walking in the light (ii. 7—11). Next it was introduced as a special form of righteousness and mark of God's children (iii. 10—18). Here it appears as a gift of the Spirit of God, a contrast to the antichristian spirit, and above all as an effluence from the very Being of God.

'Love one another' here, as in iii. 11, applies primarily to the mutual love of *Christians*. The love of Christians to unbelievers is not expressly excluded, but it is not definitely before the Apostle's mind.

love is of God] And 'we are of God' (v. 6), and 'ye are of God' (*v.* 4); therefore there should be the family bond of love between us.

every one that loveth is born of God] This follows from the preceding statement. If God is the source of all love, then whatever love a man has in him comes from God; and this part of his moral nature is of Divine origin. Of '*every one* that loveth' is this true, whether he be heathen or Christian: there is no limitation. If a Socrates or a Marcus Aurelius loves his fellow-men, it is by the grace of God that he does so. See concluding note on iii. 4.

knoweth God. He that loveth not, knoweth not God; for 8
God is love. In this was manifested the love of God 9

knoweth God] He comes by experience to know Him by thus sharing the Divine nature.
8. *knoweth not God*] Literally, *knew not God*, i.e. never attained to a knowledge of Him. This is a remarkable instance of S. John's habit of not making the second part of an antithesis the exact counterpart of the first, but an advance beyond it. Instead of saying 'is not born of God' he says 'never knew God', which is much stronger. Not to have known love is not to have known God.
God is love] This is the third of S. John's great statements respecting the Nature of God: 'God is Spirit' (John iv. 24); 'God is light' (1 John i. 5), and 'God is love'. See on i. 5. Here, as in the other cases, the predicate has no article, and expresses not a quality which He *possesses*, but one which embraces all that He *is*. This is clear from S. John's argument. It does not follow, because God is *full of* love, that one who does not love cannot have known God: all that follows from this is that his knowledge of God is very incomplete. Only if God *is* love, i.e. if love is Himself, is the statement true, that to have no personal knowledge of love is to have no personal knowledge of God. And here we may remark that to attain by experience to a knowledge of God (γινώσκειν τὸν Θεόν) is a very different thing from knowing something *about* Him (εἰδέναι τι περὶ αὐτοῦ). The Gnostics knew a good deal about God, but they did not know Him, for instead of loving those brethren who did not share their intellectual attainments, they had an arrogant contempt for them. They had recognised that 'God is spirit', and to some extent that 'God is light'; for they knew Him to be an immaterial Being and the highest Intelligence: but they had wholly failed to appreciate that 'God is love'. And yet of the three great truths this is the chief. The other two are incomplete without it. The first, 'God is spirit', is almost more negative than positive: God is not material; He 'dwelleth not in temples made with hands'. The second might seem in making our idea of Him more definite to remove Him further away from us: God is perfect intelligence, perfect purity, perfect holiness. The third not only makes His Nature far more clearly known, but brings Him very close to us. The spirit is shewn to be personal, the light to have warmth and life.

If no previous religion, not even the Jewish, had attained to the truth that 'God is light', still less had any attained to the truth that 'God is love'. To the heathen world God is a powerful, a terrible, and often a cruel being; one whose fierce wrath needs to be deprecated and whose ill-will needs to be propitiated, rather than one on whose love men may rely. To the Jews He was a just and a jealous, if also a merciful God, of whose inmost being all that was known was I AM THAT I AM. To the Christian alone He is known as LOVE.

As already stated, this truth, God is love, dominates the second main division of the Epistle. In no *Book* in N. T. does the substantive 'love' (ἀγάπη) occur so often as in these two and a half *chapters* (iii. 1—v. 12);

148   I. JOHN, IV.   [v. 10.

towards us, because that God sent his only begotten Son
10 into the world, that we might live through him.   Herein is

and in no Book in N. T., excepting the Fourth Gospel, does the verb
'to love' (ἀγαπᾶν) occur *half* so many times as here. No wonder that
the writer of this Epistle has been known in the Church as 'the Apostle
of Love'. "If nothing were said in praise of love throughout the pages
of this Epistle, if nothing whatever throughout the other pages of the
Scriptures, and this one thing only were all we were told by the voice
of the Spirit of God, *For God is Love;* nothing more ought we to
require" (S. Augustine).

9. *In this was manifested*] Or, for the sake of uniformity with vv.
10, 13, 17, **Herein** *was manifested:* we have the same Greek in all four
verses. 'Herein' plainly refers to what follows: comp. iii. 16 and see
on iii. 19. For 'manifest' see on i. 2. This is a second reason for our
loving one another. We must do this (1) because love is the very Being
of Him whose children we are; (2) because of the transcendent way in
which His love was manifested. The context shews that 'the love of
God', which usually in this Epistle means our love to God, here means
His love to us: comp. iii. 16.

towards us] Rather, **in** *us:* we are the sphere in which God's love is
exhibited: comp. v. 16 and John ix. 3, which is very parallel. The
latter passage tends to shew that 'in us' is to be joined with 'manifested'
rather than with 'the love of God': *Herein was the love of God manifested in us.* The rendering 'in our case' (R. V. margin) is improbable:
comp. v. 12.

because that God sent] Better, **because** *God* **hath** *sent:* we do not
need both 'because' and 'that'; and the verb is a perfect, indicating
the permanent result of Christ's mission. In the next verse we have
aorists, speaking of past acts without reference to the present.

his only begotten Son] Literally, *His Son, His only begotten:* comp.
John iii. 16. As in 'the life, the eternal life' (i. 2), the repetition of
the article makes both ideas, 'son' and 'only-begotten', prominent
and distinct. Comp. i. 3, ii. 7, 8; 2 John 11, 13. His Son was
much to send, but it was also His only Son. The word for 'only
begotten' (μονογενής) as applied to Christ is peculiar to S. John; it
occurs four times in the Gospel (i. 14, 18, iii. 16, 18) and here. 'Only-
born' would be a more accurate rendering: Christ is the only *born* Son
as distinct from the many who have *become* sons. The word occurs in
LXX. to translate a Hebrew word (*yachid*), which is elsewhere rendered
'beloved' or 'darling' (ἀγαπητός): and oddly enough where the Greek
has 'only' the A. V. has 'darling' and *vice versâ*. Contrast Gen. xxii.
2, 12, 16 with Ps. xxii. 21, xxxv. 17. The Vulgate has *unigenitus* and
unicus. Comp. Rom. v. 8, viii. 32.

that we might live through him] These are the important words,
setting forth that in which God's love is so conspicuous and so unique.
The only Son has been sent *for this purpose* (ἵνα), that we may live, and
not die, as we should otherwise have done: comp. iii. 14, v. 11; John
iii. 16, 17, 36.

love, not that we loved God, but that he loved us, and sent his Son *to be* the propitiation for our sins. Beloved, if God so loved us, we ought also to love one another. No man hath seen God at any time. If we love one another,

10. *Herein is love*] 'Herein' again refers to what follows: Love in its full perfection is seen, not in man's love to God, but in His to man, which reached a climax in His sending His Son to save us from our sins. The superiority of God's love does not lie merely in the fact of its being Divine. It is first in order of time and therefore necessarily spontaneous: ours is at best only love in return for love. His love is absolutely disinterested; ours cannot easily be so. Comp. Titus iii. 4. 'For propitiation' and 'for our sins' see on ii. 2. 'To be the propitiation' is literally 'as a propitiation'; it is parallel to 'that we might live through Him' in the previous verse; but at the same time is an expansion of it. It states the manner in which life is won for us.

11. *Beloved*] For the sixth and last time the Apostle uses this appropriate address: see on iii. 2. No address of any kind occurs again until the last verse of the Epistle.

if God so loved us] As in iii. 13, v. 9, the fact is stated gently, but without any doubt (εἰ with the indicative): here 'if' is almost equivalent to 'since'; 'If, as is manifest, to *this* extent God loved us'. Comp. 'If I then, the Lord and the Master, have washed your feet, ye also ought to wash one another's feet' (John xiii. 14). 'So' refers to what is said in *vv.* 9, 10.

we ought also] Better, as R. V. *we also ought:* 'also' belongs to 'we'; we as well as God. In the spiritual family also *noblesse oblige*. As children of God we must exhibit His nature, and we must follow His example, and we must love those whom He loves. Nor is this the only way in which the Atonement forms part of the foundation of Christian Ethics. It is only when we have learned something of the infinite price paid to redeem us from sin, that we rightly estimate the moral enormity of sin, and the strength of the obligation which lies upon us to free ourselves from its pollution. And it was precisely those false teachers who denied the Atonement who taught that idolatry and every abominable sin were matters of no moral significance.

12. *No man hath seen God at any time*] Better, as R. V., *No man hath* **beheld** *God at any time:* a different verb (τεθέαται) is used here from that used in *v.* 20 and in John i. 18 (ἑώρακεν) where we have exactly the same statement. The verb used here implies something of gazing and contemplation: our word 'theatre' comes from it. Comp. 'Whom no man hath seen, nor can see' (1 Tim. vi. 16).

Once more (see on *v.* 7) the connecting lines of thought are not on the surface, and cannot be affirmed with certainty. What follows seems to give the clue to what otherwise looks like an abrupt transition. 'I say we must love one another, for by so doing we have proof of the presence of the invisible God. No amount of contemplation ever yet enabled any one to detect God's presence. Let us love one another,

13 God dwelleth in us, and his love is perfected in us. Hereby know we that we dwell in him, and he in us, because he hath given us of his Spirit. 14 And we have seen and do testify that the Father sent the 15 Son *to be* the Saviour of the world. Whosoever shall confess that Jesus is the Son of God, God dwelleth in him, and he

and then we are sure, not only that He is with us but in us, and not merely is, but abides'. Here, as in John i. 18, 'God' stands first for emphasis: *God no one hath ever yet beheld.*
God dwelleth in us] Better, as R. V., *God* **abideth** *in us* (see on ii. 24): He is not a momentary visitant but a permanent friend and guest.
his love is perfected in us] Or, **the love of Him** *is perfected in us.* 'His love' to us can scarcely be meant; for in what sense would our loving one another perfect that? Moreover, as already noticed, 'the love of God' in this Epistle commonly means man's love to Him, not His to man (ii. 5, iii. 17, v. 3). 'His love' might possibly mean the love which characterizes Him, or the love which He has implanted in us; but the other is simpler. Our love to God is developed and perfected by our loving one another. We practise and strengthen our love of the Unseen by shewing love to the seen. See on ii. 5.
13. This should be compared with iii. 24, to which it is closely parallel. There, as here, the gift of the Spirit is the proof of God's abiding presence: but there this is connected with keeping His commandments; here it is connected with the special duty of brotherly love.
he hath given us of his Spirit] We receive '*of* His Spirit' (ἐκ τοῦ πνεύματος): of Christ alone was it said in the fullest sense 'not by measure' is the Spirit given to him (John iii. 34). Christians are sometimes said to receive the Spirit (Gal. iii. 2, 3, 5, iv. 6), sometimes *of* the Spirit (see on iii. 24): only the former is true of Christ. See on 2 John 4.
14. *And we have seen and do testify*] Better, as R. V., *And we have* **beheld** *and* **bear witness**: see on *v.* 12 and i. 2. 'We' is emphatic, and, as in the Prologue, means S. John and the other Apostles. See on i. 4. With their own eyes they saw the Son working out His mission as the Saviour of the world. 'Beheld' points back to *v.* 12: 'God Himself no one hath ever yet beheld; but we have beheld His Son'.
sent the Son] Better, **hath** *sent the Son;* as in *v.* 9. 'Of the world' is important; not of the Jews only, or of the 'enlightened' Gnostics only, but of all. There is no limit but the willingness of men to accept salvation by believing on the Saviour. 'For God sent not the Son into the world to judge the world; but that the world should be saved through Him' (John iii. 17). See on ii. 2.
15. *Whosoever shall confess*] This was what the false prophets refused to do: see on *vv.* 2 and 3: also on v. 1.
dwelleth in him] Better, **abideth** *in him:* see on ii. 24.
and he in God] The communion is of the closest description: comp. iii. 24; John vi. 56, xiv. 20, xv. 5. Even Apostles, who have beheld

in God. And we have known and believed the love that 16
God hath to us. God is love; and he that dwelleth in love
dwelleth in God, and God in him. Herein is our love 17
made perfect, that we may have boldness in the day of
judgment: because as he is, so are we in this world. There 18

and borne witness, can have no more than this Divine fellowship, which is open to every believer.

16. *And we have known and believed*] Literally, *And we have* **come to know and have** *believed*. This is the natural order; progressive knowledge leads up to faith. But sometimes faith precedes knowledge (John vi. 69). In either case each completes the other. Sound faith is intelligent; sound knowledge is believing. We must be 'ready always to give answer to every man that asketh a reason concerning the hope that is in us' (1 Pet. iii. 15). This verse is a fulfilment of the conclusion of Christ's High-Priestly prayer; 'I made known unto them Thy name, and will make it known; that the love wherewith Thou lovedst Me may be in them, and I in them' (John xvii. 26).

God hath to us] Rather, *God hath* **in** *us*, as in *v.* 9; see note there.
he that dwelleth, &c.] Better, as R. V., *he that* **abideth** *in love*, **abideth** *in God, and God* **abideth** *in him*: see on ii. 24. In the true text (אBKL) the characteristic word 'abide' occurs characteristically three times: comp. *v.* 5, where 'the world' occurs three times.

17. *Herein is our love made perfect*] Better, as the margin, *Herein is* **love with us** *made perfect*; or, as R. V., *Herein is love* **made perfect with us**. Most earlier English Versions agree with the latter collocation. The meaning seems to be that love, which is of God (*v.* 7), takes up its abode *with us* and is developed until it is perfected. 'Love' here evidently means our love towards God: His love towards us can have no fear about it (*v.* 18). 'Herein' may refer to either of the two clauses which follow. 'Herein...that' (ἵνα) occurs possibly in John xv. 8, and 'Herein...because' (ὅτι) occurs 1 John iii. 16, iv. 9, 10. But it is perhaps best to make 'Herein' refer to what precedes; to our abiding in God and God in us. This avoids the awkwardness of making perfection of love in the *present* depend upon our attitude at the Judgment, which though near (ii. 18) according to S. John's view, is still *future*. In this way we can give its full meaning to 'that' (ἵνα): by close union with God our love is made perfect, *in order that* we may have boldness in the day of judgment. For 'boldness' see on ii. 28.

the day of judgment] The full phrase here used, '*the* day of *the* judgment' occurs nowhere else: the usual form is 'day of judgment' (Matt. x. 15, xi. 22, 24, xii. 36; 2 Pet. ii. 9, iii. 7). S. John elsewhere calls it 'the last day' (John vi. 39, 40, 44, 54), or 'the great day' (Rev. vi. 17; comp. xvi. 14). Other Scriptural phrases are 'the day of the Lord', 'the day of God', 'day of Christ', 'that day', 'the day'.

as he is, so are we in this world] 'He' (ἐκεῖνος) almost certainly is Christ, as probably always in this Epistle (ii. 6, iii. 3, 5, 7, 16). Our assurance with regard to the future Judgment is not presumption,

is no fear in love; but perfect love casteth out fear: because fear hath torment. He that feareth is not made perfect in

because in this world we are in character like Christ. The resemblance is marked as close, '*even* so are we' (καθώς); comp. ii. 6, iii. 3, 7. In what does this close resemblance specially consist? In love: the whole context points to this. He need not fear the judgment of Christ who by loving has become like Christ.

18. Proof of the preceding statement that perfect love will give us boldness, by shewing the mutually exclusive nature of love and fear. Love moves towards others in the spirit of self-sacrifice: fear shrinks from others in the spirit of self-preservation. The two are to be understood quite generally; neither love of God nor fear of God is specially meant. In all relations whatever, perfect love excludes fear, and fear prevents love from being perfect. And the two vary inversely: the more perfect the love, the less possibility of fear, and the more the fear, the less perfect the love. But, though as certain as any physical law, the principle, that perfect love excludes all fear, is an ideal that has never been verified in fact. Like the first law of motion, it is verified by the approximations made to it. No believer's love has ever been so perfect as entirely to banish fear; but every believer experiences that as his love increases his fear diminishes. It is worthy of note that S. John here abandons his antithetic method. He does not go on to state anything about him that feareth *not*. And rightly, for the absence of fear proves nothing: it may be the result of ignorance, or presumption, or indifference, or unbelief, or inveterate wickedness.

Tertullian quotes this verse in insisting on the duty of suffering martyrdom, adding "What fear would it be better to understand than that which gives rise to denial (of Christ)? What love does he assert to be perfect, but that which puts fear to flight, and gives courage to confess (Christ)? What penalty will he appoint as the punishment of fear, but that which he who denies is to pay, who has to be slain, body and soul, in hell" (*Scorp.* xii.). Simon Magus is said to have "freed his disciples from the danger of death" by martyrdom, "by teaching them to regard idolatry as a matter of indifference" (Origen *c. Celsum* VI. xi).

because fear hath torment] Better, as R. V., *because fear hath* **punishment.** The word for 'punishment' (κόλασις) occurs nowhere else in N. T., excepting Matt. xxv. 46, but it is not uncommon in LXX. nor in classical Greek. Its radical signification is 'pruning', and hence it gets the notions of 'checking, correcting, punishing'. 'Torment' as distinct from 'punishment' is expressed by a different word (βάσανος), which occurs Matt. iv. 24; Luke xvi. 23, 28. Both words are found together in Wisd. xix. 4; 'That they might fulfil the *punishment* which was wanting to their *torments*.' Wiclif has 'peyne' representing *poena* in the Vulgate: other English Versions have 'painfulness'. 'Fear hath punishment' is true in two ways; (1) fear involves the idea of punishment; (2) fear is a foretaste of punishment.

He that feareth] With Wiclif we must prefix 'but', or with Genevan,

love. We love him because he first loved us. If a man 19
say, I love God, and hateth his brother, he is a liar: for he 20
that loveth not his brother whom he hath seen, how can he

Rhemish, and R. V. 'and', to represent the Greek conjunction: **and
he that feareth** (ὁ δὲ φοβούμενος). The main sentence is here resumed,
'but perfect love...punishment' being parenthetical. The present tense
indicates a constant condition; the habitual fearer is necessarily imperfect in his love.

S. Paul teaches the same doctrine; 'Ye received not the *spirit of
bondage* again unto *fear;* but ye received the *spirit of adoption*, whereby
we cry, *Abba, Father*' (Rom. viii. 15). The servile fear, which perfect
love excludes, is therefore altogether different from the childlike awe,
which is a necessary element in the creature's love for its Creator.
Even servile fear is necessary as a *preparation* for perfect love. 'The
fear of the Lord is the beginning of wisdom'; and it is also the
beginning of love. The sinner must begin by fearing the God against
whom he has sinned. Bengel gives the various stages thus: 'neither
love nor fear; fear without love; both fear and love; love without
fear'. Fear is the child of bondage; love of freedom. In this case
also the bondwoman and her son must be cast out (Gal. iv. 30).

19. *We love him*] Omit 'Him', which is a later addition to the
true text: some authorities for 'Him' add 'God', and some have
'God' for 'He' in the next clause. No accusative is expressed, and
none, whether 'God' or 'one another', is to be understood: Christian
love of every kind is meant. Authorities are much divided between
'we love' and 'let us love'; for the Greek (ἀγαπῶμεν) may be either
indicative or hortative subjunctive. The former is better. The Peschito
and Vulgate render 'let us love' and with Codex A insert 'therefore':
nos ergo diligamus.

because he first loved us] We shall narrow the Apostle's meaning if
we limit this to the idea of *gratitude* evoking love. The 'first', which is
the important word, means much more than that. 1. Our love owes
its very origin to God's love, from which it is an effluence (*v.* 7).
2. Love is checked by fear when it is doubtful whether it is returned.
Our love has no such check; for it knows that God's love has been
beforehand with it. Bede compares 'Ye did not choose Me, but I
chose you' (John xv. 16).

20. *If a man say*] We return to the form of statement which
was so common at the beginning of the Epistle (i. 6, 8, 10). The case
here contemplated is one form of the man that feareth *not*. His
freedom from fear is caused, however, not by the perfection of love, but
by presumption. He is either morally blind or a conscious hypocrite.
Comp. ii. 4, 9.

loveth not] As we have seen already (iii. 14, 15), S. John treats not
loving as equivalent to hating.

whom he hath seen] S. John does not say 'whom he can see', but
'whom he has continually before his eyes'. The perfect tense, as so
often, expresses a permanent state continuing from the past. His

21 love God whom he hath not seen? And this commandment have we from him, That he who loveth God love his brother also.

brother has been and remains in sight, God has been and remains out of sight. 'Out of sight, out of mind' is a saying which holds good in morals and religion as well as in society. And if a man fails in duties which are ever before his eyes and are easy, how can we credit him with performing duties which require an effort to bear in mind and are difficult? And in this case the seen would necessarily suggest the unseen: for the *brother* on earth implies the *Father* in heaven. If therefore even the seen is not loved, what must we infer as to the unseen? The seen brother and the unseen God are put in striking juxtaposition in the Greek; 'He that loveth not his brother whom he hath seen, the God whom he hath not seen cannot love'. But in English this would be misunderstood.

how can he love] With אB against AKL we should probably read **cannot love**: the 'how' is perhaps a reminiscence of iii. 17; comp. John iii. 4, 9, v. 44, vi. 52, ix. 16, xiv. 5. In a similar spirit Philo says parents may be regarded as 'visible gods', and 'it is impossible that the Invisible should be revered by those who have no reverence for the visible'.

21. *And this commandment have we*] The Apostle drives home his arguments for the practice of brotherly love by the fact that God has commanded all who love Him to love their brethren. Some take 'Him' to mean Christ. But this is unlikely, as Christ has not been mentioned for several verses: although it must be admitted that S. John is so full of the truth that 'I and My Father are one', that he makes the transition from the Father to the Son and from the Son to the Father almost unconsciously. Where has God given this commandment? In the whole Law, which is summed up in loving God with all one's heart and one's neighbour as oneself (Deut. vi, 5; Lev. xix. 18; Luke x. 27). The Apostle thus anticipates a possible objection. A man may say 'I *can* love God without loving my brother, and I can prove my love by keeping His commandments' (John xiv. 15). 'Nay', says S. John, 'your own argument shews your error: you cannot keep His commandments without loving your brother'. Thus then we have two revelations of God: our brother, who is His image; and His commandment, which is His will. Not to love our brother is a flagrant violation of both. As Pascal puts it, we must know men in order to love them, but we must love God in order to know Him.

that he who loveth God love his brother also] "The final particle (ἵνα) gives more than the simple contents of the commandment. It marks the injunction as directed to an aim" (Westcott). See on i. 9.

CHAP. V.

The chapter falls into two parts. The first twelve verses form the last section of the second main division of the Epistle, GOD IS LOVE

Whosoever believeth that Jesus is the Christ is born of **5**

(ii. 29—v. 12): the last nine verses form the conclusion and summary of the whole. Some editors break up the first part of the chapter into two sections, 1—5 and 6—12, but texts and versions seem to be right in giving the whole as one paragraph. The second part does contain two smaller sections, 13—17 and 18—21. We may analyse the chapter therefore as follows: *Faith is the Source of Love, the Victory over the World, and the Possession of Life* (1—12). Conclusion and Summary: *Intercessory Love the Fruit of Faith and of the Possession of Life* (13—17); *The Sum of the Christian's Knowledge* (18—20); *Final Practical Injunction* (21).

It will be observed that in the middle of the first section we have what looks at first sight a digression and yet is intimately connected with the main subject of the section. This main subject is *Faith*, a word which (strangely enough) occurs nowhere else in S. John's Epistles, nor in his Gospel. And faith necessarily implies *witness*. Only on the strength of testimony is faith possible. Therefore in this paragraph on Faith and its effects the Apostle gives in detail the various kinds of witness on which the Christian's faith is based (6—12). The paragraph shews plainly S. John's view of the relation of Faith to Love. The two are inseparable. Faith that does not lead to Love, Love that is not based on Faith, must come to nothing.

1—12. FAITH IS THE SOURCE OF LOVE, THE VICTORY OVER THE WORLD AND THE POSSESSION OF LIFE.

1. *Whosoever believeth*] Or, *Every one that believeth:* the construction is identical with that in ii. 29, iii. 3, 4, iv. 2, 3, 7, and in the second half of this verse. See concluding note on iii. 4. The verb 'believe', which occurs only 3 times in the rest of the Epistle, occurs 6 times in these first 13 verses. After the third verse the word 'love', which has been the keyword of the last two chapters, ceases to appear. With the first sentence comp. John i. 12.

The verse is a couple of syllogisms condensed into an irregular Sorites.

Every one who believes the Incarnation is a child of God.
Every child of God loves its Father.
∴ Every believer in the Incarnation loves God.
Every believer in the Incarnation loves God.
Every one who loves God loves the children of God.
∴ Every believer in the Incarnation loves the children of God.

To believe that Jesus is the Christ is to believe that One who was known as a man fulfilled a known and Divine commission; that He who was born and was crucified is the Anointed, the Messiah of Israel, the Saviour of the world. To believe this is to accept both the Old and the New Testaments; it is to believe that Jesus is what He claimed to be, One who is equal with the Father, and as such demands of every believer the absolute surrender of self to Him. Belief without love is, as S. Augustine remarks, the belief of a demon (James ii. 19).

God: and every one that loveth him that begat loveth him
2 also that is begotten of him. By this we know that we love
the children of God, when we love God, and keep his com-
3 mandments. For this is the love of God, that we keep his
commandments: and his commandments are not grievous.

is born of God] Better, in order to be uniform with what follows, *is*
begotten *of God:* see on v. 18.

him also that is begotten of him] Any believer. Here again the verb
(ἀγαπᾷ) may be either the indicative or the hortative subjunctive: as in
iv. 19, the indicative is preferable; 'loveth', not 'let him love'.

This verse shews that iv. 20 ought not to be interpreted to mean that
through love of the visible brother we ascend to the love of the invisible
God. On the contrary the love of the Father is the source of love of
His children. "That is the natural order; that, we may say it confidently, is the universal order" (Maurice).

2. The converse of the truth insisted upon in iv. 20, 21 is now stated.
There love and obedience to God was shewn to involve love of His
children: here love of God's children is said to follow from our love and
obedience to God. The two (or three) ideas mutually imply one another.
Love to God implies obedience, and either of these implies love of His
children, which again implies the other two. In short, love to God and
love to the brethren confirm and prove each other. If either is found
alone it is not genuine. Fellowship with God and fellowship one with
another (i. 3, 7) necessarily exist together. A man may be conscious of
kindliness towards others and yet doubt whether he is fulfilling the law
of brotherly love. For such the Apostle gives this test, 'Do you love
God? Do you strive to obey Him? If so your love of others is of the
right kind'. For the characteristic phrase 'keep His commandments'
see on ii. 3: but here the true reading seems to be **do** *His commandments*, a phrase which occurs nowhere else. This reading is supported
by B, all ancient Versions, and several Fathers. Note the 'when', or
more literally, 'whenever' (ὅταν): whenever we love and obey we have
fresh evidence that our philanthropy is Christian.

3. *For this is the love of God*] Or, *For the love of God is this*, i.e.
consists in this: see on i. 5. The truth implied in *v.* 2, that love
involves obedience, is here explicitly stated. Comp. John xiv. 15, 21,
23, xv. 10; 2 John 6.

his commandments are not grievous] For two reasons: 1. Because
He gives us strength to bear them; *juvat qui jubet* (Phil. iv. 13); 2.
Because love makes them light. They are not like the 'burdens
grievous to be borne' which the legal rigour of the Pharisees laid on
men's consciences. Here again we have an echo of the Master's words;
'My yoke is easy, and My burden is light' (Matt. xi. 30).

4. Reason why keeping even the difficult commandment of loving
others rather than oneself is not a grievous burden. It is the world and
its ways which makes the Divine commands grievous, and the new birth
involved in faith gives us a new unworldly nature and a strength which
conquers the world.

For whatsoever is born of God overcometh the world: and 4
this is the victory that overcometh the world, *even* our faith.
Who is he that overcometh the world, but he that believeth 5
that Jesus is the Son of God? This is he that came by 6

For whatsoever is born of God] Or, Because *whatsoever is* **begotten** *of God:* see on v. 1. The collective neuter, '*what*soever', gives the principle a wide sweep by stating it in its most abstract form: comp. John vi. 37, xvii. 2. Moreover, whereas the masculine would make the victorious *person* prominent, the neuter emphasizes rather the victorious *power*. It is not the man, but his birth from God, which conquers. In v. 1 we had the masculine and in v. 18 return to the masculine again. In all three cases we have the perfect, not the aorist, participle. It is not the mere fact of having received the Divine birth that is insisted on, but the permanent results of the birth. Comp. John iii. 6, 8, where we have the same tense and a similar change from neuter to masculine.

this is the victory that overcometh] Better, *the victory that* **overcame** *the world is this* (see on i. 5): aorist, of a victory won once for all. Faith, which is 'the proof of things not seen' (Heb. xi. 1) which 'are eternal' (2 Cor. iv. 18), has conquered the world which is visible and 'is passing away' (ii. 17). Faith is both the victory and the victor. Under the influence of the Vulgate's *vincit*, Wiclif, Luther, Tyndale and many others all have the present tense here. In the faith which has won a decisive victory the believer goes on conquering. 'Victory' (νίκη) occurs nowhere else in N.T.

5. *Who is he that overcometh*] Here the present tense is right. The Apostle appeals to the daily experience of every victorious Christian.

that Jesus is the Son of God] The faith that conquers is no mere vague belief in the existence of God, but a definite belief in the Incarnation: comp. v. 1, ii. 22, iii. 23, iv. 2, 3. For the form of question comp. ii. 22: this verse shews that 'the liar' (ὁ ψεύστης) there does not mean 'the supreme liar', for 'he that overcometh' (ὁ νικῶν) cannot mean 'the supreme conqueror'. The one sole Victor, who is such in the highest and unique sense, is Christ. Comp. 'Thanks be to God, which giveth us the victory through our Lord Jesus Christ' (1 Cor. xv. 57). Belief in Christ is at once belief in God and in man. It lays a foundation for love and trust towards our fellow men. Thus the instinctive distrust and selfishness, which reign supreme in the world, are overcome.

6. *This is he that came*] Closely connected with what precedes: 'This *Son of God* is He that came'. The identity of the historic person Jesus with the eternal Son of God is once more insisted upon as the central and indispensable truth of the Christian faith. Faith in this truth is the only faith that can overcome the world and give eternal life. And it is a truth attested by witness of the highest and most extraordinary kind.

by water and blood] Literally, **by means of** or **through** *water and blood*. This is the most perplexing passage in the Epistle and one of the most perplexing in N. T. A very great variety of interpretations

water and blood, *even* Jesus Christ; not by water only, but

have been suggested. It would be simply confusing to discuss them all; but a few of the principal explanations, and the reasons for adopting the one preferred, may be stated with advantage. The water and the blood have been interpreted to mean:—

(1) The Baptism by means of water in the Jordan and the Death by means of blood upon the Cross.

(2) The water and blood which flowed from Christ's pierced side.

(3) Purification and Redemption.

(4) The Sacraments of Baptism and of the Eucharist.

These are fairly representative interpretations; the first two making the water and blood refer to facts in the earthly career of the Messiah; the last two making them symbolical of mysteries. It will be observed that these explanations are not all exclusive one of another: either of the last two may be combined with either of the first two; and in fact the fourth is not unfrequently combined with the second. The second, which is S. Augustine's, has recently received the support of the *Speaker's Commentary* and of Canon F. W. Farrar in *The Early Days of Christianity*: but in spite of its attractiveness it appears to be scarcely tenable. The difficult passage in John xix. 34 and the difficult passage before us do not really explain one another. That "*in these two passages alone, of all Scripture, are blood and water placed together,*" would, if true, amount to nothing more than a presumption that one may be connected with the other. And such a presumption would be at once weakened by the change of order: instead of the 'blood and water' of the Gospel we have 'water and blood' here. But the statement is not true; e.g. 'He shall cleanse the house with the *blood* of the bird, and with the running *water*' (Lev. xiv. 52); 'He took the *blood* of the calves and the goats, with *water* and scarlet wool and hyssop, &c.' (Heb. ix. 19). And is it credible that S. John would speak of effusions from the dead body of Jesus as the Son of God 'coming through water and blood'? Moreover, what, on this interpretation, can be the point of the emphatic addition, 'not in the water only, but in the water and in the blood'? At the piercing of the side it was the water, not the blood, that was so marvellous. So that, to make the reference clear, the whole ought to run somewhat in this manner: 'This is He that shed forth blood and water, even Jesus Christ; not the blood only, but the blood and the water'.

The first of the four explanations is far more tenable, and is adopted by Bede, but not to the entire exclusion of the second. So also Dr Westcott, who thinks the additional reference to John xix. 34 "beyond question". The Baptism in the water of Jordan and the Death by the shedding of blood sum up the work of redemption. Christ's Baptism, with the Divine proclamation of Him as the Son of God and the Divine outpouring of the Spirit upon Him, is not merely the opening but the explanation of the whole of His Ministry. The bloody death upon the Cross is not merely the close but the explanation of His Passion.

by water and blood. And it is the Spirit that beareth

'Coming' when spoken of the Christ includes the notion of His *mission* (John i. 15, 27, 30, iii. 31, vi. 14, vii. 27, 31, 41, &c., &c.). Therefore, when we are told that the Son of God '*came* by means of *water* and *blood*,' we may reasonably understand this as meaning that He fulfilled His mission by the Baptism with which His public work began and the bloody Death with which He finished it (John xix. 30). (1) This interpretation explains the *order;* 'water and blood', not 'blood and water'. (2) It explains the *first preposition;* 'through' or 'by means of' (διά with the genitive: comp. the remarkable parallel Heb. ix. 12). (3) It also explains the *second preposition;* 'in' (ἐν, of the element *in* which, without the notion of means: comp. the remarkable parallel Heb. ix. 25). Christ's Baptism and Death were in one sense the *means by which,* in another sense the *spheres in which* His work was accomplished. (4) Above all it explains the emphatic addition, 'not in water only, but in the water and in the blood'. The Gnostic teachers, against whom the Apostle is writing, admitted that the Christ came 'through' and 'in' *water:* it was precisely at the Baptism, they said, that the Divine Word united Himself with the man Jesus. But they denied that the Divine Person had any share in what was effected 'through' and 'in' *blood:* for according to them the Word departed from Jesus at Gethsemane. S. John emphatically assures us that there was no such separation. It was the Son of God who was baptized; and it was the Son of God who was crucified: and it is faith in this vital truth that produces brotherly love, that overcomes the world, and is eternal life.

It may reasonably be admitted, however, that there is this large amount of connexion between the 'water and blood' here and the 'blood and water' in the Gospel. Both in a symbolical manner point to the two great sacraments. Thus Tertullian says; "He had *come by means of water and blood,* just as John had written; that He might be baptized by the water, glorified by the blood; to make us in like manner *called* by water, *chosen* by blood. These two baptisms He sent out from the wound in His pierced side, in order that they who believed in His blood might be bathed in the water; they who had been bathed in the water might likewise drink the blood" (*De Bapt.* XVI.).

not by water only, but by water and blood] Better as R.V., *not* **with the** *water only, but* **with the** *water and* **the** *blood.* 'With' is literally 'in', of the element or sphere in which a thing is done. The use of 'in' in this connexion both here and Heb. ix. 25 perhaps comes direct from LXX. In Lev. xvi. 3 we have 'He shall *come* into the holy place *in* a young bullock' (ἐν μόσχῳ ἐκ βοῶν), i.e. *with* one. The Hebrew may mean 'in', 'with', 'by'. The article in all three cases simply means 'the water' and 'the blood' already mentioned.

As applied to *us* these words will mean, 'Christ came not merely to purify by His baptism, but to give new life by His blood; 'for the blood is the life'.' In short, all that is said in the Gospel, especially in chapters iii. and vi., respecting water and blood may be included here. The Epistle is the companion treatise of the Gospel.

7 witness, because the Spirit is truth. For there are three
that bear record *in heaven, the Father, the Word, and the*

And it is the Spirit that beareth witness] Here again there are great
diversities of interpretation. S. Augustine, who makes the water and
blood refer to the effusions of Christ's side, takes 'the spirit' to mean
the spirit which He committed to His Father at His death (John xix. 30;
Luke xxiii. 46). But in what sense could Christ's human spirit be said
to be 'the Truth'? Far more probably it is the Holy Spirit that is
meant (iii. 24, iv. 13; John i. 32, 33, vii. 39; Rev. ii. 7, 11, 17, 29, &c.).
Bede takes this view and understands the witness of the Spirit at
Christ's baptism to be meant. The *form* of the sentence is exactly
parallel to ' It is the spirit that giveth life' (John vi. 63). We might
render in each case; 'The spirit is the life-giver', 'And the Spirit is the
witness-bearer'.

that beareth witness] We have seen already (note on i. 2) that
witness to the truth in order to produce faith is one of S. John's leading
thoughts in Gospel, Epistles, and Revelation. Here it becomes the
dominant thought: the word 'witness' (verb or substantive) occurs ten
times in five verses. In the Gospel we have seven witnesses to Christ;
scripture (v. 39—47), *the Baptist* (i. 7), *the Disciples* (xv. 27, xvi. 30),
Christ's works (v. 36, x. 25, 38), *Christ's words* (viii. 14, 18, xviii. 37),
the Father (v. 37, viii. 18), *the Spirit* (xv. 26). Of these seven three are
specially mentioned in the Epistle, *the Disciples* in i. 2, *the Father* in
vv. 9, 10, and *the Spirit* here; but to these are added two more, *the
water* and *the blood*.

because the Spirit is truth] It would be possible to translate ' It
is the Spirit that beareth witness *that* the Spirit is the truth': but this
self-attestation of the Spirit would have no relation to the context. It
is the witnesses to Christ, to the identity of Jesus with the Son of God,
that S. John is marshalling before us. It is **because** *the Spirit is the
Truth* that His testimony is irrefragable: He can neither deceive nor
be deceived. He is 'the Spirit of Truth' (John xiv. 16, xv. 26), and
He glorifies the Christ, taking of His and declaring it unto the Church
(John xvi. 14).

There is a remarkable Latin reading, *quoniam Christus est veritas*,
'It is the Spirit that beareth witness that *the Christ* is the Truth', but it
has no authority.

7. *For there are three that bear record in heaven*] If there is one thing
that is certain in textual criticism, it is that this famous passage is not
genuine. The Revisers have only performed an imperative duty in
excluding it from both text and margin. External and internal evidence
are alike overwhelmingly against the passage. A summary of both will
be found in Appendix D. But there are three facts, which every one
should know, and which alone are enough to shew that the words are
an interpolation. (1) They are not found in a single Greek MS. earlier
than the fourteenth century. (2) Not one of the Greek or Latin
Fathers who conducted the controversies about the doctrine of the
Trinity in the third, fourth, and first half of the fifth centuries ever

Holy Ghost: and these three are one. And there are three that bear witness in earth, the Spirit, and the water, and the blood: and *these* three agree in one. If we receive the

quotes the words. (3) The words occur first towards the end of the fifth century in Latin, and are found in no other language until the fourteenth century. The only words which are genuine in this verse are, *For there are three that bear record*, or more accurately, *For those who bear* **witness** *are three:* 'three' is the predicate; for 'witness' see on i. 2.

8. *And there are three that bear witness in earth*] These words also are part of the spurious insertion. The true text of *vv.* 7, 8 runs: *For those who bear witness are three, the Spirit, and the water, and the blood; and* **the** *three agree in one*. S. John says 'those who bear witness', not simply 'the witnesses': they are not merely witnesses who might be called, or who have once been called, but who are perpetually delivering their testimony. The masculine (οἱ μαρτυροῦντες) is evidence of the personality of the Spirit. The Apostle is answering the misgivings of those who fancied that when he, the last of the Apostles, was taken from them, the Church would possess only second-hand evidence, and a tradition ever growing fainter, as to the Person and Mission of the Christ. 'Nay', says he, 'evidence at first-hand is ever present, and each believer has it in himself' (*v.* 10). Comp. John xv. 26.

are three] It is very doubtful whether the Trinity is even remotely symbolized. Perhaps S. John wishes to give the full complement of evidence recognized by law (Matt. xviii. 16; 2 Cor. xiii. 1; Deut. xix. 15; comp. John viii. 17).

the water, and the blood] These of course have the same meaning as before; Christ's Baptism and Death. "The real value of our Lord's baptism and His death may be estimated by supposing that neither had taken place, and that our Lord had appeared on His mission without openly professing His mission from God in submitting to the baptism of John; or that He had died quietly, as other men die" (Jelf).

agree in one] Literally, *are* (united) *into the one;* or, *are for the one* object of establishing this truth. This may mean either that they are joined so as to become one witness, or that they co-operate in producing one result. "The trinity of witnesses furnish one testimony". 'To be one (ἓν εἶναι) occurs John x. 30, xvii. 11, 21, 22; and (εἷς ἐστε) 1 Cor. iii. 23: 'into one' (εἰς ἕν) occurs John xi. 52, xvii. 23: but 'to be into one' or 'to be into the one' occurs nowhere else in N. T. 'The one' here has been made into an argument for the genuineness of *v.* 7. It is said that '*the* one' plainly implies that 'one' has preceded. But this lands us in absurdity by making 'one' in *v.* 8 mean the same as 'one' in *v.* 7. 'One' in *v.* 7 means 'one Substance', the 'Unity in Trinity'. But what sense can 'The spirit, the water, and the blood agree in the Unity in Trinity' yield?

9—11. S. John's characteristic repetition of the word 'witness' is

162   I. JOHN, V.   [V. 10.

witness of men, the witness of God is greater: for this is
10 the witness of God which he hath testified of his Son. He
that believeth on the Son of God hath the witness in him-

greatly weakened in A.V. by the substitution of 'testify' in *v.* 9 and
'record' in *vv.* 10, 11: see on i. 2, ii. 15, 24, iv. 5.

9. *If we receive the witness of men*] And it is notorious that we
do so: comp. 'if God so loved us' (iv. 11), and see on 2 John 10. The
argument reads like an echo of that of Christ to the Pharisees, 'In
your law it is written that the witness of two *men* is true' (John viii.
17); how much more therefore the witness of the Father and the Son?
For 'receive' in the sense of 'accept as valid' comp. John iii. 11,
32, 33.

for] Or, *because*. Something is evidently to be understood; e.g. 'I
say, the witness of God, *because*...', or 'I use this argument, *because*...'.

this is the witness of God] Better, as R.V., *the witness of God is
this:* 'this' is the predicate and refers to what follows (see on i. 5).
His witness consists in His having borne witness about His Son.

which he hath testified] According to the better reading and rendering, **that** *He hath borne* **witness**. 'I appeal to the witness of
God, because the witness of God is this, even the fact that He hath
borne witness concerning His Son'. The perfect tense indicates the
permanence of the testimony. Comp. 'He that hath seen hath borne
witness' (John xix. 35).

10. *He that believeth on the Son of God*] For the first time in this
Epistle we have the full phrase 'to believe *on*', of which S. John is so
fond in his Gospel, where it occurs nearly 40 times. Elsewhere in
N.T. it occurs only about 10 times. It expresses the strongest confidence and trust; faith moves towards and reposes on its object.
Whereas 'to believe a person' (πιστεύειν τινί) need mean no more than
to believe what he says (iv. 1), 'to believe *on* or *in* a person' (πιστεύειν
εἴς τινα) means to have full trust in his character.

hath the witness] Some authorities add 'of God,' which is right as
an interpretation, though not as part of the text. He has it as an
abiding possession (John v. 38; Heb. x. 34): 'hath' does not mean
merely 'he accepts it'. Comp. 'The Spirit Himself beareth witness
with our spirit, that we are children of God' (Rom. viii. 16); 'God
sent forth the Spirit of His Son into our hearts, crying, Abba, Father'
(Gal. iv. 6).

in himself] According to the revised reading, *in* **him**. Wiclif has
'in him', Luther, *bei ihm:* Tyndale added the 'self', and most English
Versions have followed him. But 'in him' in this context cannot
mean anything but 'in himself'. The external witness faithfully accepted becomes internal certitude. Our faith in the Divinity of Christ
attests its own Divine origin, for we could not have obtained it otherwise than from God. "The human mind is made for truth, and so
rests in truth, as it cannot rest in falsehood. When then it once becomes possessed of a truth, what is to dispossess it? but this is to be
certain; therefore once certitude, always certitude. If certitude in any

self: he that believeth not God hath made him a liar; because he believeth not the record that God gave of his Son. And this is the record, that God hath given to us 11 eternal life, and this life is in his Son. He that hath the 12

matter be the termination of all doubt or fear about its truth, and an unconditional conscious adherence to it, it carries with it an inward assurance, strong though implicit, that it shall never fail" (J. H. Newman).

he that believeth not God] He that has not even enough faith to induce him to believe what God says (see first note on this verse). There are great diversities of reading here; 'God', 'the Son', 'the Son of God', 'His Son', 'Jesus Christ': of these 'God' (ℵBKLP) is certainly to be preferred. The others have arisen from a wish to make 'he that believeth not' more exactly balance 'he that believeth'. But, as we have repeatedly seen, S. John's antitheses seldom balance exactly. Yet it is by no means impossible that all five are wrong, and that we ought simply to read '*He that believeth not* hath made Him a liar': comp. John iii. 18, of which this verse seems to be an echo. In 'he that believeth not', the case is stated quite generally and indefinitely (ὁ μὴ πιστεύων): the Apostle is not pointing at some one person who was known as not believing (ὁ οὐ πιστεύων); comp. iii. 10, 14, iv. 8, 20, v. 12.

hath made him a liar] See on i. 10.

believeth not the record that God gave] Better, as R.V., **hath not believed in the witness** *that God* **hath** *borne*: see on i. 2. The perfect in both cases indicates a permanent result: he has been and remains an unbeliever in the witness which God has given and continually supplies concerning His Son. 'To believe *in* (on) the witness' occurs nowhere else. See on iii. 23.

11. *And this is the record*] Better, as R.V., **And the witness is this**, as in v. 9: this is what the external witness of God, when it is internally appropriated by the believer, consists in; viz. the Divine gift of eternal life.

eternal life] See on i. 2 and on John iii. 36, v. 24. 'Hath given' is more literally **gave**; but perhaps this is a case in which the English perfect may represent the Greek aorist. But at any rate 'gave' must not be weakened into 'offered', still less into 'promised'. The believer already possesses eternal life.

this life is in his Son] This is a new independent statement, coordinate with the first clause: it is not, like the second clause, dependent upon the first. Eternal life has its seat and source in the Son, who is the 'Prince' or 'Author of life' (Acts iii. 15): see on John i. 4, v. 26.

12. A deduction from the preceding clause. If the Son has the life in Himself, then whoever has the Son has the life, and no man can have the one without the other. 'To have the Son' must be compared with 'to have the Father' in ii. 23. In both cases 'have' signifies possession in living union through faith.

11—2

Son hath life; *and* he that hath not the Son of God hath not life.

hath life] Better, as R.V., *hath* the *life;* not merely 'the life just mentioned', 'the life which God has given', but 'the life which in the full sense of the word is such'.

he that hath not] As in verse 10, the negative alternative is stated generally and indefinitely (ὁ μὴ ἔχων). The addition of 'of God' is neither fortuitous nor pleonastic. Those who possess Him know that He is the Son of God; those who do not, need to be reminded Whose Son it is that they reject.

The verse constitutes another close parallel with the Gospel: comp. the last words of the Baptist (John iii. 36).

13—21. CONCLUSION AND SUMMARY.

Some modern writers consider that *v.* 13 constitutes the conclusion of the Epistle, the remainder (14—21) being a postscript or appendix, analogous to chap. xxi. of the Gospel, and possibly by another hand. Some go so far as to conjecture that the same person added chap. xxi. to the Gospel and the last nine verses to the Epistle after the Apostle's death.

Not much can be urged in favour of these views. No MS. or version seems to exist in which these concluding verses are wanting. Tertullian quotes *vv.* 16, 17, 18 (*De Pudicitia* xix.) and *v.* 21 (*De Corona* x.): Clement of Alexandria quotes *vv.* 16, 17 (*Strom.* II. xv.); and both these writers in quoting mention S. John by name. This shews that at the end of the second century these verses were an integral part of the Epistle. Against such evidence as this, arbitrary statements that the division of sins into sins unto death and sins not unto death, the sternness of *v.* 19, and the warning against idolatry, are unlike S. John, will not have much weight. The diction is S. John's throughout, and some of the fundamental ideas of the Epistle reappear in these concluding verses. Moreover, the connexion with the first half of the chapter is so close, that there is no reason for supposing that, while unquestionably by S. John himself, yet it is, like chap. xxi. of the Gospel, a subsequent addition to the original work. Indeed so close is the connexion with what precedes that some commentators consider only the last four verses, or even only the last verse, to be the proper Conclusion of the Epistle.

The Conclusion, as here arranged, falls into three parts. In the first, three main thoughts are retouched; faith in the Son of God, eternal life, and love of the brethren shewing itself in intercession (13—17). In the second, three great facts of which believers have certain knowledge are restated (18—20). In the third, a farewell practical warning is given (*v.* 21).

13—17. INTERCESSORY LOVE THE FRUIT OF FAITH AND OF THE POSSESSION OF LIFE.

13—17. Eternal life, faith, and brotherly love shewing boldness

These *things* have I written unto you that believe on the 13
name of the Son of God; that ye may know that ye have
eternal life, and that ye may believe on the name of the
Son of God. And this is the confidence that we have in 14

in intercession, are the leading ideas of this section. We have had most of these topics before, and the section is more or less of a recapitulation. But S. John "cannot even recapitulate without the introduction of new and most important thoughts" (F. W. Farrar); and the combination of the idea of boldness in prayer (iii. 21, 22) with that of love of the brethren leads to very fruitful results.

13. *These things have I written unto you*] 'These things' will cover the whole Epistle, and such is probably the meaning, as in i. 4, where S. John states the purpose of his Epistle in words which are explained by what he says here: there is nothing there or here, as there is in ii. 26, to limit 'these things' to what immediately precedes. As in ii. 21, 26, 'I have written' is literally, 'I wrote': it is the epistolary aorist, which may be represented in English either by the present or the perfect.

In the remainder of the verse the divergences of reading are very considerable, and authorities are much divided. The original text seems to be that represented by $\aleph^1$ B, which has been adopted in R. V. *These things have I written unto you,* that ye may know that ye have eternal life,—unto you that believe on the name of the Son of God. The awkwardness of the explanatory clause added at the end has led to various expedients for making the whole run more smoothly. Comp. the similarly added explanation in *v.* 16;—'them that sin not unto death.'

that ye may know that ye have eternal life] At the opening of the Epistle S. John said 'These things we write that our joy may be fulfilled' (i. 4). The context there shews what constitutes this joy. It is the consciousness of fellowship with God and His Son and His saints; in other words it is the conscious possession of eternal life (John xvii. 3). Thus the Introduction and Conclusion of the Epistle mutually explain one another. This verse should also be compared with its parallel in the Gospel (xx. 31), a passage which has probably influenced some of the various readings here. We see at once the similar yet not identical purposes of Gospel and Epistle. S. John writes his Gospel, 'that ye may *have life*'; he writes his Epistle 'that ye may *know* that ye have life.' The one leads to the obtaining of the boon; the other to the joy of knowing that the boon has been obtained. The one is to produce faith; the other is to make clear the fruits of faith.

believe on the name] See on *v.* 10 and on iii. 23.

14. *And this is the confidence that we have in him*] Better, *And the* **boldness** *that we have* **towards** *Him is this:* see on i. 5 and ii. 28. For the fourth and last time in the Epistle the Apostle touches on the subject of the Christian's 'boldness.' Twice he speaks of it in connexion with the Day of Judgment (ii. 28, iv. 17); twice in connexion with approaching God in prayer (iii. 21, 22 and here). In the present case

him, that, if we ask any *thing* according to his will, he
15 heareth us: and if we know that he hear us, whatsoever we
ask, we know that we have the petitions that we desired of
16 him. If any *man* see his brother sin a sin *which is* not

it is with special reference to intercessory prayer that the subject is
retouched. Thus two more leading ideas of the Epistle meet in this
recapitulation, boldness towards God and brotherly love; for it is love
of the brethren which induces us to pray for them.
according to his will] This is the only limitation, and it is a very
gracious limitation. His will is always for His children's good, and
therefore it is only when they ignorantly ask for what is not for their
good that their prayers are denied. Comp. S. Paul's case, 2 Cor. xii. 9.
'Heareth' of course means that He hears and *grants* what we ask
(John ix. 31, xi. 41, 42). Comp. 'The desire of the righteous shall be
granted' (Prov. x. 24).

15. *if we know that he hear us...we know that we have*] The one
certitude depends upon the other: if we trust God's goodness, we are
perfectly certain that our trust is not misplaced. Comp. 'All things
whatsoever ye pray and ask for, *believe that ye have received them*, and
ye shall have them' (Mark xi. 24). 'Whatsoever we ask' belongs
to the conditional clause.

that we have] Not merely that we *shall* have: our prayers are
already granted, although no results may be perceptible. 'Everyone
that asketh, *receiveth;* and he that seeketh, *findeth*' (Matt. vii. 8).

that we desired of him] Better, *that we* **have asked** *of Him:* it
is the perfect tense of the same verb as is used in 'whatsoever we ask.'
Comp. Matt. xx. 20. 'Of Him' or 'from Him' (ἀπ' αὐτοῦ) can be
taken with 'that we have'.

16. 'The prayer of faith' is all-prevailing when it is in accordance
with God's will. This is the sole limit as regards prayer on our own
behalf. Is there any other limit in the case of prayer on behalf of
another? Yes, there is that other's own will: this will prove a further
limitation. Man's will has been endowed by God with such royal
freedom, that not even His will coerces it. Still less, therefore, can a
brother's prayer coerce it. If a human will has deliberately and obstinately resisted God, and persists in doing so, we are debarred from
our usual certitude. Against a rebel will even the prayer of faith in
accordance with God's will (for of course God desires the submission of
the rebel) may be offered in vain.—For exhortations to intercession
elsewhere in N. T. see 1 Thess. v. 25; Heb. xiii. 18, 19; James v. 14—
20; comp. Phil. i. 4.

If any man see his brother] Here it is obvious that 'brother' must
mean 'fellow-*Christian*', not any one whether Christian or not.

sin a sin] More accurately, as R. V., **sinning** *a sin:* the supposed
case is one in which the sinner is seen in the very act. The phrase 'to
sin a sin' occurs nowhere else in N.T. Comp. Lev. v. 6, 10, 13; Ezek.
xviii. 24.

unto death, he shall ask, and he shall give him life for
them that sin not unto death. There is a sin unto death:

he shall ask] Future for imperative; or, *he* will *ask*, i.e. a Christian
in such a case is sure to pray for his erring brother. The latter seems
preferable.

and he shall give him life] The Greek is ambiguous. 'He' may
mean either God or the intercessor, and 'him' may mean either the
intercessor or the sinner for whom he intercedes. If the latter alternatives be taken, we may compare 'he shall save a soul from death'
(James v. 20). Commentators are much divided. On the one hand
it is urged that throughout Scripture asking is man's part and giving
God's; but, on the other hand, when two verbs are connected so
closely as these, 'will ask and will give' (αἰτήσει καὶ δώσει), it seems
rather violent to give them different nominatives; 'he will ask and
God will give'. It seems better to translate; *he will ask and will
give him life,—them that sin not unto death.* 'Them' is in apposition
to 'him', the clause being an explanation rather awkwardly added,
similar to that at the end of *v.* 13. If 'God' be inserted, 'them'
is the *dativus commodi;* 'God will grant the intercessor life *for* those
who sin'. The change to the plural makes the statement more
general: 'sinning not unto death' is not likely to be an isolated case.
The Vulgate is here exceedingly free; *petat, et dabitur ei vita peccanti
non ad mortem*. Tertullian also ignores the change of number; *postu-
labit, et dabit ei vitam dominus qui non ad mortem delinquit.*

There is a sin unto death] Or, *There* is sin *unto death;* we have no
τις or μία in the Greek, a fact which is against the supposition that any
act of sin is intended. In that case would not S. John have named it,
that the faithful might avoid it, and also know when it had been committed? The following explanations of 'sin unto death' may be safely
rejected. 1. Sin punished by the law with death. 2. Sin punished by
Divine visitation with death or sickness. 3. Sin punished by the
Church with excommunication. As a help to a right explanation we
may get rid of the idea which some commentators assume, that 'sin
unto death' is a sin which can be *recognised* by those among whom the
one who commits it lives. S. John's very guarded language points the
other way. He implies that *some* sins may be known to be '*not* unto
death': he neither says nor implies that all 'sin unto death' can be
known as such. As a further help we may remember that no sin, if
repented of, can be too great for God's mercy. Hence S. John does
not speak even of this sin as 'fatal' or 'mortal', but as '*unto* death'
(πρὸς θάνατον). Death is its natural, but not its absolutely inevitable
consequence. It is possible to close the heart against the influences of
God's Spirit so obstinately and persistently that repentance becomes a
moral impossibility. Just as the body may starve itself to such an extent
as to make the digestion, or even the reception, of food impossible; so
the soul may go on refusing offers of grace until the very power to receive grace perishes. Such a condition is necessarily sin, and 'sin unto
death'. No passing over out of death into life (iii. 14) is any longer

17 I do not say that he shall pray for it. All unrighteousness is
18 sin: and there is a sin not unto death. We know that

(without a miracle of grace) possible. 'Sin unto death', therefore, is not any *act* of sin, however heinous, but a *state* or *habit* of sin wilfully chosen and persisted in: it is constant and consummate opposition to God. In the phraseology of this Epistle we might say that it is the deliberate preference of darkness to light, of falsehood to truth, of sin to righteousness, of the world to the Father, of spiritual death to eternal life.

I do not say that he shall pray for it] More accurately, **not concerning that do I say that he should make request.** This reproduces the telling order of the Greek; it avoids the ambiguity which lurks in 'pray for it'; it preserves the emphatic 'that'; and marks better the difference between the verb (αἰτεῖν) previously rendered 'ask' (*vv*. 14, 15, 16) and the one (ἐρωτᾶν) here rendered 'pray'. Of the two verbs the latter is the *less* suppliant (see on John xiv. 16), whereas 'pray' is *more* suppliant than 'ask'. Two explanations of the change of verb are suggested. 1. The Apostle does not advise request, much less does he advise urgent supplication in such a case. 2. He uses the less humble word to express a request which seems to savour of presumption. See on 2 John 5.

(1) Note carefully that S. John, even in this extreme case, *does not forbid intercession:* all he says is that he does not command it. For one who sins an ordinary sin we may intercede in faith with certainty that a prayer so fully in harmony with God's will is heard. The sinner will receive grace to repent. But where the sinner has made repentance morally impossible S. John does not encourage us to intercede. Comp. Jer. vii. 16, xiv. 11.

(2) Note also that, while distinguishing between deadly and not deadly sin, *he gives us no criterion by which we may distinguish the one from the other.* He thus condemns rather than sanctions those attempts which casuists have made to tabulate sins under the heads of 'mortal' and 'venial'. Sins differ indefinitely in their intensity and effect on the soul, ending at one end of the scale in 'sin unto death'; and the gradations depend not merely or chiefly on the sinful *act*, but on the *motive* which prompted it, and the *feeling* (whether of sorrow or delight) which the recollection of it evokes. Further than this it is not safe to define or dogmatize. This seems to be intimated by what is told us in the next verse. Two facts are to be borne in mind, and beyond them we need not pry.

17. *All unrighteousness is sin*] A warning against *carelessness* about breaches of duty, whether in ourselves or in others. All such things are sin and need the cleansing blood of Christ (i. 9, ii. 2). Here, therefore, is a wide enough field for brotherly intercession. The statement serves also as a farewell declaration against the Gnostic doctrine that to the enlightened Christian declensions from righteousness involve no sin. Comp. the definition of sin as lawlessness in iii. 4.

there is a sin not unto death] Or, as before, *there* **is sin** *not unto*

whosoever is born of God sinneth not; but he that is
begotten of God keepeth himself, and *that* wicked one

death : Wiclif, Tyndale, Cranmer, and the Genevan here omit the
indefinite article, though they all insert it in *v.* 16. A warning against
despair, whether about ourselves or about others. Not all sin is
mortal:—an answer by anticipation to the unchristian rigour of Montanism and Novatianism.

18—20. THE SUM OF THE CHRISTIAN'S KNOWLEDGE.

18—20. The Epistle now draws rapidly to a close. Having briefly,
yet with much new material, retouched some of the leading ideas of the
Epistle, eternal life, faith in Christ and boldness in prayer united with
brotherly love (13—17), the Apostle now goes on to emphasize once
more three great facts about which Christians have sure knowledge,
facts respecting themselves, their relations to the evil one and his kingdom, and their relations to the Son of God. Each verse is a condensation of what has been said elsewhere. *V.* 18 is a combination of iii. 9
with ii. 13; *v.* 19 a combination of the substance of i. 6, ii. 8, 15 and
iii. 10, 13: *v.* 20 condenses the substance of iv. 9—iv. and v. 1—12.
"Hence we have in these last verses a final emphasis laid on the fundamental principles on which the Epistle rests; that *through the mission
of the Lord Jesus Christ we have fellowship with God;* that *this fellowship protects us from sin;* and that *it establishes us in a relation of utter
opposition to the world"* (Haupt). Fellowship with one another is not
mentioned again, but is included in the threefold '*we* know'.

18. *We know*] This confident expression of the certitude of Christian
faith stands at the beginning of each of these three verses and is the link
which binds them together. We have had it twice before (iii. 2, 14;
comp. ii. 20, 21, iii. 5, 15): and perhaps in all cases it is meant to mark
the contrast between the real knowledge of the believer, which is based
upon Divine revelation in Christ, and the spurious knowledge of the
Gnostic, which is based upon human intelligence.

The triple 'we know' at the close of the Epistle confirms the view
that John xxi. 24 is by the Apostle's own hand, and not added by the
Ephesian elders.

whosoever is born of God] Better, as R.V., *whosoever is* **begotten** *of
God.* It is the same verb, though not the same tense, as is used in the
next clause: A.V. changes the verb and does not change the tense.
The sentence is a return to the statement made in iii. 9, where see
notes. Once more the Apostle is not afraid of an apparent contradiction (see on ii. 15). He has just been saying that if a Christian sins his
brother will intercede for him; and now he says that the child of God
does not sin. The one statement refers to possible but exceptional
facts; the other to the habitual state. A child of God may sin; but
his normal condition is one of resistance to sin.

but he that is begotten of God keepeth himself] Rather, *but* **the
Begotten** *of God keepeth* **him.** The first change depends upon a question
of interpretation, the second on one of reading; and neither can be

19 toucheth him not. *And* we know that we are of God, and

determined with certainty. The latter is the easier question and it throws light on the former. 'Him' (αὐτόν), on the high authority of A¹B and the Vulgate, seems to be rightly preferred by most editors to 'himself' (ἑαυτόν). This 'him' is the child of God spoken of in the first clause: who is it that 'keepeth him'? Not the child of God himself, as A.V. leads us to suppose and many commentators explain, but the Son of God, the Only-Begotten. On any other interpretation S. John's marked change of tense appears arbitrary and confusing. Recipients of the Divine birth are always spoken of by S. John both in his Gospel and in his Epistle in the *perfect* participle (ὁ γεγεννημένος or τὸ γεγεννημένον); iii. 9, v. 1, 4; John iii. 6, 8; also the first clause here. In the present clause he abruptly changes to the *aorist* participle (ὁ γεννηθείς), which he uses nowhere else (comp. Matt. i. 20; Gal. iv. 29). The force of the two tenses here seems to be this: the perfect expresses a permanent relation begun in the past and continued in the present; the aorist expresses a timeless relation, a mere fact: the one signifies the child of God as opposed to those who have not become His children; the other signifies the Son of God as opposed to the evil one. It is some confirmation of this view that in the Constantinopolitan Creed, commonly called the Nicene Creed, 'begotten of the Father' (τὸν ἐκ τοῦ Πατρὸς γεννηθέντα) is the same form of expression as that used here for 'begotten of God' (ὁ γεννηθεὶς ἐκ τοῦ Θεοῦ). Moreover this interpretation produces another harmony between Gospel and Epistle. Christ both directly by His power and indirectly by His intercession 'keepeth' the children of God : 'I *kept* them in Thy Name' (xvii. 12); 'I pray not that Thou shouldest take them out of the world but that Thou shouldest *keep them from the evil one*' (xvii. 15).

that wicked one toucheth him not] Better, **the evil one** *toucheth him not*: see on i. 2 and ii. 13. Strangely enough the Genevan Version has 'that wycked *man.*' The original is perhaps less strong than the English; 'layeth not hold on him' (ἅπτεται); see on John xx. 17. The evil one does assault him, but he gets no hold. 'No one shall snatch them out of My hand' (John x. 28). 'The ruler of the world cometh: and he hath nothing in Me' (John xiv. 30). Therefore whoever is in Christ is safe.

19. *And we know*] The conjunction must be omitted on abundant authority. This introduces the second great fact of which the believer has sure knowledge. And, as so often, S. John's divisions are not sharp, but the parts intermingle. The second fact is partly anticipated in the first; the first is partly repeated in the second. Christians know that as children of God they are preserved by His Son from the devil. Then what do they know about the world, and their relation to the world? *They know that they are of God and the whole world lieth in* **the evil one.** It remains in his power. It has *not* passed over, as they have done, out of death into life; but it abides in the evil one, who is its ruler (John xii. 31, xiv. 30, xvi. 11), as the Christian abides in Christ. It is clear therefore that the severance between the Church and the world

the whole world lieth in wickedness. And we know that 20
the Son of God is come, and hath given us an understanding,
that we may know him *that is* true, and we are in him *that*

ought to be, and tends to be, as total as that between God and the evil
one. The preceding verse and the antithesis to God, to say nothing of
ii. 13, 14, iv. 4, make it quite clear that 'the evil' (τῷ πονηρῷ) is here
masculine and not neuter. The Vulgate has *in maligno*, not *in malo*.
Tyndale and Cranmer have 'is altogether set on wickedness,' which is
doubly or trebly wrong. Note once more that the opposition is not
exact, but goes beyond what precedes. The evil one doth not obtain
hold of the child of God: he not only obtains hold over the world, but
has it wholly within his embrace. No similar use of 'to lie in' occurs
in N. T. Comp. Sophocles *Oed. Col.* 248.

20. *And we know*] This introduces the third great fact of which
believers have certain knowledge. The first two Christian certitudes
are that the believer as a child of God progresses under Christ's protec-
tion towards the sinlessness of God, while the unbelieving world lies
wholly in the power of the evil one. Therefore the Christian knows
that both in the moral nature which he inherits, and in the moral
sphere in which he lives, there is an ever-widening gulf between him
and the world. But his knowledge goes beyond this. Even in the
intellectual sphere, in which the Gnostic claims to have such advantages, the Christian is, by Christ's bounty, superior.

The 'and' (δέ) brings the whole to a conclusion: comp. Heb.
xiii. 20, 22. Or it may mark the opposition between the world's evil
case and what is stated here; in which case δέ should be rendered 'but.'

is come] This includes the notion of 'is here' (ἥκει); but it is the
coming at the Incarnation rather than the perpetual presence that is
prominent in this context.

hath given us an understanding] Or, *hath given us understanding*,
i.e. the capacity for receiving knowledge, intellectual power. The word
(διάνοια) occurs nowhere else in S. John's writings.

that we may know] Literally, 'that we may continue to recognise, as
we do now' (ἵνα with the indicative; see on John xvii. 3). It is the
appropriation of the knowledge that is emphasized; hence 'recognise'
(γινώσκομεν) rather than 'know' (οἴδαμεν). The latter word is used at
the opening of these three verses: there it is the *possession* of the
knowledge that is the main thing.

him that is true] God; another parallel with Christ's Prayer; '*that
they should know* Thee the only *true God*' (John xvii. 3), where some
authorities give ἵνα with the indicative, as here. 'True' does not mean
'that cannot lie' (Titus i. 2), but 'genuine, real, *very*,' as opposed to the
false gods of *v.* 21. See on ii. 8. What is the Gnostic's claim to
superior knowledge in comparison with this? We know that we have
the Divine gift of intelligence by means of which we attain to the knowledge of a personal God who embraces and sustains us in his Son.

and we are in him] A fresh sentence, not dependent on either
preceding 'that'. 'Him that is true' again means God. It is arbitrary

is true, *even* in his Son Jesus Christ. This is the true God, 21 and eternal life. Little children, keep yourselves from idols. Amen.

to change the meaning and make this refer to Christ. 'The Son has given us understanding by which to attain to knowledge of the Father.' Instead of resuming 'And we *do know* the Father,' the Apostle makes an advance and says: 'And we *are in* the Father.' Knowledge has become fellowship (i. 3, ii. 3—5). God has appeared as man; God has spoken as man to man; and the Christian faith, which is the one absolute certainty for man, the one means of re-uniting him to God, is the result.

even in his Son Jesus Christ] Omit 'even' which has been inserted in A.V. and R.V. to make 'in Him that is true' refer to Christ. This last clause explains how it is that we are in the Father, viz. by being in the Son. Comp. ii. 23; John i. 18, xiv. 9, xvii. 21, 23. Tyndale boldly turns the second 'in' into 'through'; 'we are *in* him that is true, *through* his sonne Jesu Christ.' We have had similar explanatory additions in *vv.* 13, 16.

This is the true God] It is impossible to determine with certainty whether 'This' (οὗτος) refers to the Father, the *principal* substantive of the previous sentence, or to Jesus Christ, the *nearest* substantive. That S. John teaches the Divinity of Jesus Christ both in Epistle and Gospel is so manifest, that a text more or less in favour of the doctrine need not be the subject of heated controversy. The following considerations are in favour of referring 'This' to *Christ*. 1. Jesus Christ is the subject last mentioned. 2. The Father having been twice called 'the true One' in the previous verse, to proceed to say of Him 'This is the true God' is somewhat tautological. 3. It is Christ who both in this Epistle (i. 2, v. 12) and also in the Gospel (xi. 25, xiv. 6) is called the Life. 4. S. Athanasius three times in his *Orations against the Arians* interprets the passage in this way, as if there was no doubt about it (III. xxiv. 4, xxv. 16; IV. ix. 1). The following are in favour of referring 'This' to the Father. 1. The Father is the leading subject of all that follows 'understanding.' 2. To repeat what has been already stated and add to it is exactly S. John's style. He has spoken of 'Him that is true': and he now goes on 'This (true One) is the true *God and eternal life.*' 3. It is the Father who is the source of that life which the Son has and is (John v. 26). 4. John xvii. 3 supports this view. 5. The Divinity of Christ has less special point in reference to the warning against idols: the truth that God is the true God is the basis of the warning against false gods: comp. 1 Thess. i. 9. But see the conclusion of the note on 'from idols' in the next verse: see also note *k* in Lect. V. of Liddon's *Bampton Lectures*.

21. FAREWELL WARNING.

Little children] As usual (ii. 1, 12, 28, iii. 7, 18, iv. 4), this refers to all his readers.

keep yourselves] Better, as R. V., **guard** *yourselves*. It is not the verb used in v. 18 (τηρεῖν) but that used 2 Thess. iii. 3 (φυλάσσειν); 'shall *guard* you *from* the evil one'. Both verbs occur John xvii. 12: comp. xii. 25, 47. Here the verb is in the aorist imperative; 'once for all be on your guard and have nothing to do with'. The use of the reflexive pronoun instead of the middle voice intensifies the command to personal care and exertion (φυλάξατε ἑαυτά). This construction is frequent in S. John: i. 8, iii. 3; John vii. 4, xi. 33, 55, xiii. 4, xxi. 1; Rev. vi. 15, viii. 6, xix. 7.

from idols] Or perhaps, *from* **the** *idols;* those with which Ephesus abounded: or again, *from* **your** *idols;* those which have been, or may become, a snare to you. This is the last of the contrasts of which the Epistle is so full. We have had light and darkness, truth and falsehood, love and hate, God and the world, Christ and Antichrist, life and death, doing righteousness and doing sin, the children of God and the children of the devil, the spirit of truth and the spirit of error, the believer untouched by the evil one and the world lying in the evil one; and now at the close we have what in that age was the ever present and pressing contrast between the true God and the idols. There is no need to seek far-fetched figurative explanations of 'the idols' when the literal meaning lies close at hand, is suggested by the context, and is in harmony with the known circumstances of the time. Is it reasonable to suppose that S. John was warning his readers against "systematising inferences of scholastic theology; theories of self-vaunting orthodoxy... tyrannous shibboleths of aggressive systems", or against superstitious honour paid to the "Madonna, or saints, or pope, or priesthood", when every street through which his readers walked, and every heathen house they visited, swarmed with idols in the literal sense; above all when it was its magnificent temples and groves and seductive idolatrous rites which constituted some of the chief attractions at Ephesus? Acts xix. 27, 35; Tac. Ann. iii. 61, iv. 55. Ephesian coins with idolatrous figures on them are common. 'Ephesian letters' ('Ἐφέσια γράμματα) were celebrated in the history of magic, and to magic the 'curious arts' of Acts xix. 19 point. Of the strictness which was necessary in order to preserve Christians from these dangers the history of the first four centuries is full. Elsewhere in N. T. the word is *invariably* used literally: Acts vii. 41, xv. 20; Rom. ii. 22; 1 Cor. viii. 4, 7, x. 19, xii. 2; 2 Cor. vi. 16; 1 Thess. i. 9; Rev. ix. 20. Moreover, if we interpret this warning literally, we have another point of contact between the Epistle and the Apocalypse (Rev. ix. 20, xxi. 8). Again, as we have seen, some of the Gnostic teachers maintained that idolatry was harmless, or that at any rate there was no need to suffer martyrdom in order to avoid it. This verse is a final protest against such doctrine. Lastly, this emphatic warning against the worship of creatures intensifies the whole teaching of this Epistle; the main purpose of which is to establish the truth that the Son of God has come in the flesh in the Man Jesus. Such a Being was worthy of worship. But if, as Ebionites and Cerinthians taught, Jesus was a creature, the son of Joseph and Mary, then worship of such an one would be only one more of those idolatries from which S. John in his farewell injunction bids Christians once and for ever to guard themselves.

Amen] Here, as at the end of the Gospel and the Second Epistle, 'Amen' is the addition of a copyist. ℵAB and most Versions omit it. Such conclusions, borrowed from liturgies, have been freely added throughout N. T. Perhaps that in Gal. vi. 18 is the only final 'Amen' that is genuine; but that in 2 Pet. iii. 8 is well supported.

THE SECOND EPISTLE OF
JOHN.

THE elder unto the elect lady and her children, whom 1
I love in the truth; and not I only, but also all they

THE SECOND EPISTLE OF JOHN] This title, like that of the First
Epistle and of the Gospel, exists in various forms both ancient and
modern, and is not original: and here again the oldest authorities give
it in the simplest form. 1. *Of John B*; 2. *Second Epistle of John*; 3.
Second Catholic Epistle of John; 4. *Second Epistle of the Holy Apostle
John the Divine*. In our Bibles the epithet 'Catholic' or 'General' has
wisely been omitted. The Epistle is not addressed to the Church at
large, but either to an individual, or to a particular Church.

1—3. ADDRESS AND GREETING.

1—3. Like most of the Epistles of S. Paul, the Epistles of S. Peter,
S. James, and S. Jude, and unlike the First Epistle, this letter has a
definite address and greeting. In its fulness the salutation reminds us of
the elaborate openings of the Epistles to the Romans, Galatians, and to
Titus.

1. *The Elder*] It is probably on account of his age that the Apostle
styles himself thus: and it is a designation which a writer personating
S. John would scarcely have chosen, as being too indistinct. On the
other hand an Elder, who did *not* wish to personate the Apostle, would
hardly call himself '*The* Elder.' It is in addressing Elders that S.
Peter calls himself a 'fellow-elder' (1 Pet. v. 1). "The use of the
word in this Epistle shews that he cannot have understood this title in
the usual ecclesiastical sense, as though he were only one among many
presbyters of a community. Clearly the writer meant thereby to express the singular and lofty position he held in the circle around him,
as the teacher venerable for his old age, and the last of the Apostles"
(Döllinger). "In this connexion there can be little doubt that it
describes not age simply but official position" (Westcott). See Appendix E.

unto the elect Lady] Or possibly, *unto the elect* **Kyria** : but the other
is better, as leaving open the question, which cannot be determined
with any approach to certainty, whether the letter is addressed to an
individual or to a community. There is no article in the Greek, so

176 II. JOHN. [vv. 2, 3.

2 that have known the truth; for the truth's sake, which
3 dwelleth in us, and shall be with us for ever. Grace be
with you, mercy, *and* peace, from God the Father, and from

that 'to *an* elect lady' is a possible translation. If we make κυρία a proper name (and no doubt there was such a name in use), we are committed to the former alternative. The rendering 'to the *lady Electa*' may be safely dismissed, if only on account of *v.* 13. If Electa is a proper name here, it is a proper name there; which involves two sisters each bearing the same extraordinary name. Comp. 'to *the elect* who are sojourners of the Dispersion' (1 Pet. i. 1), and 'for the *elect's* sake' (2 Tim. ii. 10). Every Christian is elect or chosen out of the antichristian world into the kingdom of God.

and her children] Either the children of the lady, or the members of the community, addressed in the Epistle. For the Church as a mother comp. Gal. iv. 26.

whom I love in the truth] Omit the article, and comp. 'let us *love* in deed and *truth*' (1 John iii. 18): 'whom I love in all Christian sincerity', or in a Christian temper. In the Greek 'the lady' is feminine, 'the children' are neuter, 'whom' is masculine. No argument can be drawn from this as to whether a Christian family or a Church is to be understood.

but also all they that have known] Better, as R. V., *but also all they that know*: literally, *that have come to know* (see on 1 John ii. 3). At first sight this looks like a strong argument in favour of the view that 'the elect Lady' is a Church. "How could the children of an individual woman be regarded as an object of the love of all believers"? The First Epistle is the answer to the question. Every one who 'has come to know the truth' enters that 'Communion of Saints' of which the love of each for every other is the very condition of existence. The Apostle speaks first in his own name, and then in the name of every Christian. "For all Catholics throughout the world follow one rule of truth: but all heretics and infidels do not agree in unanimous error; they impugn one another not less than the way of truth itself" (Bede).

2. *For the truth's sake*] The repetition of the word 'truth' is quite in S. John's style. 'The truth' here and at the end of *v.* 1 means the truth as revealed in Christ and the Spirit.

which dwelleth in us] Better, as R.V., *which* **abideth** *in us*: see on 1 John ii. 24.

and shall be with us for ever] 'With us' is emphatic: *and with us it shall be for ever.* An echo of Christ's farewell discourses: 'He shall give you another Advocate, that He may be *with you for ever*, even the Spirit of *truth*' (John xiv. 16). Comp. 'I am...the Truth' (John xiv. 6) and 'The Spirit is the Truth' (1 John v. 6). The Apostle and all believers love the elect lady and her children on account of the ever-abiding presence of Christ in the gift of the Spirit. 'For ever' is literally 'unto the age': see on 1 John ii. 17.

3. *Grace be with you, mercy, and peace*] Rather, as R. V., *Grace, mercy, and peace* **shall be** *with* **us**. It is not so much a prayer or a

the Lord Jesus Christ, the Son of the Father, in truth and love.
I rejoiced greatly that I found of thy children walking in 4

blessing, as the confident assurance of a blessing; and the Apostle includes himself within its scope. This triplet of heavenly gifts occurs, and in the same order, in the salutations to Timothy (both Epistles) and Titus. The more common form is 'grace and peace'. In Jude 2 we have another combination; 'mercy, peace, and love'. In secular letters we have simply 'greeting' (χαίρειν) instead of these Christian blessings. 'Grace' is the *favour* of God towards sinners (see on John i. 14); 'mercy' is the *compassion* of God for the misery of sinners; 'peace' is the result when the guilt and misery of sin are removed. 'Grace' is rare in the writings of S. John; elsewhere only John i. 14, 16, 17; Rev. i. 4, xxii. 21.

from God the Father] Literally, '*from the presence of*, or *from the hand of* (παρά) *God the Father*': see on John i. 6, xvi. 27: the more usual expression is simply 'from' (ἀπό), as in Rom. i. 7; 1 Cor. i. 3; 2 Cor. i. 2, &c.

and from the Lord Jesus Christ the Son of the Father] Omit 'the Lord' with AB and the Vulgate; the title of 'Lord' for Jesus Christ, though found in the Gospel and in the Revelation, does not occur in S. John's Epistles. The repetition of the preposition marks the separate Personality of Christ; whose Divine Sonship is emphasized with an unusual fulness of expression, perhaps in anticipation of the errors condemned in vv. 7 and 10.

in truth and love] These two words, so characteristic of S. John (see on 1 John i. 8, ii. 8, iii. 1), are key-notes of this short Epistle, in which 'truth' occurs five times, and 'love' twice as a substantive and twice as a verb. 'Commandment' is a third such word.

4. THE OCCASION OF THE EPISTLE.

4. The Apostle has met with some of the elect lady's children (or some members of the particular Church addressed), probably in one of his Apostolic visits to some Church in Asia Minor. Their Christian life delighted him and apparently prompted him to write this letter.

I rejoiced greatly] Or, *I have rejoiced greatly*, or perhaps, as R. V., *I rejoice greatly*, if it is the epistolary aorist, as in 1 John ii. 26, v. 13. The same phrase occurs 3 John 3 and Luke xxiii. 8. The word for 'rejoice' (χαίρω) is cognate with 'grace' (χάρις) in v. 3. 'Grace' is originally 'that which causes joy': but there is no connexion between the two words here. Like S. Paul, the Elder leads up to his admonition by stating something which is a cause of joy and thankfulness: comp. Philem. 4; 2 Tim. i. 3; Rom. i. 8; &c.

that I found] Better, *that I have found*, or **because** *I* **have** *found*. There is nothing in 'I have found' (εὕρηκα) to shew that there had been any *seeking* on the part of the Apostle, still less that there had been any *examination* as to the rightness of their conduct.

of thy children] This elliptical mode of expression (ἐκ τῶν τέκνων)

178 II. JOHN. [v. 5.

truth, as we have received a commandment from the Father.
5 And now I beseech thee, lady, not as though I wrote a new
commandment unto thee, but *that* which we had from the

is rather common in S. John (John i. 24, vii. 40, xvi. 17; Rev. ii. 10, v. 9, xi. 9; see on 1 John iv. 13). It is impossible to say whether the expression is a delicate way of intimating that only some of the children were walking in truth, or whether it merely means that the Apostle had fallen in with only some of the children. The expression of affection in *v.* 1 is in favour of the latter supposition; but the strong warnings against intercourse with heretical teachers favours the former: some of her children were already contaminated. 'Walking' indicates the activity of human life (see on 1 John i. 7): 'in truth' is in Christian truth, as in *vv.* 1 and 3; in Christian tone and temper.

as we have received a commandment] The changes made in R. V., **even as we received commandment**, are all improvements in the direction of accuracy. 'Even as' (καθώς) points to the completeness of their obedience: comp. 1 John ii. 6, 27, iii. 3, 7, 23, iv. 17. The aorist points to the definite occasion of their reception of the commandment: comp. 'heard' 1 John ii. 7, 24, iii. 11; and 'gave' iii. 23, 24. 'Commandment' is the third key-word of the Epistle, in which it occurs four times. Love, truth, and obedience; these are the three leading ideas, which partly imply, partly supplement one another. Obedience without love becomes servile; love without obedience becomes unreal: neither of them can flourish outside the realm of truth.

from the Father] Literally, as in *v.* 3, *from the hand of the Father* (παρὰ τοῦ Πατρός). The Divine command has come direct from the Giver.

5—11. We now enter upon the main portion of the Epistle, which has three divisions: *Exhortation to Love and Obedience* (5, 6); *Warnings against False Doctrine* (7—9); *Warnings against False Charity* (10, 11). As usual, the transitions from one subject to another are made gently and without any marked break.

5, 6. EXHORTATION TO LOVE AND OBEDIENCE.

5. *And now*] As in 1 John ii. 28 (see note there), this introduces a practical exhortation depending on what precedes. 'It is my joy at the Christian life of some of thy children, and my anxiety about the others, that move me to exhort thee'.

I beseech thee] S. John uses the same verb (ἐρωτῶν) as that used of making request about 'sin unto death' (1 John v. 16). It perhaps indicates that he begs as an equal or superior rather than as an inferior. In both passages the Vulgate rightly has *rogo*, not *peto*. In classical Greek the verb = *interrogo*, 'I ask a question', a meaning which it frequently has in N. T. S. Paul uses it very seldom, and always in the sense of 'I request'; his usual word is παρακαλῶ, which S. John never employs.

a new commandment] See on 1 John ii. 7.

beginning, that we love one another. And this is love, that 6
we walk after his commandments. This is the commandment,
That, as ye have heard from the beginning, ye should walk in

from the beginning] See on 1 John ii. 7.
that we love one another] 'That' (ἵνα) introduces the *purport* of the command; but perhaps the notion of *purpose* is not wholly absent (see on 1 John i. 8 and comp. iii. 23). It is doubtful whether 'that we love' depends upon 'commandment' or upon 'I beseech thee'.
6. *And this is love*] Or, *And* **the love is this**: the love which I mean consists in this (see on 1 John i. 5). In *v.* 5 obedience prompts love; here love prompts obedience. This is no vicious logical circle, but a healthy moral connexion, as is stated above on *v.* 4. Love divorced from duty will run riot, and duty divorced from love will starve. See on 1 John v. 3. The Apostle has no sympathy with a religion of pious emotions: there must be a *persevering walk according to God's commands*. In writing to a woman it might be all the more necessary to insist on the fact that love is not a mere matter of feeling.
This is the commandment] Or, as before, *The commandment is this*, i.e. consists in this. We had a similar transition from plural to singular, 'commandments' to 'commandment' in 1 John iii. 22, 23.
In these verses (5, 6) S. John seems to be referring to the First Epistle, which she would know.
as ye have heard] Better, as R. V., **even as ye heard**, referring to the time when they were first instructed in Christian Ethics. See on 'received' in *v.* 4. R. V. is also more accurate in placing 'that' after, instead of before, 'even as ye heard'. But A. V. is not wrong, for 'even as ye heard' belongs to the apodosis, not to the protasis: still, this is interpretation rather than translation.
ye should walk in it] In brotherly love; not, in the commandment, as the Vulgate implies. S. John speaks of walking *in* (ἐν) truth, *in* light, *in* darkness; but of walking *according to* (κατά) the commandments. S. Paul speaks both of walking *in* love (Eph. v. 2) and *according to* love (Rom. xiv. 15). Neither speaks of walking *in* commandments: and in Luke i. 6 a different verb is used. Moreover the context here is in favour of 'in it' meaning in love.

7—9. WARNINGS AGAINST FALSE DOCTRINE.

7—9. The third element in the triplet of leading thoughts once more comes to the front, but without being named. Love and obedience require, as the condition of their existence, truth. It is in truth that 'the Elder' and all who love the truth love the elect lady and her children; and they love them for the truth's sake. Truth no less than love is the condition of receiving the threefold blessing of grace, mercy, and peace. And it was the fact that some of her children were walking in truth, while others seemed to be deserting it, which led the Apostle in the fulness of his heart to write to her. All this tends to shew the preciousness of the truth. Love of the brethren and loyal obedience

7 it. For many deceivers are entered into the world, who confess not that Jesus Christ is come in the flesh. This is a

to God's commands will alike suggest that we should jealously guard against those who by tampering with the truth harm the brethren and dishonour God and His Son.

7. *For*] Or, *Because*. Some would make this conjunction introduce the reason for v. 8: 'Because many deceivers have appeared...... look to yourselves.' But this is altogether unlike S. John's simple manner; to say nothing of the very awkward parenthesis which is thus made of 'This is......Antichrist.' 'For' or 'Because' points backwards to vv. 5 and 6, not forwards to v. 8. 'I am recalling our obligations to mutual love and to obedience of the Divine command, because there are men with whom you and yours come in contact, whose teaching strikes at the root of these obligations.'

many deceivers] The word for 'deceiver' (πλάνος) reaches that meaning in two ways. 1. 'Making to wander, leading astray.' 2. 'Vagabond,' and hence 'a charlatan' or 'impostor.' The former meaning is predominant here. It is rare in N. T. Comp. Matt. xxvii. 63. S. John uses it nowhere else, but not unfrequently uses the cognate verb, 'to lead astray' (1 John i. 8, ii. 26, iii. 7).

are entered into the world] Rather, are **gone forth** (NAB and Versions) *into the world:* literally, *went forth;* but here the English perfect idiomatically represents the Greek aorist : in 1 John iv. 1 we have the perfect in the Greek. 'The world' here may mean 'the earth' or 'human society': or we may take it in S. John's special sense of what is external to the Church and antichristian; see on 1 John ii. 2. The meaning may be that, like the many antichrists in 1 John ii. 18, they went out from the Church into the unchristian world. Possibly the same persons are meant in both Epistles. Irenaeus (A. D. 180) by a slip of memory quotes this passage as from the First Epistle (*Haer.* III. xvi. 8).

who confess not] More accurately, as R. V., *even they that confess not:* the many deceivers and those who confess not are the same group, and this is their character,—unbelief and denial of the truth. 'Confess not'=deny.

that Jesus Christ is come in the flesh] This is not quite accurate; nor does R. V., 'that Jesus Christ *cometh* in the flesh', seem to be more than a partial correction. Rather, *that confess not Jesus Christ* as **coming** *in the flesh*, or possibly, *that confess not Jesus* as **Christ coming** *in the flesh.* See on 1 John iv. 2, where the Greek is similar, but with perfect instead of present participle. These deceivers denied not merely the fact of the Incarnation, but its possibility. In both passages A. V. and R. V. translate as if we had the infinitive mood instead of the participle. The difference is, that with the participle the denial is directed against the *Person*, 'they deny *Jesus*'; with the infinitive it is directed against the *fact*, 'they deny that He *cometh*' or '*has come.*' Note that Christ is never said to come *into* the flesh; but either, as here and 1 John iv. 2, to come *in* the flesh; or, to

deceiver and an antichrist. Look to yourselves, that we lose 8
not *those things* which we have wrought, but *that* we receive
a full reward. Whosoever transgresseth, and abideth not in 9

become flesh (John i. 14). To say that Christ came *into* the flesh would
leave room for saying that the Divine Son was united with Jesus after
He was born of Mary; which would be no true Incarnation.
 This is a deceiver and an Antichrist] Rather, *This is* the *deceiver
and* the *Antichrist:* a good example of inadequate treatment of the
Greek article in A. V. (see on 1 John i. 2). Luther is more accurate;
'Dieser ist *der* Verführer und *der* Widerchrist'. The transition from
plural to singular (see on *v.* 6) may be explained in two ways; 1. The
man who acts thus is the deceiver and the Antichrist; 2. These men
collectively are the deceiver and the Antichrist. In either case the
article means 'him of whom you have heard': 'the deceiver' in reference to his fellow men; 'the Antichrist' in reference to his Redeemer.
 This completes the series of condemnatory names which S. John uses
in speaking of these false teachers; liars (1 John ii. 22), seducers
(1 John ii. 26), false prophets (1 John iv. 1), deceivers (2 John 7), antichrists (1 John ii. 18, 22; iv. 3; 2 John 7). On the Antichrist of S.
John see Appendix B.
 8. *Look to yourselves*] Exactly as in Mark xiii. 9, excepting the
emphatic pronoun; 'But look *ye* to yourselves'.
 that we lose not] The persons of the three verbs are much varied
in our authorities. The original reading probably was, as R. V., ye
lose...**we** *have wrought*...**ye** *receive*. To make the sentence run more
smoothly some have made all the verbs in the first person, others have
made them all in the second. For the construction comp. 1 Cor. xvi.
10. The meaning is, 'Take heed that these deceivers do not undo
the work which Apostles and Evangelists have wrought in you, but
that ye receive the full fruit of it'.
 a full reward] Eternal life. The word 'reward' has reference to
'have wrought'. 'Apostles have done the work, and you, if you take
heed, will have the reward'. Eternal life is called a *full* reward in
contrast to real but incomplete rewards which true believers receive
in this life; peace, joy, increase of grace, and the like. Comp. Mark
x. 29, 30.
 9. Explains more fully what is at stake; no less than the possession
of the Father and the Son.
 Whosoever transgresseth] This is a simplification (KL) of a much
more difficult reading (ℵAB), *Whosoever*, or *Every one that* (see on
1 John iii. 16) **goeth before** (πᾶς ὁ προάγων) or *that* **goeth onwards**.
The verb is fairly common in the Synoptists and the Acts, but occurs
nowhere else in S. John's writings. It may be interpreted in two ways:
1. Every one who sets himself up as a leader; 2. Every one who goes
on beyond the Gospel. The latter is perhaps better. These antichristian
Gnostics were *advanced* thinkers: the Gospel was all very well for the
unenlightened; but they knew something higher. This agrees very
well with what follows: by advancing they did not abide. There is an

the doctrine of Christ, hath not God. He that abideth in the doctrine of Christ, he hath both the Father and the Son. 10 If there come any unto you, and bring not this doctrine, receive him not into *your* house, neither bid him God

advance which involves desertion of first principles; and such an advance is not progress but apostasy.

in the doctrine] 'In the teaching', as R.V., is no improvement. Of the two words used in N.T., διδαχή (as here) and διδασκαλία (which S. John does not use), the former should be rendered 'doctrine', the latter, as being closer to διδάσκαλος and διδάσκειν, should be rendered 'teaching'. But no hard and fast line can be drawn.

of Christ] The doctrine which He taught (John xviii. 19; Rev. ii. 14, 15), rather than the doctrine which teaches about Him.

hath not God] This must not be watered down to mean 'does not know God': it means that he has Him not as his God; does not possess Him in his heart as a Being to adore, and trust, and love.

he that abideth] The opposite case is now stated, and as usual the original idea is not merely negatived but expanded. 'Of Christ' in this half of the verse must be omitted: it has been inserted in some authorities to make the two halves more exactly correspond.

hath both the Father and the Son] This shews that 'hath not God' implies 'hath neither the Father nor the Son'. See on 1 John ii. 23.

10, 11. WARNINGS AGAINST FALSE CHARITY.

10. *If there come any unto you*] Better, as R.V., *If any one cometh unto you*: it is εἰ with the indicative, not ἐάν with the subjunctive. It is implied that such people do come; it is no mere hypothesis: comp. 1 John v. 9; John vii. 4, 23, viii. 39, 46, xviii. 8. 'Cometh' probably means more than a mere visit: it implies coming on a mission as a teacher; comp. 3 John 10; John i. 7, 30, 31, iii. 2, iv. 25, v. 43, vii. 27, &c.; 1 Cor. ii. 1, iv. 18, 19, 21, xi. 34, &c.

and bring not this doctrine] Better, *and bringeth not this doctrine*. The negative (οὐ not μή) should be emphasized in reading: it "does not coalesce with the verb, as some maintain, but sharply marks off from the class of faithful Christians all who are *not* faithful" (Speaker's Commentary on 1 Cor. xvi. 22). The phrase 'to bring doctrine' occurs nowhere else in N.T., but it is on the analogy of 'to bring a message, to bring word' (Hom. *Il.* xv. 15, 175 &c.): comp. 'What accusation *bring* ye'? (John xviii. 29).

receive him not into your house] 'Refuse him the hospitality which as a matter of course you would shew to a faithful Christian'. Charity has its limits: it must not be shewn to one man in such a way as to do grievous harm to others; still less must it be shewn in such a way as to do more harm than good to the recipient of it. If these deceivers were treated as if they were true Christians, (1) their opportunities of doing harm would be greatly increased, (2) they might never be brought to

speed: for he that biddeth him God speed is partaker of his 11
evil deeds.

see their own errors. "S. John is at once earnestly dogmatic and earnestly philanthropic; for the Incarnation has taught him both the preciousness of man and the preciousness of truth" (Liddon). The famous story respecting S. John and Cerinthus in the public baths is confirmed in its main outlines by this injunction to the elect lady, which it explains and illustrates. See the Introduction, p. 24.

The greatest care will be necessary before we can venture to act upon the injunction here given to the elect lady. We must ask, *Are the cases really parallel?* Am I quite sure that the man in question is an unbeliever and a *teacher* of infidelity? Will my shewing him hospitality aid him in teaching infidelity? Am I and mine in any danger of being infected by his errors? Is he more likely to be impressed by severity or gentleness? Is severity likely to create sympathy in others, first for him, and then for his teaching? In not a few cases the differences between Christianity in the first century and Christianity in the nineteenth would at once destroy the analogy between these antichristian Gnostics visiting Kyria and an Agnostic visiting one of ourselves. Let us never forget the way in which the Lord treated Pharisees, publicans and sinners.

neither bid him God speed] 'Give him no greeting' is perhaps too narrow, whether as translation or interpretation. **And do not bid him, God speed** will perhaps be a better rendering; and the injunction will cover any act which might seem to give sanction to the false doctrine or shew sympathy with it. The word for 'God speed' ($\chi\alpha\acute{\iota}\rho\epsilon\iota\nu$) is used in a similar sense Acts xv. 23, xxiii. 26; James i. 1 : comp. John xix. 3, &c.

11. *For he that biddeth him God speed*] Much more, therefore, he that by receiving him into his house affords a home and head-quarters for false teaching.

is partaker of his evil deeds] More accurately, as R. V., **partaketh in his evil works** : literally, with much emphasis on 'evil', *partaketh in his works, his evil (works)*. The word for 'partake' ($\kappa o \iota \nu \omega \nu \epsilon \tilde{\iota} \nu$) occurs nowhere else in S. John, but is cognate with the word for 'fellowship' ($\kappa o \iota \nu \omega \nu \acute{\iota} \alpha$), 1 John i. 3, 6, 7. The word for 'evil' ($\pi o \nu \eta \rho \acute{o} s$) is the same as that used of 'the evil one', 1 John ii. 13, 14, iii. 12, v. 18, 19. What is involved, therefore, in having fellowship with such men is obvious. At a Council of Carthage (A.D. 256), when Cyprian uttered his famous invective against Stephen, Bishop of Rome,—Aurelius, Bishop of Chullabi, quoted this passage with the introductory remark, "John the Apostle laid it down in his Epistle": and Alexander, Bishop of Alexandria (c. A.D. 315), quotes the passage as an injunction of "the blessed John" (Socrates *H. E.* 1. vi.). The change from 'deeds' to 'works' may seem frivolous and vexatious, but it is not unimportant. 'Works' is a wider word and better represents $\xi\rho\gamma\alpha$: words no less than deeds are included, and here it is specially the words of these deceivers that is meant. Moreover in 1 John iii. 12 the same word is rendered 'works'

12 Having many *things* to write unto you, I would not *write* with paper and ink: but I trust to come unto you, and

of the 'evil works' of Cain. See on John v. 20, vi. 27, 29. Wiclif and the Rhemish have 'works' here.

At the end of this verse some Latin versions insert, 'Lo I have told you beforehand, that ye be not confounded (or, condemned) in the day of the Lord (or, of our Lord Jesus Christ)'. Wiclif admits the insertion, but the Rhemish does not: Cranmer puts it in italics and in brackets. It has no authority.

12, 13. CONCLUSION.

12, 13. The strong resemblance to the Conclusion of the Third Epistle seems to shew that the two letters are nearly contemporaneous.

12. *Having many things to write*] The First Epistle will give us some idea of what these were.

I would not write with paper and ink] There is here no 'write' in the Greek; and in the first clause 'write' is almost too limited in meaning for γράφειν, which like our 'say' covers a variety of methods of communication. *Having many things to say to you, I would not (say them) by means of paper and ink*. Perhaps we may here trace a sign of the failing powers of an old man, to whom writing is serious fatigue.

'Paper' (χάρτης) occurs nowhere else in N.T.; but it occurs in LXX. of Jer. xxxvi. 23; and its diminutive (χαρτίον) is frequent in that chapter. In 3 Macc. iv. 20 we have a cognate word (χαρτήρια), which probably, like 'paper' here, means Egyptian papyrus, as distinct from the more expensive 'parchment' (μεμβράναι) mentioned 2 Tim. iv. 13. But both papyrus and parchment were costly, which may account for the Apostle's brevity. See *Dict. of the Bible*, WRITING, and *Dict. of Antiquities*, LIBER.

'Ink' (μέλαν) is mentioned again 3 John 13; elsewhere in N.T. only 2 Cor. iii. 3: comp. LXX. of Jer. xxxvi. 18. It was made of lamp-black and gall-juice, or more simply of soot and water.

but I trust] Or, as R.V., *but I* **hope**: the verb (ἐλπίζω) is frequent in N.T., and there seems to be no reason for changing the usual rendering: comp. 1 Tim. iii. 14; Phil. ii. 19, 23. A.V. wavers needlessly between 'hope' and 'trust'.

to come unto you] More exactly, according to the true reading (γενέσθαι πρὸς ὑμᾶς), *to* **appear before** *you*: literally, 'to come to be in your presence'. Comp. 1 Cor. ii. 3, xvi. 10. The phrase is used of words as well as of persons: John x. 35; Acts x. 13, and as a various reading, vii. 31. In all these cases the coming is expressed with a certain amount of solemnity.

The 'you' (ὑμῖν, ὑμᾶς) in this verse includes the children mentioned in v. 1. This, when contrasted with 'thee' (σε, σοί) in v. 5, seems to be in favour of understanding the 'lady' literally. The change from 'thee' to 'you' seems more in harmony with a matron and her family than with a Church and its members.

speak face to face, that our joy may be full. The children 13
of thy elect sister greet thee. Amen.

face to face] Literally, *mouth to mouth:* it is not the phrase which is used in 1 Cor. xiii. 12 and Gen. xxxii. 31. Comp. Num. xii. 8; Jer. xxxix. (xxxii.) 4.

that our joy may be full] Better, as R. V., *that your* (AB and Vulgate) *joy may be* fulfilled : see on 1 John i. 4. "The high associations with which" the phrase "is connected lead us to suppose that it would scarcely have been applied by S. John to any meeting but one of peculiar solemnity after a cruel and prolonged separation which had threatened to be eternal" (Bishop Alexander). Comp. Rom. i. 12.

13. *The children of thy elect sister greet thee*] Better, for the sake of uniformity with 3 John 14, salute *thee:* the same verb is used in both passages. That the elect sister herself sends no greeting is taken as an argument in favour of the 'elect lady' being a Church, and the 'elect sister' a sister Church, which could send no greeting other than that of its members or 'children'. But the verse fits the other hypothesis equally well. Kyria's nephews may be engaged in business at Ephesus under S. John's Apostolic care : their mother may be living elsewhere, or be dead. It was perhaps from these children of her sister that the Apostle had knowledge of the state of things in the elect lady's house. Their sending a salutation through him may intimate that they share his anxiety respecting her and hers.

Amen] As in 1 John v. 21 (where see note), this is the addition of a copyist.

THE THIRD EPISTLE OF
JOHN.

1, 2   THE elder unto the wellbeloved Gaius, whom I love in the truth. Beloved, I wish above all *things* that thou

The Third Epistle of John]   This title, like that of the Gospel and of the other two Epistles, is not original, and is found in various forms, the most ancient being the simplest. 1. *Of John* I'; 2. *Third Epistle of John*; 3. *Third Catholic Epistle of John*; 4. *Third Catholic Epistle of the Apostle John*. This letter has still less reason than the second to be styled 'Catholic' or 'General.' The Second Epistle may *possibly* be addressed to a local Church and be intended to be encyclical; but beyond all reasonable doubt this one is addressed to an individual.

1. THE ADDRESS.

1. This Epistle, like the Second, and most others in N.T., has a definite address, but of a very short and simple kind: comp. James i. 1. It has no greeting, properly so called, the prayer expressed in *v.* 2 taking its place.

The Elder]   See on 2 John 1. From the Apostle's using this title in both Epistles we may conclude that he commonly designated himself thus. If not, it is additional evidence that the two letters were written about the same time: see on *vv.* 13, 14.

unto the wellbeloved Gaius]   More exactly, **to Gaius the beloved**: the epithet is the same word as we have had repeatedly in the First Epistle (ii. 7, iii. 2, 21, iv. 1, 7, 11) and have again in *vv.* 2, 5, 11. The name Gaius being perhaps the most common of all names in the Roman Empire, it is idle to speculate without further evidence as to whether the one here addressed is identical with either Gaius of Macedonia (Acts xix. 29), Gaius of Derbe (Acts xx. 4), or Gaius of Corinth (Rom. xvi. 23). See Introduction, Chap. IV. sect. ii. pp. 60, 61.

whom I love in the truth]   Better, *whom I love* **in truth**: see on 2 John 1. This is not mere tautology after 'the beloved;' nor is it mere emphasis. 'The beloved' gives a common sentiment respecting Gaius: this clause expresses the Apostle's own feeling. There is no need, as in the Second Epistle, to enlarge upon the meaning of loving in truth. In this letter the Apostle has not to touch upon defects which a less true love might have passed over in silence.

mayest prosper and be in health, even as thy soul prospereth. For I rejoiced greatly, when *the* brethren came and testified 3 of the truth *that is* in thee, even as thou walkest in the truth. I have no greater joy than to hear that my children 4

2—4. PERSONAL GOOD WISHES AND SENTIMENTS.

2. *I wish above all things that*] Rather, **I pray that in all respects**; literally, *concerning all things*. It might well surprise us to find S. John placing health and prosperity *above* all things; and though the Greek phrase (περὶ πάντων) has that meaning sometimes in Homer, yet no parallel use of it has been found in either N.T. or LXX.

prosper] The word (εὐοδοῦσθαι) occurs elsewhere in N.T. only Rom. i. 10 and 1 Cor. xvi. 2, but is frequent in LXX. Etymologically it has the meaning of being prospered in a *journey*, but that element has been lost in usage, and should not be restored even in Rom. i. 10.

and be in health] Bodily health, the chief element in all prosperity: Luke vii. 10, xv. 27; comp. v. 31. We cannot conclude from these good wishes that Gaius had been ailing in health and fortune: but it is quite clear from what follows that 'prosper and be in health' do not refer to his spiritual condition, and this verse is, therefore, good authority for praying for temporal blessings for our friends. In the Pastoral Epistles 'to be in health' (ὑγιαίνειν) is always used figuratively of faith and doctrine.

The order of the Greek is striking, 'all things' at the beginning being placed in contrast to 'soul' at the end of the sentence: *in all things I pray that thou mayest prosper and be in health, even as prospereth thy soul.* The verse is a model for all friendly wishes of good fortune to others.

3. *For*] 'I know that thy soul is in a prosperous condition, *for* I have it on good authority.'

I rejoiced greatly] See on 2 John 4. This cannot so well be the epistolary aorist, but rather refers to the definite occasions when information was brought. Of course if 'rejoiced' becomes present as epistolary aorist, 'came' and 'bare witness' must be treated in like manner.

testified of the truth that is in thee] Better, **bare witness** (see on 1 John i. 2) **to thy truth** (see on *v.* 6). The whole, literally rendered, runs thus; *For I rejoiced greatly at brethren coming and witnessing to thy truth.* John v. 33 is wrongly quoted as a parallel. There the Baptist 'hath borne witness to the truth,' i.e. to the Gospel or to Christ. Here the brethren bare witness to Gaius's truth, i.e. to his Christian life, as is shewn by what follows. The 'thy' is emphatic, as in *v.* 6; perhaps in contrast to the conduct of Diotrephes. Comp. Luke iv. 22.

even as thou walkest in the truth] Omit '*the*,' as in 2 John 4. This is part of what the brethren reported, explaining what they meant by Gaius's truth.

4. *I have no greater joy*] In the Greek 'greater' is put first for emphasis, and this is worth preserving; **Greater joy have I none than this.** 'Joy' should perhaps rather be **grace** (χάριν), i.e. favour from

5 walk in truth. Beloved, thou doest faithfully whatsoever **6** thou doest to the brethren, and to strangers; which have borne witness of thy charity before the church: whom if

God. The Greek for 'greater' is a double comparative (μειζοτέραν), like 'lesser' in English. In Eph. iii. 8 we have a comparative superlative. Such things belong to the later stage of a language, when ordinary forms are losing their strength. 'Than *this*' is literally 'than *these*,' where 'these' either means 'these *joys*,' or more likely 'these *things*,' viz. the frequent reports of the brethren. Comp. John xv. 13.

to hear that my children walk in truth] Better, as R.V., *to hear of my children* **walking** *in* **the** *truth*. Similarly in Acts vii. 12; 'When Jacob heard of corn being in Egypt.' 'My children' means in particular members of the Churches in Asia which were under S. John's Apostolic care.

5—8. GAIUS PRAISED FOR HIS HOSPITALITY: ITS SPECIAL VALUE.

5. *Beloved*] The affectionate address marks a new section (comp. *vv.* 3, 11), but here again the fresh subject grows quite naturally out of what precedes, without any abrupt transition. The good report, which caused the Apostle such joy, testified in particular to the Christian hospitality of Gaius.

thou doest faithfully] So the Vulgate; *fideliter facis*: Wiclif, Tyndale, and other English Versions take the same view. So also Luther: *du thust treulich*. The Greek is literally, *thou doest* **a faithful (thing),** *whatsoever thou* **workest** (same verb as is rendered 'wrought' in 2 John 8) *unto the brethren:* which is intolerably clumsy as a piece of English. R.V. makes a compromise; *thou doest a faithful work in whatsoever thou doest;* which is closer to the Greek than A.V., but not exact. 'To do a faithful act' (πιστὸν ποιεῖν) *possibly* means to do what is worthy of a faithful man or of a believer, *ostendens ex operibus fidem* (Bede); and 'to do faithfully' expresses this fairly well: *thou doest faithfully* **in all** *thou* **workest towards** *the brethren*. But this use of πιστὸν ποιεῖν is unsupported by examples, and therefore Westcott would translate *Thou* **makest sure** *whatsoever thou workest;* i.e. 'such an act will not be lost, will not fail of its due issue and reward'. The change of verb should at any rate be kept, not only on account of 2 John 8, but also of Matt. xxvi. 10, where 'she hath wrought a good work upon Me' (εἰργάσατο εἰς ἐμέ) is singularly parallel to 'thou workest toward the brethren' (ἐργάσῃ εἰς τοὺς ἀδελφούς).

and to the strangers] The true text (אABC) gives, *and that strangers* (καὶ τοῦτο ξένους); i.e. towards the brethren, and those brethren strangers. Comp. 1 Cor. vi. 6; Phil. i. 28; Eph. ii. 8. The brethren and the strangers are not two classes, but one and the same. It enhanced the hospitality of Gaius that the Christians whom he entertained were personally unknown to him: *Fideliter facis quidquid operaris in fratres, et hoc in peregrinos*. Comp. Matt. xxv. 35.

6. *Which have borne witness of thy charity*] Rather, as R.V., **who bare witness to thy love**. There is no need here to turn the aorist into

thou bring forward on their journey after a godly sort, thou
shalt do well: because that for his name's sake they went 7
forth, taking nothing of the Gentiles. We therefore ought 8

the perfect; and certainly in S. John's writings (whatever may be our
view of 1 Cor. xiii.) ἀγάπη must always be rendered 'love.' In a text
like this, moreover, 'charity' is specially likely to be understood in the
vulgar sense of almsgiving.

before the church] Probably at Ephesus; but wherever S. John was
when he wrote the letter. Only in this Third Epistle does he use the
word 'church.'

whom...thou shalt do well] The verb comes immediately after the
relative in the Greek, and may as well remain there; *whom* **thou wilt
do well to forward** *on their journey:* literally, *whom thou wilt do well
having sent on.* The word for 'send on' or 'forward' occurs Acts
xv. 3, xx. 38, xxi. 5; Rom. xv. 24; 1 Cor. xvi. 6, 11; 2 Cor. i. 16;
Tit. iii. 13. There would be abundant opportunity in the early Church
for such friendly acts; and in telling Gaius that he will do a good deed
in helping Christians on their way the Apostle gently urges him to continue such work. Comp. Phil. iv. 14; Acts x. 33.

after a godly sort] This is vague and rather wide of the Greek, which
means, **worthily of God** (R.V.), or, **in a manner worthy of God**
(Rhemish), or *as it beseemeth God* (Tyndale and Genevan). 'Help them
forward in a way worthy of Him whose servants they and you are.'
Comp. 1 Thess. ii. 12; Col. i. 10.

7. *Because that for his Name's sake*] Much more forcibly the true
text (אABCKL), For *for the sake of* **the** *Name:* the 'His' is a weak amplification in several versions. A similar weakening is found in Acts
v. 41, which should run, 'Rejoicing that they were counted worthy to
suffer dishonour for *the* Name.' 'The Name' of course means the
Name of Jesus Christ: comp. James ii. 7. This use of 'the Name' is
common in the Apostolic Fathers; Ignatius, *Eph.* iii., vii.; *Philad.* x.;
Clem. Rom. ii., xiii.; Hermas, *Sim.* viii. 10, ix. 13, 28.

they went forth] Comp. Acts xv. 40.

taking nothing of the Gentiles] Hence the necessity for men like
Gaius to help. These missionaries declined to 'spoil the Egyptians'
by taking from the heathen, and therefore would be in great difficulties
if Christians did not come forward with assistance. We are not to
understand that the Gentiles offered help which these brethren refused,
but that the brethren never asked them for help. 'The Gentiles' (οἱ
ἐθνικοί) cannot well mean Gentile *converts*. What possible objection
could there be to receiving help from them? Comp. Matt. v. 47, vi. 7,
xviii. 17, the only other places where the word occurs. There was
reason in not accepting money or hospitality at all, but working for
their own living, as S. Paul loved to do. And there was reason in not
accepting help from heathen. But there would be no reason in accepting from Jewish converts, but not from Gentile ones.

Some expositors render this very differently. 'For for the Name's
sake they went forth from the Gentiles, taking nothing;' i.e. they were

to receive such, that we might be fellowhelpers to the truth.

driven out by the heathen, penniless. But 'went forth' is too gentle a word to mean this; and the negative (μηδέν not οὐδέν) seems to imply that it was their *determination* not to accept anything, not merely that as a matter of *fact* they received nothing. For 'receive from' in a similar sense comp. Matt. xvii. 25.

8. *We therefore*] 'We' is in emphatic contrast to the heathen just mentioned. The Apostle softens the injunction by including himself: comp. 1 John ii. 1.

ought to receive such] Or, *ought to* **support** *such*, to *undertake* for them: the verb (ὑπολαμβάνειν not ἀπολαμβάνειν) occurs elsewhere in N.T. only in S. Luke's writings, and there with a very different meaning. Comp. Xen. *Anab.* I. i. 7. There is perhaps a play upon words between the missionaries *taking* nothing *from* the Gentiles, and Christians being therefore bound to *undertake* for them.

that we might be fellowhelpers to] Rather, *that we* **may become** *fellow-***workers with**. 'Fellow-workers' rather than 'fellow-helpers' on account of v. 5; see also on 2 John 11. Cognate words are used in the Greek, and this may as well be preserved in the English. 'Fellow-workers' with what? Not with the truth, as both A.V. and R.V. lead us to suppose; but with the missionary brethren. In N.T. persons are invariably said to be 'fellow-workers *of*' (Rom. xvi. 3, 9, 21; 1 Cor. iii. 9; 2 Cor. i. 24; Phil. ii. 25, iv. 3; [1 Thess. iii. 2;] Philem. i. 24), never 'fellow-workers *to*' or 'fellow-workers *with:*' those with whom the fellow-worker works are put in the genitive, not in the dative. The dative here is the *dativus commodi*, and the meaning is; *that we may become* **their** *fellow-workers* **for** *the truth*. Sometimes instead of the dative we have the accusative with a preposition (Col. iv. 11; comp. 2 Cor. viii. 23).

9, 10. DIOTREPHES CONDEMNED FOR HIS ARROGANCE AND HOSTILITY.

This is the most surprising part of the letter; and of the internal evidence this is the item which seems to weigh most heavily against the Apostolic authorship. That any Christian should be found to act in this manner towards the last surviving Apostle is nothing less than astounding. Those who opposed S. Paul, like Alexander the coppersmith (2 Tim. iv. 14), afford only remote parallels (1 Tim. i. 20; 2 Tim. i. 15). They do not seem to have gone the lengths of Diotrephes: the authority of Apostles was less understood in S. Paul's time: and his claim to be an Apostle was at least open to question; for he was not one of the Twelve, and he had himself been a persecutor. But from the very first the N.T. is full of the saddest surprises. And those who accept as historical the unbelief of Christ's brethren, the treachery of Judas, the flight of all the Disciples, the denial of S. Peter, the quarrels of Apostles both before and after their Lord's departure, and the flagrant abuses in the Church of Corinth, with much more of the same

I wrote unto the church : but Diotrephes, who loveth to 9
have the preeminence among them, receiveth us not. Where- 10
fore, if I come, I will remember his deeds which he doeth,
prating against us with malicious words: and not content
therewith, neither doth he himself receive the brethren, and

kind, will not be disposed to think it incredible that Diotrephes acted
in the manner here described even towards the Apostle S. John.

9. *I wrote unto the Church*] The best authorities give *I wrote* **somewhat** *to the Church;* i. e. 'I wrote a short letter, a something on which
I do not lay much stress'. There is yet another reading; *I would have
written to the Church:* but this is an obvious corruption to avoid the
unwelcome conclusion that an official letter from S. John has been lost.
The reference cannot be to either the First or the Second Epistle,
neither of which contains any mention of this subject. There is nothing
surprising in such a letter having perished: and Diotrephes would be
likely to suppress it. That the brethren whom Gaius received were the
bearers of it, and that his hospitality was specially acceptable on
account of the violence of Diotrephes, does not seem to fit in well with
the context. 'To the Church' probably means 'to the Church' of
which Diotrephes was a prominent member: that he was *presbyter* of
it cannot be either affirmed or denied from what is stated here.

who loveth to have the preeminence] The expression (ὁ φιλοπρωτεύων)
occurs nowhere else in N.T.; but it comes very close to "whosoever
willeth to be first among you" (Matt. xx. 28). Perhaps the meaning is
that Diotrephes meant to make his Church independent: hitherto it
had been governed by S. John from Ephesus, but Diotrephes wished to
make it autonomous to his own glorification. Just as the antichristian
teachers claimed to be first in the intellectual sphere (2 John 9), so the
unchristian Diotrephes claimed to be first in influence and authority.

10. *Wherefore*] Or, **For this cause**: see on 1 John iii. 1.

I will remember] I will direct public attention to the matter, 'will
bear witness of it before the Church' (*v.* 6). It is the word used in
John xiv. 26, 'He shall bring all things to your remembrance.'

his deeds which he doeth] Or, *his* **works** *which he doeth:* see on
2 John 11.

with malicious words] Or, *with* **evil** *words:* it is the same adjective
(πονηρός) as is used throughout the First Epistle of 'the evil one.' The
word for 'prate' (φλυαρεῖν) occurs nowhere else in N.T. It is frequent
in Aristophanes and Demosthenes, and means literally 'to talk nonsense.' Its construction here with an accusative after it is quite exceptional. 'Prates against us,' *garriens in nos*, cannot well be improved:
it conveys the idea that the words were not only wicked, but senseless.
Comp. 'And not only idle, but *tattlers* (φλύαροι) also and busybodies,
speaking things which they ought not' (1 Tim. v. 13). Other renderings
are 'chiding against us' (Wiclif), 'jesting on us' (Tyndale and Cranmer), 'pratteling against us' (Genevan), 'chatting against us' (Rhemish),
plaudert wider uns (Luther).

neither doth he himself receive the brethren] The same word (ἐπιδέ-

forbiddeth them that would, and casteth *them* out of the
11 church. Beloved, follow not *that which is* evil, but *that
which is* good. He that doeth good is of God: but he that
12 doeth evil hath not seen God. Demetrius hath good report

χεται) is used here and at the end of *v.* 9. It occurs nowhere else in
N.T. but is common in classical Greek. In *v.* 9 the meaning probably
is 'admits not our authority,' or 'ignores our letter.' Here of course
it is 'refuses hospitality to.' But perhaps 'closes his doors against'
may be the meaning in both places; 'us' being S. John's friends. By
saying 'us' rather than 'me', the Apostle avoids the appearance of a
personal quarrel.

casteth them out of the Church] He excommunicates those who are
willing to receive the missionary brethren. The exact meaning of this
is uncertain, as we have not sufficient knowledge of the circumstances.
The natural meaning is that Diotrephes had sufficient authority or
influence in some Christian congregation to exclude from it those who
received brethren of whom he did not approve. For the expression
comp. John ix. 34, 35.

11, 12. THE MORAL.

11, 12. This is the main portion of the Epistle. In it the Apostle
bids Gaius beware of imitating such conduct. And if an example of
Christian conduct is needed there is Demetrius.

11. *Beloved*] The address again marks transition to a new subject,
but without any abrupt change. The behaviour of Diotrephes will at
least serve as a warning.

follow not that which is evil, but that which is good] More simply,
imitate *not* the ill, *but* **the good.** The word for 'evil' or 'ill' is not
that used in the previous verse (πονηρός), but a word, which, though
one of the most common in the Greek language to express the idea of
'bad,' is rarely used by S. John (κακός). Elsewhere only John xviii.
23; Rev. ii. 2, xvi. 2: in Rev. xvi. 2 both words occur. Perhaps 'ill'
is hardly strong enough here, and the 'evil' of A.V. had better be
retained. Nothing turns on the change of word, so that it is not absolutely necessary to mark it. For 'imitate' comp. 2 Thess. iii. 7, 9;
Heb. xiii. 7: the word occurs nowhere else in N.T.

He that doeth good is of God] He has God as the source (ἐκ) of
his moral and spiritual life; he is a child of God. In its highest sense
this is true only of Him who 'went about doing good;' but it is true
in a lower sense of every earnest Christian. See on 1 John ii. 16, 29,
iii. 8, 9, iv. 4, 6, 7.

hath not seen God] See on 1 John iii. 6. Of course doing good and
doing evil are to be understood in a wide sense: the particular cases of
granting and refusing hospitality to missionary brethren are no longer
specially in question.

12. While Diotrephes sets an example to be abhorred, Demetrius
sets one to be imitated. We know of him, as of Diotrephes, just what
is told us here and no more. Perhaps he was the bearer of this letter.

of all *men*, and of the truth itself: yea, and we also bear record; and ye know that our record is true.

That Demetrius is the silversmith of Ephesus who once made silver shrines for Artemis (Acts xix. 24) is a conjecture, which is worth mentioning but cannot be said to be probable.

Demetrius hath good report, &c.] Literally, **Witness** *hath been borne to Demetrius by all men and by the truth itself;* or less stiffly, as R. V., *Demetrius hath the* **witness** *of all men.* See on 1 John i. 2. 'All men' means chiefly those who belonged to the Church of the place where Demetrius lived, and the missionaries who had been there in the course of their labours. The force of the perfect is the common one of present result of past action: the testimony has been given and still abides.

and of the truth itself] A great deal has been written about this clause; and it is certainly a puzzling statement. Of the various explanations suggested these two seem to be best. 1. 'The Truth' means "the divine rule of the walk of all believers:" Demetrius walked according to this rule and his conformity was manifest to all who knew the rule: thus the rule bore witness to his Christian life. This is intelligible, but it is a little far-fetched. 2. 'The Truth' is the Spirit of truth (1 John v. 6) which speaks in the disciples. The witness which 'all men' bear to the Christian conduct of Demetrius is not mere human testimony which may be the result of prejudice or of deceit: it is given under the direction of the Holy Spirit. This explanation is preferable. The witness given respecting Demetrius was that of disciples, who reported their own experience of him: but it was also that of the Spirit, who guided and illumined them in their estimate. See note on John xv. 27, which is a remarkably parallel passage, and comp. Acts v. 32, xv. 28, where as here the human and Divine elements in Christian testimony are clearly marked.

yea, and we also bear record] Better, as R. V., *yea, we also bear* **witness** (see on 1 John i. 2): the 'and' of A.V. is redundant. The Apostle mentions his own testimony in particular as corroborating the evidence of 'all men.'

and ye know that our record is true] Rather, as R.V., *and* **thou knowest** *that our* **witness** *is true*. The evidence for the singular, οἶδας (אABC and most Versions), as against the plural, οἴδατε (KL), is quite decisive: a few authorities, under the influence of John xxi. 24, read '*we* know:' comp. John xix. 35. The plural has perhaps grown out of the belief that the Epistle is not private but Catholic.

John xxi. is evidently an appendix to the Gospel, and was possibly written long after the first twenty chapters. It may have been written after this Epistle; and (if so) xxi. 24 may be "an echo of this sentence" (Westcott).

13, 14. CONCLUSION.

13, 14. The marked similarity to the Conclusion of the Second Epistle is strong evidence that the two letters were written about the same time. See notes on 2 John 12, 13.

S. JOHN (F.P.) 13

13 I had many *things* to write, but I will not with ink and
14 pen write unto thee: but I trust *I* shall shortly see thee,
and we shall speak face to face. Peace *be* to thee. *Our*
friends salute thee. Greet the friends by name.

13. *I had many things to write*] With R. V., following ℵABC and all ancient Versions, we must add **to thee**. 'I had' is imperfect: at the time of my writing there were many things which I had to communicate to thee.

but I will not] 'Will' is not the sign of the future tense auxiliary to 'write,' but the present of the verb 'to will:' *but I will not to write to thee; I do not care to write.* See on John vi. 67, vii. 17, viii. 44.

with ink and pen] In the Second Epistle we had 'with *paper* and ink.' The word for 'pen' (κάλαμος) occurs in this sense nowhere else in N. T. It signifies the reed, *calamus*, commonly used for the purpose. In LXX. of Ps. xliv. 2, 'My tongue is the pen of a ready writer,' the same word is used; so also in Matt. xi. 7 and Rev. xi. 1, but in the sense of reed, not of pen.

14. *But I trust I shall shortly see thee*] More closely, *but* **I hope immediately** *to see thee*. The punctuation of this passage should be assimilated to the parallel passage in the Second Epistle. There is no reason for placing a comma before 'but I hope' in the one case, and a full stop in the other.

face to face] As in 2 John 12, this is literally 'mouth to mouth.'

Peace be to thee] Instead of the usual 'Farewell' we have an ordinary blessing with Christian fulness of meaning.

Pax interna conscientiae,
Pax fraterna amicitiae,
Pax superna gloriae.

Comp. John xx. 19, 26. The concluding blessing 1 Pet. v. 14 is similar; comp. Eph. vi. 23; 2 Thess. iii. 16; Gal. vi. 16.

Our friends salute thee] Rather, **The** *friends salute thee:* there is no authority for 'our' either as translation or interpretation. If any pronoun be inserted, it should be 'thy': the friends spoken of are probably the friends of Gaius. It is perhaps on account of the private character of the letter, as addressed to an individual and not to a Church, that S. John says 'the friends' rather than 'the brethren.' Comp. 'Lazarus, our *friend*, is fallen asleep' (John xi. 11); and 'Julius treated Paul kindly, and gave him leave to go unto *the friends* and refresh himself' (Acts xxvii. 3), where 'the friends' probably means '*his* friends,' just as it probably means '*thy* friends' here. In 'Lazarus, *our* friend' the pronoun is expressed in the Greek.

Greet the friends by name] Better, as R. V., **Salute** *the friends by name:* the same verb is used as in the previous sentence and in 2 John 13 (ἀσπάζεσθαι): 'greet' may be reserved for the verb used Acts xv. 23, xxiii. 26; James i. 1; comp. 2 John 10, 11 (χαίρειν). The former is much the more common word in N. T. to express salutation. For other instances of capricious changes of rendering in the same passage in A.V. comp. 1 John ii. 24, iii. 24, v. 10, 15; John iii. 31.

by name] The phrase (κατ' ὄνομα) occurs in N. T. in only one other passage (John x. 3); 'He calleth His own sheep *by name*.' The salutation is not to be given in a general way, but to each individual separately. S. John as shepherd of the Churches of Asia would imitate the Good Shepherd and know all his sheep by name.

APPENDICES.

A. THE THREE EVIL TENDENCIES IN THE WORLD.

THE three forms of evil 'in the world' mentioned in 1 John ii. 16 have been taken as a summary of sin, if not in all its aspects, at least in its chief aspects. 'The lust of the flesh, the lust of the eyes, and the vainglory of life' have seemed from very early times to form a synopsis of the various modes of temptation and sin. And certainly they cover so wide a field that we cannot well suppose that they are mere examples of evil more or less fortuitously mentioned. They appear to have been carefully chosen on account of their typical nature and wide comprehensiveness.

There is, however, a wide difference between the views stated at the beginning and end of the preceding paragraph. It is one thing to say that we have here a very comprehensive statement of three typical forms of evil; quite another to say that the statement is a summary of all the various kinds of temptation and sin.

To begin with, we must bear in mind what seems to be S. John's purpose in this statement. He is not giving us an account of the different ways in which Christians are tempted, or (what is much the same) the different sins into which they may fall. Rather, he is stating the principal forms of evil which are exhibited 'in the world,' i.e. in those who are *not* Christians. He is insisting upon the evil origin of these desires and tendencies, and of the world in which they exist, in order that his readers may know that the world and its ways have no claim on their affections. All that is of God, and especially each child of God, has a claim on the love of every believer. All that is not of God has no such claim.

It is difficult to maintain, without making some of the three heads unnaturally elastic, that all kinds of sin, or even all of the principal kinds of sin, are included in the list. Under which of the three heads are we to place unbelief, heresy, blasphemy, or persistent impenitence? Injustice in many of its forms, and especially in the most extreme form of all—murder, cannot without some violence be brought within the sweep of these three classes of evil.

Two positions, therefore, may be insisted upon with regard to this classification.

1. It applies to forms of evil which prevail in the non-Christian world rather than to forms of temptation which beset Christians.
2. It is very comprehensive, but it is not exhaustive.

It seems well, however, to quote a powerful statement of what may be said on the other side. The italics are ours, to mark where there seems to be over-statement. "I think these distinctions, the lust of the flesh, the lust of the eye, and the pride of life, prove themselves to be very accurate and very complete distinctions in practice, though an ordinary philosopher may perhaps adopt some other classification of those tendencies which connect us with the world and give it a dominion over us. To the lust of the flesh may be referred *the crimes and miseries which have been produced by* gluttony, drunkenness, and the irregular intercourse of the sexes; an appalling catalogue, certainly, which no mortal eye could dare to gaze upon. To the lust of the eye may be referred all worship of visible things, *with the divisions, persecutions, hatreds, superstitions, which this worship has produced in different countries and ages*. To the pride or boasting of life,—where you are not to understand by life, for the Greek words are entirely different, either natural or spiritual life, such as the Apostle spoke of in the first chapter of the Epistle, but all that belongs to the outside of existence, houses, lands, whatever exalts a man above his fellow,—to this head we must refer *the oppressor's wrongs*, and that contumely which Hamlet reckons among the things which are harder to bear even than the 'slings and arrows of outrageous fortune.' In these three divisions I suspect all the mischiefs which have befallen our race may be reckoned, and each of us is taught by the Apostle, and may know by experience that the seeds of the evils so enumerated are in himself" (Maurice).

Do we not feel in reading this that S. John's words have been somewhat strained in order to make them cover the whole ground? One sin produces so many others in its train, and these again so many more, that there will not be much difficulty in making the classification exhaustive, if under each head we are to include all the crimes and miseries, divisions and hatreds, which that particular form of evil has produced.

Some of the *parallels* and *contrasts* which have from early times been made to the Apostle's classification are striking, even when somewhat fanciful. Others are both fanciful and unreal.

The three forms of evil noticed by S. John in this passage are only partially parallel to those which are commonly represented under the three heads of the world, the flesh, and the devil. Strictly speaking those particular forms of spiritual evil which would come under the head of the devil, as distinct from the world and the flesh, are not included in the Apostle's enumeration at all. 'The vainglory of life' would come under the head of the world; 'the lust of the flesh' of course under that of 'the flesh;' while 'the lust of the eyes' would belong partly to the one and partly to the other.

There is more reality in the parallel drawn between S. John's classification and the three elements in the temptation by which Eve was overcome by the evil one, and again the three temptations in which Christ overcame the evil one. 'When the woman saw that the tree was good for food (the lust of the flesh), and that it was pleasant to the eyes (the lust of the eyes), and a tree to be desired to make one wise (the vainglory of life), she took of the fruit thereof, and did eat'

(Gen. iii. 6). Similarly, the temptations (1) to work a miracle in order to satisfy the cravings of the flesh, (2) to submit to Satan in order to win possession of all that the eye could see, (3) to tempt God in order to win the glory of a miraculous preservation (Luke iv. 1—12).

Again, there is point in the contrast drawn between these three forms of evil 'in the world' and the three great virtues which have been the peculiar creation of the Gospel (Liddon *Bampton Lectures* VIII. iii. B), purity, charity, and humility, with the three corresponding 'counsels of perfection,' chastity, poverty, and obedience.

But in all these cases, whether of parallel or contrast, it will probably be felt that the correspondence is not perfect throughout, and that the comparison, though striking, is not quite satisfying, because not quite exact.

It is surely both fanciful and misleading to see in this trinity of evil any contrast to the three Divine Persons in the Godhead. Is there any sense in which we can say with truth that a lust, whether of the flesh or of the eyes, is more opposed to the attributes of the Father than to the attributes of the Son? Forced analogies in any sphere are productive of fallacies; in the sphere of religious truth they may easily become profane.

B. ANTICHRIST.

In the notes on 1 John ii. 18 it has been pointed out that the term 'Antichrist' is in N. T. peculiar to the Epistles of S. John (1 John ii. 18, 22, iv. 3; 2 John 7), and that in meaning it seems to combine the ideas of a mock Christ and an opponent of Christ, but that the latter idea is the prominent one. The false claims of a rival Christ are more or less included in the signification; but the predominant notion is that of hostility.

It remains to say something on two other points of interest. I. Is the Antichrist of S. John a person or a tendency, an individual man or a principle? II. Is the Antichrist of S. John identical with the great adversary spoken of by S. Paul in 2 Thess. ii.? The answer to the one question will to a certain extent depend upon the answer to the other.

I. It will be observed that S. John introduces the term 'Antichrist,' as he introduces the term 'Logos' (1 John i. 1; John i. 1), without any explanation. He expressly states that it is one with which his readers are familiar; 'even as ye heard that Antichrist cometh.' Certainly this, the first introduction of the name, looks like an allusion to a person. All the more so when we remember that the Christ was 'He that cometh' (Matt. xi. 3; Luke xix. 20). Both Christ and Antichrist had been the subject of prophecy, and therefore each might be spoken of as 'He that cometh.' But it is by no means conclusive. We may understand 'Antichrist' to mean an impersonal power, or principle, or tendency, exhibiting itself in the words and conduct of individuals, without doing violence to the passage. In the one case the 'many antichrists' will be forerunners of the great personal opponent; in the other the antichristian spirit which they exhibit may be regarded as Antichrist.

APPENDICES.

But the balance of probability seems to be in favour of the view that the Antichrist, of which S. John's readers had heard as certain to come shortly before the end of the world, is a person.

Such is not the case with the other three passages in which the term occurs. 'Who is the liar but he that denieth that Jesus is the Christ? This is the Antichrist, even he that denieth the Father and the Son' (1 John ii. 22). There were many who denied that Jesus is the Christ and thereby denied not only the Son but the Father of whom the Son is the revelation and representative. Therefore once more we have many antichrists, each one of whom may be spoken of as 'the Antichrist,' inasmuch as he exhibits the antichristian characteristics. No doubt this does not exclude the idea of a person who should have these characteristics in the highest possible degree, and who had not yet appeared. But this passage *taken by itself* would hardly suggest such a person.

So also with the third passage in the First Epistle. 'Every spirit which confesseth not Jesus is not of God : and this is the (spirit) of the Antichrist, whereof ye have heard that it cometh, and now is in the world already' (iv. 3). Here it is no longer 'the Antichrist' that is spoken of, but 'the spirit of the Antichrist.' This is evidently a principle; which again does not exclude, though it would not necessarily suggest or imply, the idea of a person who would embody this antichristian spirit of denial.

The passage in the Second Epistle is similar to the second passage in the First Epistle. 'Many deceivers are gone forth into the world, even they that confess not Jesus Christ as coming in the flesh. This is the deceiver and the Antichrist' (*v.* 7). Here again we have many who exhibit the characteristics of Antichrist. Each one of them, and also the spirit which animates them, may be spoken of as 'the Antichrist;' the further idea of an individual who shall exhibit this spirit in an extraordinary manner being neither necessarily excluded, nor necessarily implied.

The first of the four passages, therefore, will have to interpret the other three. And as the interpretation of that passage cannot be determined beyond dispute, we must be content to admit that the question as to whether the Antichrist of S. John is personal or not cannot be answered with certainty. The probability seems to be in favour of an affirmative answer. In the passage which *introduces* the subject (1 John ii. 18) the Antichrist, of which the Apostle's little children had heard as coming, appears to be a person of whom the 'many antichrists' with their lying doctrine are the heralds and already existing representatives. And it may well be that, having introduced the term with the personal signification familiar to his readers, the Apostle goes on to make other uses of it ; in order to warn them that, although the personal Antichrist has not yet come, yet his spirit and doctrine are already at work in the world.

Nevertheless, we must allow that, if we confine our attention to the passages of S. John in which the term occurs, the balance in favour of the view that he looked to the coming of a personal Antichrist is far from conclusive. This balance, however, whatever its amount, is considerably augmented when we take a wider range and consider—(*a*) The origin of the doctrine which the Apostle says that his readers had already heard respecting Antichrist; (*b*) The treatment of the question by those who followed S. John as teachers in the Church; (*c*) Other passages in the N. T. which seem to bear upon the question. The discussion of this third point is placed last because it involves the second question to be investigated in this Appendix;—Is the Antichrist of S. John identical with S. Paul's 'man of sin.'

(*a*) There can be little doubt that the *origin* of the primitive doctrine respecting Antichrist is *the Book of Daniel*, to which our Lord Himself had drawn attention in speaking of the 'abomination of desolation' (Matt. xxiv. 15; Dan. ix. 27, xii. 11). The causing the daily sacrifice to cease, which was one great element of this desolation, at once brings these passages into connexion with the 'little horn' of Dan. viii. 9—14, the language respecting which seems almost necessarily to imply an individual potentate. The prophecies respecting the 'king of fierce countenance' (viii. 23—25) and 'the king' who 'shall do according to his will' (xi. 36—39) strongly confirm this view. And just as it has been in individuals that Christians have seen realisations, or at least types, of Antichrist (Nero, Julian, Mahomet), so it was in an individual (Antiochus Epiphanes) that the Jews believed that they saw such. It is by no means improbable that S. John himself considered Nero to be a type, indeed the great type, of Antichrist. When Nero perished so miserably and obscurely in A.D. 68, Romans and Christians alike believed that he had only disappeared for a time. Like the Emperor Frederick II. in Germany, and Sebastian 'the Regretted' in Portugal, this last representative of the Caesars was supposed to be still alive in mysterious retirement: some day he would return. Among Christians this belief took the form that Nero was to come again as the Antichrist (Suet. *Nero* 40, 56; Tac. *Hist.* ii. 8). All this will incline us to believe that the Antichrist, of whose future coming S. John's 'little children' had heard, was not a mere principle, but a person.

(*b*) "That Antichrist is one individual man, not a power, not a mere ethical spirit, or a political system, not a dynasty, or a succession of rulers, was *the universal tradition of the early Church.*" This strong statement seems to need a small amount of qualification. The Alexandrian School is not fond of the subject. "Clement makes no mention of the Antichrist at all; Origen, after his fashion, passes into the region of generalizing allegory. The Antichrist, the 'adversary,' is 'false doctrine;' the temple of God in which he sits and exalts himself, is the written Word; men are to flee, when he comes, to 'the mountains of truth' (*Hom. xxix. in Matt.*). Gregory of Nyssa (*Orat. xi. c. Eunom.*) follows in the same track." Still the general tendency is all the other way. Justin Martyr (*Trypho* XXXII.) says "He whom Daniel foretells would have dominion for a time, and times, and an half, is even already at the door, about to speak blasphemous and daring things against the Most High." He speaks of him as 'the man of sin.' Irenaeus (v. xxv. 1, 3), Tertullian (*De Res. Carn.* XXIV., XXV.), Lactantius (*Div. Inst.* VII. xvii.), Cyril of Jerusalem (*Catech.* XV. 4, 11, 14, 17), and others take a similar view, some of them enlarging much upon the subject. Augustine (*De Civ. Dei*, xx. xix.) says "Satan shall be loosed, and by means of that Antichrist shall work with all power in a lying but wonderful manner." Jerome affirms that Antichrist "is one man, in whom Satan shall dwell bodily;" and Theodoret that "the Man of Sin, the son of perdition, will make every effort for the seduction of the pious, by false miracles, and by force, and by persecution." From these and many more passages that might be cited it is quite clear that the Church of the first three or four centuries almost universally regarded Antichrist as an individual. The evidence, beginning with Justin Martyr in the sub-Apostolic age, warrants us in believing that in this stream of testimony we have a belief which prevailed in the time of the Apostles and was possibly shared by them. But as regards this last point it is worth remarking how reserved the Apostles seem to have been with regard to the interpretation of prophecy. "What the Apostles disclosed concerning the future was for the most part disclosed by them in private, to individuals—not committed to writing, not intended for the edifying of the body of Christ,—and was soon lost" (J. H. Newman).

(*c*) Besides the various passages in N.T. which point to the coming of false Christs and false prophets (Matt. xxiv. 5, 24; Mark xiii. 22, 23; Acts xx. 29; 2 Tim. iii. 1; 2 Pet. ii. 1), there are two passages which give a detailed description of a great power, hostile to God and His people, which is to arise hereafter and have great success;—Rev. xiii. and 2 Thess. ii. The second of these passages will be considered in the discussion of the second question. With regard to the first this much may be asserted with something like certainty, that the correspondence between the 'beast' of Rev. xiii. and the 'little horn' of Dan. vii. is too close to be accidental. But in consideration of the difficulty of the subject and the great diversity of opinion it would be rash to affirm positively that the 'beast' of the Apocalypse is a person. The correspondence between the 'beast' and the 'little horn' is not so close as to compel us to interpret both images alike. The wiser plan will be to leave Rev. xiii. out of consideration as neutral, for we cannot be at all sure whether the beast (1) is a person, (2) is identical with Antichrist. We shall find that 2 Thess. ii. favours the belief that Antichrist is an individual.

II. There is a strong preponderance of opinion in favour of the view that *the Antichrist of S. John is the same as the great adversary of S. Paul* (2 Thess. ii. 3). 1. Even in the name there is some similarity; the Antichrist (ὁ ἀντίχριστος) and 'he that opposeth' (ὁ ἀντικείμενος). And the idea of being a rival Christ which is included in the name Antichrist and is wanting in 'he that opposeth,' is supplied in S. Paul's description of the great opponent: for he is a '*man*,' and he 'setteth himself forth as *God*.' 2. Both Apostles state that their readers had previously been instructed about this future adversary. 3. Both declare that his coming is preceded by an apostasy of many nominal Christians. 4. Both connect his coming with the Second Advent of Christ. 5. Both describe him as a liar and deceiver. 6. S. Paul says that this 'man of sin exalteth himself against all that is called God.' S. John places the spirit of Antichrist as the opposite of the Spirit of God.

7. S. Paul states that his 'coming is according to the working of Satan.' S. John implies that he is of the evil one. 8. Both Apostles state that, although this great opponent of the truth is still to come, yet his spirit is already at work in the world. With agreement in so many and such important details before us, we can hardly be mistaken in affirming that the two Apostles in their accounts of the trouble in store for the Church have one and the same meaning.

Having answered, therefore, this second question in the affirmative we return to the first question with a substantial addition to the evidence. It would be most unnatural to understand S. Paul's 'man of sin' as an impersonal principle; and the widely different interpretations of the passage for the most part agree in this, that the great adversary is an individual. If, therefore, S. John has the same meaning as S. Paul, then the Antichrist of S. John is an individual.

To sum up:—Although none of the four passages in S. John's Epistles are conclusive, yet the first of them (1 John ii. 18) inclines us to regard Antichrist as a person. This view is confirmed (*a*) by earlier Jewish ideas on the subject, (*b*) by subsequent Christian ideas from the sub-Apostolic age onwards, (*c*) above all by S. Paul's description of the 'man of sin,' whose similarity to S. John's Antichrist is of a very close and remarkable kind.

For further information on this difficult subject see the articles on Antichrist in Smith's *Dictionary of the Bible* (Appendix), and *Dictionary of Christian Biography*, with the authorities there quoted; also four lectures on *The Patristical Idea of Antichrist* in J. H. Newman's *Discussions and Arguments*.

C. THE SECT OF THE CAINITES.

The name of this extravagant Gnostic sect varies considerably in different authors who mention them: Cainistae, Caiani, Cainani, Cainaei, Caimiani, Caini, and possibly other varieties, are found. The Cainites were a branch of the Ophites, one of the oldest forms of Gnosticism known to us. Other branches of the Ophites known to us through Hippolytus are the *Naassenes* (*Naash*) or 'Venerators of the serpent,' the *Peratae* (πέραν or περᾷν) 'Transmarines' or 'Transcendentalists,' the *Sethians* or 'Venerators of Seth,' and the *Justinians* or followers of Justin, a teacher otherwise unknown. Of these the Naassenes, as far as name goes, are the same as the Ophites, the one name being Hebrew, and the other Greek (ὄφις) in origin, and both meaning 'Serpentists' or 'Venerators of the serpent.'

All the Ophite sects make the serpent play a prominent part in their system, and that not out of sheer caprice or extravagance, but as part of a reasoned and philosophical system. In common with almost all Gnostics they held that matter is radically evil, and that therefore the Creator of the material universe cannot be a perfectly good being. The Ophites regarded the Creator as in the main an evil being, opposed to the Supreme God. From this it followed that Adam in disobeying his Creator did not fall from a high estate, nor rebelled against the

APPENDICES. 203

Most High, but defied a hostile power and freed himself from its thraldom: and the serpent who induced him to do this, so far from being the author of sin and death, was the giver of light and liberty. It was through the serpent that the human race were first made aware that the being who created them was not supreme, but that there were higher than he; and accordingly the serpent became the symbol of intelligence and enlightenment.

Logically carried out, such a system involved a complete inversion of all the moral teaching of the Old Testament. All that the Creator of the world (who is the God of the Jews) commands, must be disobeyed, and all that He forbids must be done. The negative must be struck out of the Ten Commandments, and everything that Moses and the Prophets denounced must be cultivated as virtues. From this monstrous consequence of their premises most of the Ophites seem to have recoiled. Some modified their premises and made the Creator to be, not an utterly evil being, but an inferior power, who through ignorance sometimes acted in opposition to the Supreme God. Others, while retaining the Ophite doctrine that the serpent was a benefactor and deliverer of mankind in the matter of the temptation of Eve, endeavoured to bring this into harmony with Scripture by declaring that he did this service to mankind unwittingly. His intention was evil; he wished to do a mischief to the human race. But it was overruled to good; and what the serpent plotted for the ruin of man turned out to be man's enlightenment.

The Cainites, however, accepted the Ophite premises without qualification, and followed them without shrinking to their legitimate conclusion. Matter and the Creator of everything material are utterly evil. The revolt of Adam and Eve against their Creator was a righteous act, the breaking up of a tyranny. The serpent who suggested and aided this emancipation is a good being, as worthy of veneration, as the Creator is of abhorrence. The redemption of man begins with the first act of disobedience to the Creator. Jesus Christ is not the redeemer of the human race. He merely completed what the serpent had begun. Indeed some Cainites seem to have identified Jesus with the serpent. Others again, with more consistency, seem to have maintained that Jesus was an enemy of the truth and deserved to die.

The moral outcome of such a system has been already indicated, and the Cainites are said to have openly accepted it. Everything that the God of the Old Testament forbids must be practised, and everything that He orders abjured. Cain, the people of Sodom, Esau, Korah, Dathan and Abiram, are the characters to be imitated as saints and heroes; and in the New Testament, Judas. These are the true martyrs, whom the Creator and His followers have persecuted. About Judas, as about Jesus Christ, they seem not to have been agreed, some maintaining that he justly caused the death of one who perverted the truth; others, that having higher knowledge than the Eleven, he saw the benefits which would follow from the death of Christ, and therefore brought it about. These benefits, however, were not such as Christians commonly suppose, viz. the deliverance of mankind from the power of the serpent, but the final extinction of the dominion of the Creator. Irenaeus

(*Haer.* I. xxxi. 1) tells us that they had a book called the *Gospel of Judas.* In the next section he states the practical result of these tenets. "They say, like Carpocrates, that men cannot be saved until they have gone through all kinds of experience. They maintain also that in everyone of their sinful and foul actions an angel attends them and listens to them as they work audacity and incur pollution. According to the nature of the action they invoke the name of the angel, saying, 'O thou angel, I use thy work. O thou great power, I accomplish thy action.' And they declare that this is 'perfect knowledge,'—fearlessly to rush into such actions as it is not right even to name."

These are developments of those 'depths of Satan' of which S. John speaks in the Apocalypse (ii. 24) as a vaunted form of knowledge. Into the fantastic details of the system it is not necessary to enter. Suffice to say, that taking an inverted form of the Old Testament narrative as their basis, they engrafted upon it whatever took their fancy in the Egyptian rites of Isis and Osiris, the Greek mysteries of Eleusis, the Phoenician cultus of Adonis, the speculative cosmogony of Plato, or the wild orgies of Phrygian Cybele. *Purpurei panni* from all these sources find place in the patchwork system of the Ophite Gnostics. Christianity supplied materials for still further accretions, and probably acted as a considerable stimulus to the development of such theories. In several of its Protean forms we trace what appear to be adaptations of the Christian doctrine of the Trinity.

"The first appearance of the Ophite heresy in connexion with Christian doctrines," says Dean Mansel (*The Gnostic Heresies* p. 104), "can hardly be placed later than the latter part of the first century;" which brings us within the limits of S. John's lifetime. It is not probable that the monstrous system of the Cainites was formulated as early as this. But the first beginnings of it were there; and it is by no means impossible that 1 John iii. 10—12 was written as a condemnation of the principles on which the Cainite doctrine was built. Be this as it may, the prodigious heresy, although it probably never had very many adherents and died out in the third century, is nevertheless very instructive. It shews us to what results the great Gnostic principle, that matter is utterly evil, when courageously followed to its logical consequences, leads. And it therefore helps us to understand the stern and uncompromising severity with which Gnostic principles are condemned, by implication in the Fourth Gospel, and in express terms in these Epistles.

D. THE THREE HEAVENLY WITNESSES.

The outcry which has been made in some quarters against the Revisers for omitting the disputed words in 1 John v. 7, and without a hint in the margin that there is any authority for them, is not creditable to English scholarship. The veteran scholar Döllinger expressed his surprise at this outcry in a conversation with the present writer in July, 1882: and he expressed his amazement and amusement that anyone in these days should *write a book* in defence of the passage, in a conversation in September, 1883. The Revisers' action is a very tardy act of

APPENDICES. 205

justice; and we may hope that, whether their work as a whole is authorised or not, leave will before long be granted to the clergy to omit these words in reading 1 John v. as a Lesson at Morning or Evening Prayer, or as the Epistle for the First Sunday after Easter. The insertion of the passage in the first instance was quite indefensible, and it is difficult to see upon what sound principles its retention can be defended. There would be no difficulty in treating this case by itself and leaving other disputed texts to be dealt with hereafter. The passage stands absolutely alone (*a*) in the completeness of the evidence against it, (*b*) in the momentous character of the insertion. A summary of the evidence at greater length than could conveniently be given in a note will convince any unprejudiced person that (as Dr Döllinger observed) nothing in textual criticism is more certain than that the disputed words are spurious.

(i) *The External Evidence.*

1. **Every Greek uncial MS.** omits the passage.
2. *Every Greek cursive MS. earlier than the fifteenth century* omits the passage.
3. Out of about 250 known cursive MSS. only *two* (No. 162 of the 15th century and No. 34 of the 16th century) contain the passage, and in them it is *a manifest translation from a late recension of the Latin Vulgate.*

Erasmus hastily promised that if he could find the words in a single Greek MS. he would insert them in his text; and on the authority of No. 34 he inserted them in his third edition; Beza and Stephanus inserted them also: and hence their presence in all English Versions until the Revised Version of 1881.

4. **Every Ancient Version of the first four centuries** omits the passage.
5. *Every Version earlier than the fourteenth century, except the Latin*, omits the passage.
6. **No Greek Father** quotes the passage in any of the numerous discussions on the doctrine of the Trinity. Against Sabellianism and Arianism it would have been almost conclusive.

It has been urged that the orthodox Fathers did not quote *v*. 7 because in conjunction with *v*. 8 it might be used in the interests of Arianism. But in that case why did not the Arians quote *v*. 7? Had they done so, the orthodox would have replied and shewn the true meaning of both verses. Evidently both parties were ignorant of its existence.

Again, it has been urged that the Greek Synopsis of Holy Scripture printed in some editions of the Greek Fathers, and also the so-called *Disputation with Arius*, "*seem* to betray an acquaintance with the disputed verse." Even if this 'seeming' could be shewn to be a reality, the fact would prove no more than that the interpolation existed in a Greek as well as a Latin form about the fifth century. Can we seriously defend a text which does not even 'seem' to be known to a single Greek Father until 350 years or more after S. John's death. Could we defend a passage as Chaucer's which was never quoted until the nineteenth century, and was in no edition of his works of earlier date than that?—And the 'seeming' can *not* be shewn to be a reality.

7. *No Latin Father earlier than the fifth century* quotes the passage.

It is sometimes stated that Tertullian possibly, and S. Cyprian certainly, knew the passage. Even if this were true, it would prove nothing for the genuineness of the words against the mass of testimony mentioned in the first six of these paragraphs. Such a fact would only prove that the insertion, which is obviously of Latin origin, was made at a very early date. But the statement is not true. "Tertullian and Cyprian use language which makes it morally certain that they would have quoted these words had they known them" (Westcott and Hort Vol. II. p. 104).

Tertullian's words are as follows:—'*De meo sumet,*' *inquit, sicut ipse de Patris. Ita connexus Patris in Filio, et Filii in Paracleto, tres efficit cohaerentes alterum ex altero: qui tres unum sunt, non unus; quomodo dictum est, 'Ego et Pater unum sumus,' ad substantiae unitatem, non ad numeri singularitatem.* "He saith, *He shall take of Mine* (John xvi. 14), even as He Himself of the Father. Thus the connexion of the Father in the Son, and of the Son in the Paraclete, maketh Three that cohere together one from the other: which Three are one Substance, not one Person; as it is said, *I and My Father are one* (John x. 30), in respect to unity of essence, not to singularity of number" (*Adv. Praxean.* xxv.).

S. Cyprian writes thus; *Dicit Dominus. 'Ego et Pater unum sumus'; et iterum de Patre et Filio et Spiritu Sancto scriptum est, 'Et tres unum sunt.'* "The Lord saith, *I and the Father are one;* and again it is written concerning the Father, Son, and Holy Spirit, *And three are one*" (*De Unit. Eccl.* vi.).

It is very difficult to believe that Tertullian's words contain any allusion to the disputed passage. The passage in S. Cyprian seems at first sight to look like such an allusion; but in all probability he has in his mind the passage which follows the disputed words; 'the spirit, the water, and the blood: and the three agree in one'; the Latin Version of which runs, *spiritus et aqua et sanguis; et hi tres unum sunt.* For the Vulgate makes no difference between the conclusions of *vv.* 7 and 8; in both cases the sentence ends with *et hi tres unum sunt.* That S. Cyprian should thus positively allude to 'the spirit, the water, and the blood' as 'the Father, the Son, and the Holy Spirit' will seem improbable to no one who is familiar with the extent to which the Fathers make any triplet found in Scripture, not merely suggest, but *signify* the Trinity. To take an example from Cyprian himself: "We find that the three children with Daniel, strong in faith and victorious in captivity, observed the third, sixth, and ninth hour, as it were, for a sacrament of the Trinity, which in the last times had to be manifested. For both the first hour in its progress to the third shews forth the consummated number of the Trinity, and also the fourth proceeding to the sixth declares another Trinity; and when from the seventh the ninth is completed, the perfect Trinity is numbered every three hours" (*Dom. Orat.* xxxiv).

APPENDICES. 207

But perhaps the most conclusive argument in favour of the view that Cyprian is alluding to 'the spirit, the water and the blood,' and not to 'the Three that bear witness in heaven, the Father, the Word, and the Holy Spirit,' is S. Augustine's treatment of the passage in question. *In all his voluminous writings there is no trace of the clause about the Three Heavenly Witnesses;* but about 'the spirit, the water and the blood' he writes thus;—" Which three things if we look at as they are in themselves, they are in substance several and distinct, and not one. But if we will inquire into the things signified by these, there not unreasonably comes into our thoughts the Trinity itself, which is the one, only, true, supreme God, Father, and Son and Holy Spirit, of whom it could most truly be said, *There are Three Witnesses, and the Three are One.* So that by the term 'spirit' we should understand God the Father to be signified; as indeed it was concerning the worshipping of Him that the Lord was speaking, when He said, *God is spirit.* By the term 'blood,' the Son; because *the Word was made flesh.* And by the term 'water,' the Holy Spirit; as, when Jesus spake of the water which He would give to them that thirst, the Evangelist saith, *But this said He of the Spirit, which they that believed on Him were to receive.* Moreover, that the Father, Son, and Holy Spirit are witnesses, who that believes the Gospel can doubt, when the Son saith, *I am one that bear witness of Myself, and the Father that sent Me, He beareth witness of Me?* Where, though the Holy Spirit is not mentioned, yet He is not to be thought separated from them" (*Contra Maxim.* II. xxii. 3). Is it credible that S. Augustine would go to S. John's Gospel to prove that the Father and the Son might be called witnesses if in the very passage which he is explaining they were called such? His explanation becomes fatuous if the disputed words are genuine. A minute point of some significance is worth remarking, that in these passages both S. Cyprian and S. Augustine invariably write 'the Son,' not 'the Word,' which is the expression used in the disputed passage.

Facundus of Hermiana in his *Defense* of the "Three Chapters" (c. A.D. 550) explains 1 John v. 8 in the same manner as S. Augustine, quoting the verse several times and evidently knowing nothing of *v.* 7. This shews that late in the sixth century the passage was not generally known even in North Africa. Moreover *he quotes the passage of S. Cyprian* as authority for this mystical interpretation of *v.* 8. This shews how (300 years after he wrote) S. Cyprian was still understood by a Bishop of his own Church, even after the interpolation had been made. Attempts have been made to weaken the evidence of Facundus by asserting that Fulgentius, who is a little earlier in date, understood Cyprian to be referring to *v.* 7, not to *v.* 8. It is by no means certain that this is the meaning of Fulgentius; and, even if it is, it proves no more than that in the sixth century, as in the nineteenth, there were some persons who believed that Cyprian alludes to 1 John v. 7. Even if such persons were right, it would only shew that this corruption, like many other corruptions of the text, was in existence in the third century.

This may suffice to shew that the passage in Cyprian probably refers to 1 John v. 8 and gives no support to *v.* 7. And this probability becomes something like a certainty when we consider the extreme unlikelihood of his knowing a text which was wholly unknown to S. Hilary, S. Ambrose, and S. Augustine; which is absent from the earliest MSS. of the Vulgate (and consequently was not known to Jerome); and which is not found in Leo I.[1]

The anonymous treatise *On Rebaptism* (which begins with a fierce attack on the view of S. Cyprian that heretics ought to be rebaptized, and was therefore probably written before the martyrdom of the bishop) twice quotes the passage (xv. and xix.), and in each case says nothing about the Three bearing witness in heaven, but mentions only the spirit, the water, and the blood. This confirms the belief that the words were not found in the Latin Version in use in north Africa at that time.

Lastly, the letter of Leo the Great to Flavianus in B.C. 449, shortly before the Council of Chalcedon, "supplies positive evidence to the same effect for the Roman text by quoting *vv.* 4—8 without the inserted words" (Westcott and Hort Vol. II. p. 104).

Therefore the statement, that *No Latin Father earlier than the fifth century quotes the passage*, is strictly correct. The words in question first occur in some Latin controversial writings towards the end of the fifth century, but are not often quoted until the eleventh. The insertion appears to have originated in North Africa, which at the close of the fifth century was suffering from a cruel persecution under the Arian Vandals. The words are quoted in part in two of the works attributed to Vigilius of Thapsus, and a little later in one by Fulgentius of Ruspe. They are also quoted in a confession of faith drawn up by Eugenius, Bishop of Carthage, and presented to Hunneric c. A.D. 484. But it is worth noting that in these first appearances of the text the wording of it varies: the form has not yet become set. The *Prologus Galeatus* to the Catholic Epistles, falsely written in the name of Jerome, blames the Latin translators of the Epistle for omitting *Patris et Filii et Spiritus testimonium*. But not until some centuries later are the inserted words often cited even by Latin writers. Bede, the representative scholar of Western Christendom in the eighth century, omits all notice of them in his commentary, and probably did not know them; he comments on every other verse in the chapter.

The external evidence against them could not well be much stronger. If S. John had written the words, who would wish to expel such conclusive testimony to the doctrine of the Trinity from Scripture? If anyone had wished to do so, how could he have kept the words out of every MS. and every Version for four centuries? And had he succeeded in doing this, how could they have been recovered?

In short, we may use in this case the argument which Tertullian uses with such force in reference to the Christian faith. "Is it credible that so many and such important authorities should have *strayed* into giving unanimous testimony?" *Ecquid verisimile est ut tot et tantae ecclesiae in unam fidem erraverint?*

---

[1] The passage (sometimes quoted as from S. Cyprian) in the Epistle to Jubaianus may be omitted. 1. S. Augustine doubted the genuineness of the Epistle. 2. The important words *cum tres unum sunt* are not found in all, if any, early editions of the Epistle. 3. Even if they are genuine, they come from *v.* 8, not from *v.* 7.

(ii) *Internal Evidence.*

But it is sometimes said, that, although the external evidence is no doubt exceedingly strong, yet it is not the whole of the case. The internal evidence also must be considered, and that tells very powerfully the other way. Let us admit for the sake of argument that the internal evidence is very strongly in favour of the genuineness of the disputed words. Let us assume that the passage, though making sense without the words (as is indisputably the case), makes far better sense with the words. Let us suppose that the sense of the passage when thus enlarged is so superior to the shorter form of it, that it would be incredible that anyone to whom the longer form had occurred would ever write the shorter one. Can all this prove, in the teeth of abundant evidence to the contrary, that the longer and vastly superior passage was written, and not the shorter and inferior one? If twenty reporters quite independently represent an orator as having uttered a very tame and clumsy sentence, which the insertion of a couple of short clauses would make smooth and far more telling, would this fact convince us that the orator must have spoken the two clauses, and that twenty reporters had all accidentally left just these two clauses out? The fact that in a few out of many editions of the orator's collected speeches, published many years after his death, these two clauses were found, but not always in exactly the same words, would hardly strengthen our belief that they were actually uttered at the time. No amount of internal probability, supplemented by subsequent evidence of this kind, ought to shake our confidence in the reports of the twenty writers who took down the speaker's words at the moment. Where the external evidence is *ample, harmonious,* and *credible,* considerations of internal evidence are out of place. If the authorities which omit the words in question had united in representing S. John as having written nonsense or blasphemy, then, in spite of their number and weight and unanimity, we should refuse to believe them. But here no such doubts are possible; and the abundance and coherence of the external evidence tell us that the internal evidence, whatever its testimony, cannot be allowed any weight.

And here it is very important to bear in mind an obvious but not always remembered truth. Although internal evidence by itself may be sufficient to decide what an author did *not* write, it can never by itself be sufficient to decide what he *did* write. Without any external evidence we may be certain that S. John did not write 'The Word cannot come in the flesh;' but without external evidence we cannot know what he did write. And if the external evidence amply testifies that he wrote 'The Word became flesh,' it is absurd to try and ascertain from the internal evidence what (in our judgment) he must have written. So also in the present case it is absurd to say that the internal evidence (even if altogether in favour of the disputed words) can prove that S. John wrote the words.

The case has been discussed on this basis for the sake of argument and to meet the extraordinary opinion that the internal evidence is in favour of the inserted words. But as a matter of fact internal considerations require us to expel the clauses in question almost as imperatively as does the testimony of MSS., Versions, and Fathers.

1. The inserted words break the sense. In *v.* 6 we have the water, the blood, and the spirit mentioned; and they are recapitulated in S. John's manner in *v.* 8. The spurious words in *v.* 7 make an awkward parenthesis, in order to avoid which, *v.* 7 is sometimes inserted *after v.* 8.

2. S. John nowhere speaks of 'the *Father*' and 'the *Word*' together. He either says '*God*' and 'the *Word*' (John i. 1, 2, 13, 14; Rev. xix. 13), or 'the *Father*' and 'the *Son*' (1 John ii. 22, 23, 24, &c. &c.). John i. 14 is no exception; 'father' in that passage has no article in the Greek, and should not have a capital letter in English. S. John *never* uses πατήρ for the Father without the article; and the meaning of the clause is 'the glory as of an only son on a mission from a father.' Contrast, as marking S. John's usage, John i. 1 with i. 18.

3. Neither in his Gospel, nor in the First Epistle, does S. John use the theological term 'the Word' in the body of the work: in both cases this expression, which is peculiar to himself in N.T., is confined to the Prologue or Introduction.

4. The inserted words are in the theological language of a later age. No Apostle or Evangelist writes in this sharp, clear cut style respecting the Persons in the Trinity. The passage is absolutely without anything approaching to a parallel in N.T. If they were original, they would throw the gravest doubt upon the Apostolic authorship of the Epistle. As Haupt observes, "No one can deny that in the whole compass of Holy Writ there is no passage even approaching the dogmatic precision with which, in a manner approximating to the later ecclesiastical definitions, this one asserts the immanent Trinity. Such a verse could not have been omitted by inadvertence; for even supposing such a thing possible in a text of such moment, the absence of the words ἐν τῇ γῇ of *v.* 8 would still be inexplicable. The omission must then have been intentional, and due to the hand of a heretic. But would such an act have remained uncondemned? And were all our MSS. produced by heretics or framed from heretical copies?"

5. The incarnate Son bears witness to man; and the Spirit given at Pentecost bears witness to man; and through the Son, and the Spirit, and His messengers in Old and New Testament, the Father bears witness to man;—respecting the Sonship and Divinity of Jesus Christ. But in what sense can the Three Divine Persons be said to bear witness *in heaven?* Is there not something almost irreverent in making Them the counterpart of the triple witness on earth? And for whose benefit is the witness in heaven given? Do the angels need it? And if they do, what has this to do with the context? Nor can we avoid this difficulty by saying that the Three *are* in heaven, but *bear witness* on earth. It is expressly stated that the Three *bear witness in heaven*, while three *other* witnesses do so on earth.

6. The addition 'and these Three are one,' though exactly what was required by the interpolators for controversial purposes, is exactly what is not required here by the context. What is required is, not

that the Three Witnesses should in essence be only One, which would *reduce* the value of the testimony; but that the Three should agree, which would *enhance* the value of the testimony.

On this part of the evidence the words of F. D. Maurice respecting the passage are worth considering. "If it was genuine, we should be bound to consider seriously what it meant, however much its introduction in this place might puzzle us, however strange its phraseology might appear to us. Those who dwell with awe upon the Name into which they have been baptized; those who believe that all the books of the Bible, and St John's writings more than all the rest, reveal it to us; those who connect it with Christian Ethics, as I have done; might wonder that an Apostle should make a formal announcement of this Name in a parenthesis, and in connexion with such a phrase as *bearing record*, one admirably suited to describe the intercourse of God with us, but quite unsuitable, one would have thought, as an expression of His absolute and eternal being. Still, if it was really one of St John's utterances, we should listen to it in reverence, and only attribute these difficulties to our own blindness. As we have the best possible reasons for supposing it is not his, but merely the gloss of some commentator, which crept into the text, and was accepted by advocates eager to confute adversaries, less careful about the truth they were themselves fighting for,—we may thankfully dismiss it" (*Epistles of St John* pp. 276, 277).

We have, therefore, good grounds for saying that the internal evidence, no less than the external, requires us to banish these words from the text. They are evidence of the form which Trinitarian doctrine assumed in North Africa in the fifth century, and possibly at an earlier date. They are an old gloss on the words of S. John; valuable as a specimen of interpretation, but without the smallest claim to be considered original. Had they not found a place in the *Textus Receptus*, few people not bound (as Roman Catholics are) to accept the later editions of the Vulgate without question, would have dreamed of defending them. Had the translators of 1611 omitted them, no one (with the evidence, which we now possess, before him) would ever have dreamed of inserting them. In Greek texts the words were first printed in the Complutensian edition of A.D. 1514. Erasmus in his first two editions (1516 and 1518) omitted them; but having given his unhappy promise to insert them if they could be found in any Greek MS., he printed them in his third edition (1552), on the authority of the worthless Codex Britannicus (No. 34). Stephanus and Beza inserted them also: and thus they obtained a place in the universally used *Textus Receptus*. Luther never admitted them to his translation, and in the first edition of his commentary declared them to be spurious; but in the second edition he followed the third edition of Erasmus and admitted the words. They first appear in translations published in Switzerland without Luther's name, as in the Zürich edition of Froschover (1529). They were at first commonly printed either in different type or in brackets. The Basle edition of Bryllinger (1552) was one of the first to omit the brackets. Perhaps the last edition which omitted the words in the German Version is the quarto of Zach. Schürer (1620). Among English

Versions the Revised of 1881 has the honour of being the first to omit them. Tyndale in his first edition (1525) printed them as genuine, in his second (1534) and third (1535) he placed them in brackets, in the second edition with a difference of type. Cranmer (1539) follows Tyndale's second edition. But in the Genevan (1557) the difference of type and the brackets disappear, and are not restored in the Authorised Version (1611).

The following by no means complete list of scholars who have pronounced against the passage will be of interest. After Richard Simon had led the way in this direction towards the close of the seventeenth century he was followed in the eighteenth by Bentley, Clarke, Emlyn, Gibbon, Hezel, Matthaei, Michaelis, Sir Isaac Newton, Porson, Semler, and Wetstein. In the nineteenth century we have, among others, Alexander, Alford, J. H. Blunt, Davidson, Döllinger, Düsterdieck, F. W. Farrar, Field, Haddan, Hammond, Haupt, Hort, Huther, Lachmann, Lightfoot, Marsh, F. D. Maurice, McClellan. Meyrick, Oltramare, Renan, Sanday, Schaff, Scrivener, Scholz, Tischendorf, Tregelles, Turton, Weiss, Weizsäcker, Westcott, De Wette, Wordsworth, and the Revisers. Even the most conservative textual critics have abandoned the defence of this text.

Some will perhaps think that this Appendix is wasted labour: that it is a needlessly elaborate slaying of the slain. But so long as any educated Englishman, above all, so long as any English clergyman[1], believes, and indeed publicly maintains, that the passage is genuine, or even possibly genuine, trouble to demonstrate its spuriousness will not be thrown away.

[1] An Essex Rector has recently (Feb. 1883) thought it worth while to publish a book restating most of the old and exploded arguments in defence of the disputed text: and a member of the York Convocation (April, 1883) denounced the Revised Version as most mischievous, because people now heard words read as Scripture in Church and then went home and found that the words were omitted from the new Version as *not* being Scripture; and he gave as an instance the passage about the Three Heavenly Witnesses, which had been read in the Epistle that morning. He afterwards stated in a published letter "that the last word had not been spoken on this text, and that he was quite content himself to read it in the A. V., as required in the Church Service.... Whether the text was expunged by the Arians (!), or interpolated by the Western Athanasians, is as much a question as ever." Jerome's famous hyperbole, "The whole world groaned and was amazed to find itself Arian," fades into insignificance compared with the supposition that long before Jerome's day the Arians had acquired influence enough to expunge a decisive passage *from every copy of the Bible in every language*, so that neither Jerome, nor any Christian writer of his time, or before his time, had any knowledge of its existence! Where was the passage lying hid all those centuries? How was it rediscovered? Those who have been endeavouring upon critical principles to obtain a pure text of the Greek Testament have been accused of unsettling men's minds by shewing that certain small portions of the common text are of very doubtful authority. But what profound uncertainty must be the result if we once admit, as a legitimate hypothesis, the supposition that an heretical party in the Church could for several hundred years rob the whole Church, and for many hundred years rob all but Western Christendom, of the clearest statement of the central doctrine of Christianity. What else may not the Arians have expunged? What may they not have inserted?

E. JOHN THE PRESBYTER OR THE ELDER.

For some time past the writer of this Appendix has been disposed to doubt the existence of any such person as John the Elder as a contemporary of S. John the Apostle at Ephesus. It was, therefore, with much satisfaction that he found that Professor Salmon in the article on **Joannes Presbyter** in the *Dictionary of Christian Biography*, Vol. III. pp. 398—401, and Canon Farrar in *The Early Days of Christianity*, Vol. II. pp. 553—581, take a similar view. Dr Salmon's conclusion is this; "While we are willing to receive the hypothesis of two Johns, if it will help to explain any difficulty, we do not think the evidence for it enough to make us regard it as a proved historical fact. And we frankly own that if it were not for deference to better judges, we should unite with Keim in relegating, though in a different way, this 'Doppelgänger' of the apostle to the region of ghostland." Dr Farrar, with more confidence, concludes thus; "A credulous spirit of innovation is welcome to believe and to proclaim that any or all of S. John's writings were written by 'John the Presbyter.' They were: but 'John the Presbyter' is none other than John the Apostle." Professor Milligan, Riggenbach, and Zahn are of a similar opinion, and believe that this *personnage douteux, sorte de sosie de l'apôtre, qui trouble comme un spectre toute l'histoire de l'Église d'Éphèse*[1], has no separate existence.

The question mainly depends upon a quotation from Papias and the interpretation of it by Eusebius, who quotes it. Papias is stating how he obtained his information. "If on any occasion any one who had been a follower of the Elders came, I used to inquire about the discourses of the Elders—what Andrew or Peter *said*, or Philip, or Thomas or James, or John or Matthew, or any of the Lord's disciples; and what Aristion and the Elder John, the disciples of the Lord, *say*."

Certainly the meaning which this at first sight conveys is the one which Eusebius adopts; that Papias here gives us two Johns, the Apostle and the Elder. But closer study of the passage raises a doubt whether this is correct. With regard to most of the disciples of the Lord Papias could only get second-hand information; he could learn what each *said* (εἶπεν) in days long since gone by. But there were two disciples still living at the time when Papias wrote, Aristion and John; and about these he had contemporary and perhaps personal knowledge: he knows what they *say* (λέγουσι). Of one of these, John, he had knowledge of *both* kinds; reports of what he said long ago in the days when Philip, and Thomas, and Matthew were living, and knowledge of what he says now at the time when Papias writes. If this be the meaning intended, we may admit that it is rather clumsily expressed: but that will not surprise us in a writer, who (as Eusebius tells us) was "of very mean intellectual power, as one may state on the evidence of his own dissertations." The title 'Elder' cuts both ways, and tells

[1] Renan, *L'Antechrist*, p. xxiii. On the whole, however, Renan is disposed to believe in two Johns.

for and against either interpretation. It may be urged that 'the Elder' before the second 'John' seems to be intended to distinguish him from the Apostle. To which it may be replied, that it may quite as probably have been added in order to *identify* him with the Apostle, seeing that throughout the passage, Andrew, Philip, Peter, &c. are called 'Elders' and not Apostles. May not 'the Elder' be prefixed to John to distinguish him from Aristion, who was not an Apostle? In any case the first John is called 'elder' and 'disciple of the Lord;' and the second John is called 'elder' and 'disciple of the Lord.' So that the view of Eusebius, which *primâ facie* appears to be natural, turns out upon examination to be by no means certain, and perhaps not even the more probable of the two.

But other people besides Eusebius studied Papias. What was their view? Among the predecessors of Eusebius none is more important than **Irenaeus**, who made much use of Papias's work, and independently of it knew a great deal about Ephesus and S. John; and he makes no mention of any second John. This fact at once throws the balance against the Eusebian interpretation of Papias. **Polycrates**, Bishop of Ephesus, would be likely to know the work of Papias; and certainly knew a great deal about S. John and his later contemporaries. In the letter which he wrote to Victor, Bishop of Rome, on the Paschal Controversy he proudly enumerates the 'great lights,' who have fallen asleep and lie buried at Ephesus, Smyrna, Hierapolis, Laodicea, and Sardis, as authorities in favour of the Quartodeciman usage. Among these the Presbyter John is not named. At Ephesus there are the graves of 'John who rested on the Lord's bosom' and of the martyred Polycarp. But no tomb of a second John is mentioned. And would not the reputed author of two canonical Epistles and possibly of the Apocalypse have found a place in such a list, had such a person existed distinct from the Apostle? Whether **Dionysius of Alexandria** knew Papias or not we cannot tell; but he had heard of two tombs at Ephesus, each bearing the name of John. And yet he evidently knows nothing of the Presbyter John. For while contending that the John who wrote the Apocalypse cannot be the Apostle, he says that it is quite uncertain who this John is, and suggests as a possibility 'John whose surname was Mark,' the attendant of Paul and Barnabas (Acts xii. 25, xiii. 5). The fragments of **Leucius**, writings of unknown date, but probably earlier than Dionysius, contain many traditions respecting S. John the Apostle, but nothing respecting any other John. The fragments are sufficient to render it practically certain that the compiler of the stories which they contain knew no second John.

It would seem therefore that the predecessors of Eusebius, whether they had read Papias or not, agreed in believing in only one John, viz. the Apostle. Therefore those of them who had read Papias (and Irenaeus certainly had done so) must either have understood him to mean only one John, or must have ignored as untrue his statement respecting a second.

Indeed Eusebius himself would seem at one time to have held the same view. In his *Chronicon* (Schoene, p. 162) he states that Papias and Polycarp (to whom Jerome adds Ignatius) were disciples of John

APPENDICES. 215

the Divine and Apostle. That Papias was the disciple of another John, is a later theory of his, adopted (as there is good reason for believing) in order to discredit the Apocalypse. Eusebius was greatly opposed to the millenarian theories which some people spun out of the Apocalypse; and in order to attack them the better he wished to shew that the Apocalypse was not the work of the Apostle. But the Apocalypse claims to be written by John. Therefore there must have been some other John who wrote it. And as evidence of this other John he quotes Papias, whose language is so obscure that we cannot be certain whether he means one John or two.

The two tombs at Ephesus, each said to have borne the name of John, need not disturb us much. Polycrates, writing on the spot within a hundred years of the Apostle's death, seems to know nothing of a second tomb. Dionysius, writing a century and a half after his death and far away from Ephesus, has heard of two monuments, but (much as it would have suited his theory to do so) he does not venture to assert that they were the tombs of two Johns. Jerome, writing still later and still farther away from the spot, says that a second tomb is shewn at Ephesus as that of John the Presbyter, and that "some think that they are two monuments of the same John, viz. the Evangelist" —*nonnulli putant duas memorias ejusdem Johannis evangelistae esse* (*De Vir. Illust.* ix.). The probabilities are that these people were right. Either there were rival sites (a very common thing in topography), each claiming to be the grave of the Apostle; or there were two monuments commemorating two different things, e.g. the place of his death and the place of his burial. Very possibly they were churches (Zahn, *Acta Johannis*, clxiv.).

The evidence, therefore, of the existence of this perplexing Presbyter is of a somewhat shadowy kind. It amounts simply to the statement of Papias, as interpreted by Eusebius, and the two monuments. But the Eusebian interpretation is not by any means certainly correct, and the two monuments do not by any means necessarily imply two Johns. Moreover, Eusebius himself was not always of the same opinion, making Papias sometimes the disciple of the Apostle, sometimes the disciple of the supposed Presbyter. And in this inconsistency he is followed by Jerome. Assume the Eusebian interpretation to be correct, and it will then be very difficult indeed to explain how it is that Irenaeus and Polycrates know nothing of this second John, and how even Dionysius does seem to have heard of him. Assume that Eusebius was mistaken, and that Papias mentions the Apostle twice over, and then all runs smoothly.

Does this hypothetical Presbyter explain a single difficulty? If so, let us retain him as a reasonable hypothesis. But if, as seems to be the case, he causes a great deal of difficulty and explains nothing that cannot be quite well explained without him, then let him be surrendered as a superfluous conjecture. *Personae non sunt multiplicandae.* We may heartily welcome the wish of Zahn (*Acta Johannis*, p. cliv.) that the publication of the fragments of Leucius will "give the *coup de grace* to the erudite myth created by Eusebius about 'the Presbyter John.' The latter has quite long enough shared in the lot of the undying

Apostle. Had this doublet of the Apostle ever existed, he could not have failed to appear in Leucius: and in his pages the Apostle of Ephesus could never have been called simply John, if he had had at his side a second disciple of Jesus of this name." We, therefore, give up the second John as unhistorical.

It would seem as if 'Presbyter John' was destined to plague and perplex historians. A spectral personage of this name troubles, as we have seen, the history of the Church of Ephesus. Another equally mysterious personage of the same name confronts us in the history of Europe in the twelfth century; when the West was cheered with the news that a mighty Priest-King called Presbyter Johannes had arisen in the East, and restored victory to the Christian cause in the contest with the Saracens. For this extraordinary story, which appears first perhaps in Otto of Freisingen, see Baring Gould's *Myths of the Middle Ages*, p. 32. Probably in this case an unfamiliar oriental name was corrupted into a familiar name which happened to sound something like it.

INDICES.

I. GENERAL.

Abel as a type, 130
address, of the First Epistle, 32, 33
— of the Second Epistle, 57, 58
— of the Third Epistle, 60, 61
Alexander of Alexandria quotes the Second Epistle, 183
Alexander, Bishop, quoted, 62, 185
Alogi, 28
analysis, of the First Epistle, 44, 45
— of the Second Epistle, 59
— of the Third Epistle, 62
Antichrist, 27, 107, 198—202
Antioch, school of, rejected the Second and Third Epistles, 52
antithesis, S. John's love of, 48, 81, 83, 90, 135, 140, 143, 145, 147, 163, 171, 173, 182
antithetic parallelism, 79, 81, 83
aorist, force of the Greek, 107, 114, 115, 116, 139, 157; sometimes equivalent to the English perfect, 96, 139, 180
aorist epistolary, 98, 111, 165, 177
aorist imperative, 173
Apocalypse, date of the, 23, 27
— exhibits parallels with the First Epistle, 29
Apollonius on S. John at Ephesus, 11, 23
Apostolic first person plural, 76, 77, 145, 150
apparent contradictions in S. John, 101, 124, 169
arbitrary distinctions made in A. V., 114, 117, 195
argument *à fortiori*, 136
Aristotle quoted, 90
article, exaggerated translation of, in A. V., 114, 117
— ignored in A. V., 181
asyndeton, 83, 114, 144
Athanasius on 1 John v. 20, 172
Augustine on S. John's grave, 27; on the title of the First Epistle, 32; on its contents, 92; on hatred, 95; on the chrism, 111; on the circus and theatre, 103; on the children of the devil, 126; on the efficacy of prayer, 137; on love, 148; on belief without love, 154

authority, tone of, in S. John, 47
authorship, of the First Epistle, 28—32
— of the Second Epistle, 50—56
— of the Third Epistle, 60

Barnabas, Epistle of, quoted, 77
Bede quoted, 77, 90, 138, 142, 153
Bengel quoted, 89, 91, 119, 153, 176, 188
boldness at the judgment, 117; against the charges of conscience, 136; in prayer, 165
Butler quoted, 21

Cain's offering, 129
Cainites, Gnostic sect of the, 130, 202—204
Calvin quoted, 82
capricious changes of rendering in A. V., 114, 117, 195
Cassian, story about S. John in, 26
catholic, the First Epistle, 32, 71; the Second not, 175
Cerinthus, doctrine of, 82, 142, 173
Cerinthus and S. John, 24, 183
characteristics, of the First Epistle, 46—49, 86
— of S. John's style, 49, 74, 79, 80, 83, 89, 90, 91, 96
children of the devil, 126, 128
Claudius quoted, 46
Clement of Alexandria, employs the First Epistle, 30; quotes from the last 9 verses, 162; witnesses to the Second Epistle, 51
collective neuter gender, 157
commentaries on S. John's Epistles, 68, 69
contradictions, seeming, in S. John, 101, 124, 169
Coverdale's improvements in the English Version, 65, 66, 104, 133, 139
Cyprian, witnesses to the First Epistle, 31, 96; to the Second Epistle, 51, 183
Cyril of Jerusalem on the chrism, 111

Dante on S. John. 46
date of the Epistles, 34, 58, 61

INDICES.

dative of the instrument, 133
Davidson quoted, 57
Demetrius, 61, 192, 193
differences of reading, 80, 111, 120, 135, 143, 160, 161, 165, 170, 177, 181, 184, 193, 204
Dionysius on S. John's writings, 31, 51; on the two monuments of S. John, 214
Diotrephes, 60, 190
divisions in S. John gradual, 118, 139, 170
Docetism, 19, 72
Döllinger quoted, 175, 204, 205
double comparative, 188
Dualism, 19

Ebionites, 82, 173
Elder, meaning of the title of the, 53, 54, 175, 186, 214
Electa, 57, 176
Ephesian letters, 16, 173
Ephesus, Church of, 13; evidence for S. John's life at, 10, 11; situation and trade of, 11, 12; Temple of, 14, 15; tombs of S. John at, 214, 215
Epiphanius, 28
epistolary aorist, 98, 111, 165, 177
eternal life attainable in this world, 132, 163
Eusebius, on the First Epistle, 28; on the Second and Third, 52; on John the Presbyter, 213

finality a characteristic of the First Epistle, 47
First Epistle, a companion to the Gospel, 34, 36, 75; a summary of Christian Ethics, 35; an occasional letter, 37; a catholic letter, 32, 71; very difficult to analyse, 42

Gaius, 60, 61, 186
Genevan N.T., 66
genitive, partitive, 139; of apposition, 73
Gnostic cosmogony, 20
Gnostic denials of the Incarnation, 142, 159
Gnostic Docetism, 19, 72
Gnostic morality, 20, 21, 77, 169, 203, 204
Gnosticism, 16—21, 169, 171
Greek perfect, force of the, 85, 100, 130, 148, 153, 157, 162, 163, 170, 193
Greek text of the Epistles, 63, 64

Haupt quoted, 114, 169, 210
Heavenly Witnesses, the Three, 161, 204—212
Huther quoted, 115

idolatry, 14—16, 173; how regarded by Gnostics, 149, 152, 173
'if' with the indicative, 130, 149, 162, 182

Ignatius on the last days, 106; on a Christian's knowledge, 111
indicative or imperative, 116, 119
indicative or subjunctive, 153, 156
ink, 184
internal evidence as to the authorship of the two shorter Epistles, 53, 56
interpolations, 131, 143, 161, 177, 184
Introduction to the First Epistle, 9—49
— to the Second Epistle, 49—59
— to the Third Epistle, 59—62
Irenaeus on S. John and Polycarp, 10; on the date of the Apocalypse, 27; quotes the First and Second Epistles, 30, 50, 51, 143

Jelf quoted, 74, 107, 135, 137, 161
Jerome on S. John's old age, 26, 128; on the three Epistles, 53; on the two tombs at Ephesus, 215
John the Apostle and Cerinthus, 24; and the Parthians, 23, 32; near the partridge, 22, and the robber, 24; *ante Portam Latinam*, 22; death of, 26, 27; tomb of, 27, 214, 215; virginity of, 25, 26, 33
John the Elder, or the Presbyter, 54, 175, 213—216
Justin Martyr on the Apocalypse, 10

key-words in the Second Epistle, 177, 178
knowledge, of the Christian, 111, 169, 170, 171; of the Gnostic, 18, 19
Kyria, 57, 58, 175, 176

Leucian fragments, 26, 213
Liddon quoted, 112, 144, 183
literature of the Epistles, 68—70

Mansel quoted, 204
Maurice quoted, 86, 101, 112, 126, 140, 143, 156, 197, 211
millenarianism, 25
Montanism, 108, 169
Muratorian Fragment, testimony of, to S. John's Epistles, 30, 31, 52

Naassenes, 202
Newman quoted, 162, 163, 201
nominativus pendens, 115
Novatians, 82, 169

Ophites, 202, 203
Origen frequently quotes the First Epistle, 31; is reserved about the other two, 52

paper, 184
Papias made use of the First Epistle, 30; his account of John the Elder, 213—215

INDICES.

parallels between S. John and S. Paul, 81, 87, 104, 142, 153, 157, 162, 177, 201, 202
parallels between S. John's Gospel and First Epistle, 38—40, 75, 80, 96, 130, 137, 151, 163, 164, 165, 170, 171
parallels between the three Epistles, 54—56
partitive genitive, 139
Pascal quoted, 154
pen, 194
perfect, force of the Greek, 85, 100, 130, 148, 153, 157, 162, 163, 170, 193
Philo, use of 'Paraclete' in, 87; on Cain, 130; on love of parents, 154
plan of the First Epistle, 41—45
Polycarp quotes the First Epistle, 29, 143; replies to Marcion, 128; proclaims the Christian's knowledge, 111
Polycrates on S. John at Ephesus, 11
Presbyter Johannes, 54, 175, 213—216
purpose, S. John's fondness for constructions expressing, 84, 126, 148, 151, 154, 179

readings, differences of, 80, 111, 120, 135, 143, 160, 161, 165, 170, 177, 181, 193, 204
readings, supposed heretical, 143
reflexive pronoun, S. John's use of the, 83, 122, 173
repetition of the article, 74
Revised Version, 67, 68
Rhemish Bible, 67
rythm in S. John's writings, 48

Salmon quoted, 213
Second Epistle, authorship of, 50—56; analysis of, 59; to whom addressed, 57,

58; quoted by Irenaeus, 50, 51, 180; known to Clement of Alexandria, 51
Strabo's account of Ephesus, 11

Taverner's Bible, 66
tendencies, the three evil, 104, 196
Tertullian frequently quotes the First Epistle, 30; quotes from the last 9 verses, 164; on circus games, 103; on perseverance, 109; on martyrdom, 132, 152; on the two sacraments, 159
text of the Epistles, 63, 64
Third Epistle, authorship of, 50—56, 60; analysis of, 62; to whom addressed, 60
'this' as predicate, 78, 113, 128, 137, 156, 162, 163, 179
three evil tendencies, 104, 196
Three Heavenly Witnesses, 161, 204—212
Timothy, possibly the Angel of the Church of Ephesus, 13
traditions respecting S. John, 22—27
transitions in S. John seldom abrupt, 118, 139, 146, 149, 170, 178
Tyndale's New Testament, 64, 65

Universality of Redemption, 89, 150

Versions, Ancient, 64; English, 64—68

Westcott quoted, 41, 52, 65, 66, 67, 71, 80, 97, 120, 124, 132, 154, 175
Wiclif's New Testament, 64
Witnesses, the Three Heavenly, 160, 161, 204—212
Wordsworth quoted, 48

Zahn quoted, 215, 216
Zoroastrianism, 80

II. WORDS AND PHRASES EXPLAINED.

age, unto the, 103
abide, 114
Advocate, 86, 87
agree in one, 161
and now, 116, 178
annul, 143
anointing, 110
Antichrist, 107, 144, 198—202

be for the one, 161
be of God, 144, 145, 192
be of the truth, 112
be of the world, 145
beginning, 72, 92, 126
begotten of God, 119, 127, 169
behold, 133, 149
believe on, 162
believe the Name, 138

boldness, 117, 136, 165
brother, 94, 95, 166

catholic, 71
children, little, 85, 98
children of God, 120, 121
children of the devil, 126, 128
Comforter, 87
come, 107, 159, 182
come in the flesh, 142
coming, 117
communion, 76

darkness, 80
day of judgment, 151
deceiver, 182
destroy, 127, 143
do faithfully, 183

INDICES.

do righteousness, 125
do sin, 127
do the truth, 81
doctrine, 182

eternal life, 74, 75, 132
even as, 91, 132, 152, 178
evil one, 100

fathers, 99
fellowship, 76
for ever, 103
for this cause, 120, 121
forward, 189
fulfilled, 76

general, 71
give commandment, 138
grace, 177, 187
God speed, 183

handle, 73
have sin, 83
he that is in the world, 144
heart, 134, 135
herein, 134, 148, 149, 151

idols, 16, 173

joy be fulfilled, 76, 77, 185

keep His commandments, 90, 137
keep His word, 90
know, 89, 122, 131, 132, 145, 171

last hour, 105, 106
lawlessness, 123
lay down one's life, 132
lead astray, 83
life, 103, 104, 133
life eternal, 74, 75, 132
light, 78, 79, 93
little children, 85, 98
love, 91
love in word, 133, 134
love of God, 91, 133, 150
love of the brethren, 129
lust of the eyes, 103
lust of the flesh, 102

make request, 168, 178
manifest, 74, 117

message, 78
murderer, 131

Name, the, 189
new commandment, 93

occasion of stumbling, 95
old commandment, 92
Only-begotten, 148

Paraclete, 86, 87
partake, 183
pass over out of death, 130
prate, 191
presence, 117
pride of life, 103
propitiation, 88
prove or try, 141
punishment, 152
purify, 122

receive, 162
request, 168, 178
righteous, 84, 87, 88

seducer, 182
sin, 123, 168
sin unto death, 167, 168
slay, 129
speak of the world, 145

take nothing, 189
teaching, 182
true, 83, 93, 94
truth, 83
try or prove, 141

unction, 110

vainglory of life, 103

walk, 80, 178
walk in darkness, 80, 81
walk in truth, 178
what manner of, 120
will of God, 104
with the Father, 75, 87
witness, word, 85, 101
Word of Life, 73
works, 183
world, 89, 180
world's goods, 132

CAMBRIDGE: PRINTED BY C. J. CLAY, M.A. AND SONS, AT THE UNIVERSITY PRESS.

THE CAMBRIDGE BIBLE FOR SCHOOLS AND COLLEGES.

GENERAL EDITOR, THE VERY REV. J. J. S. PEROWNE, DEAN OF PETERBOROUGH.

Opinions of the Press.

"*It is difficult to commend too highly this excellent series.*"—Guardian.

"*The modesty of the general title of this series has, we believe, led many to misunderstand its character and underrate its value. The books are well suited for study in the upper forms of our best schools, but not the less are they adapted to the wants of all Bible students who are not specialists. We doubt, indeed, whether any of the numerous popular commentaries recently issued in this country will be found more serviceable for general use.*"—Academy.

"*One of the most popular and useful literary enterprises of the nineteenth century.*"—Baptist Magazine.

"*Of great value. The whole series of comments for schools is highly esteemed by students capable of forming a judgment. The books are scholarly without being pretentious: and information is so given as to be easily understood.*"—Sword and Trowel.

"*The value of the work as an aid to Biblical study, not merely in schools but among people of all classes who are desirous to have intelligent knowledge of the Scriptures, cannot easily be over-estimated.*"—The Scotsman.

The Book of Judges. J. J. LIAS, M.A. "His introduction is clear and concise, full of the information which young students require, and indicating the lines on which the various problems suggested by the Book of Judges may be solved."—*Baptist Magazine.*

1 Samuel, by A. F. KIRKPATRICK. "Remembering the interest with which we read the *Books of the Kingdom* when they were appointed as a subject for school work in our boyhood, we have looked with some eagerness into Mr Kirkpatrick's volume, which contains the first instalment of them. We are struck with the great improvement in character, and variety in the materials, with which schools are now supplied. A clear map inserted in each volume, notes suiting the convenience of the scholar and the difficulty of the passage, and not merely dictated by the fancy of the commentator, were luxuries which a quarter of a century ago the Biblical student could not buy."—*Church Quarterly Review.*

"To the valuable series of Scriptural expositions and elementary commentaries which is being issued at the Cambridge University Press, under the title of 'The Cambridge Bible for Schools,' has been added **The First Book of Samuel** by the Rev. A. F. KIRKPATRICK. Like other volumes of the series, it contains a carefully written historical and critical introduction, while the text is profusely illustrated and explained by notes."—*The Scotsman.*

II. Samuel. A. F. KIRKPATRICK, M.A. "Small as this work is in mere dimensions, it is every way the best on its subject and for its purpose that we know of. The opening sections at once prove the thorough competence of the writer for dealing with questions of criticism in an earnest, faithful and devout spirit; and the appendices discuss a few special difficulties with a full knowledge of the data, and a judicial reserve, which contrast most favourably with the superficial dogmatism which has too often made the exegesis of the Old Testament a field for the play of unlimited paradox and the ostentation of personal infallibility. The notes are always clear and suggestive; never trifling or irrelevant; and they everywhere demonstrate the great difference in value between the work of a commentator who is also a Hebraist, and that of one who has to depend for his Hebrew upon secondhand sources."—*Academy*.

"The Rev. A. F. KIRKPATRICK has now completed his commentary on the two books of Samuel. This second volume, like the first, is furnished with a scholarly and carefully prepared critical and historical introduction, and the notes supply everything necessary to enable the merely English scholar—so far as is possible for one ignorant of the original language—to gather up the precise meaning of the text. Even Hebrew scholars may consult this small volume with profit."—*Scotsman*.

I. Kings and Ephesians. "With great heartiness we commend these most valuable little commentaries. We had rather purchase these than nine out of ten of the big blown up expositions. Quality is far better than quantity, and we have it here."—*Sword and Trowel*.

I. Kings. "This is really admirably well done, and from first to last there is nothing but commendation to give to such honest work."—*Bookseller*.

II. Kings. "The Introduction is scholarly and wholly admirable, while the notes must be of incalculable value to students."—*Glasgow Herald*.

"It is equipped with a valuable introduction and commentary, and makes an admirable text book for Bible-classes."—*Scotsman*.

"It would be difficult to find a commentary better suited for general use."—*Academy*.

The Book of Job. "Able and scholarly as the Introduction is, it is far surpassed by the detailed exegesis of the book. In this Dr DAVIDSON'S strength is at its greatest. His linguistic knowledge, his artistic habit, his scientific insight, and his literary power have full scope when he comes to exegesis....The book is worthy of the reputation of Dr Davidson; it represents the results of many years of labour, and it will greatly help to the right understanding of one of the greatest works in the literature of the world."—*The Spectator*.

"In the course of a long introduction, Dr DAVIDSON has presented us with a very able and very interesting criticism of this wonderful book. Its contents, the nature of its composition, its idea and purpose, its integrity, and its age are all exhaustively treated of....We have not space to examine fully the text and notes before us, but we can, and do heartily, recommend the book, not only for the upper forms in schools, but to Bible students and teachers generally. As we wrote of a previous volume in the same series, this one leaves nothing to be desired. The notes are full and suggestive, without being too long, and, in itself, the introduction forms a valuable addition to modern Bible literature."—*The Educational Times.*

"Already we have frequently called attention to this exceedingly valuable work as its volumes have successively appeared. But we have never done so with greater pleasure, very seldom with so great pleasure, as we now refer to the last published volume, that on the **Book of Job**, by Dr DAVIDSON, of Edinburgh....We cordially commend the volume to all our readers. The least instructed will understand and enjoy it; and mature scholars will learn from it."—*Methodist Recorder.*

Job—Hosea. "It is difficult to commend too highly this excellent series, the volumes of which are now becoming numerous. The two books before us, small as they are in size, comprise almost everything that the young student can reasonably expect to find in the way of helps towards such general knowledge of their subjects as may be gained without an attempt to grapple with the Hebrew; and even the learned scholar can hardly read without interest and benefit the very able introductory matter which both these commentators have prefixed to their volumes. It is not too much to say that these works have brought within the reach of the ordinary reader resources which were until lately quite unknown for understanding some of the most difficult and obscure portions of Old Testament literature."—*Guardian.*

Ecclesiastes; or, the Preacher.—"Of the Notes, it is sufficient to say that they are in every respect worthy of Dr PLUMPTRE's high reputation as a scholar and a critic, being at once learned, sensible, and practical.... An appendix, in which it is clearly proved that the author of *Ecclesiastes* anticipated Shakspeare and Tennyson in some of their finest thoughts and reflections, will be read with interest by students both of Hebrew and of English literature. Commentaries are seldom attractive reading. This little volume is a notable exception."—*The Scotsman.*

"In short, this little book is of far greater value than most of the larger and more elaborate commentaries on this Scripture. Indispensable to the scholar, it will render real and large help to all who have to expound the dramatic utterances of **The Preacher** whether in the Church or in the School."—*The Expositor.*

"The '*ideal* biography' of the author is one of the most exquisite and fascinating pieces of writing we have met with, and, granting its starting-point, throws wonderful light on many problems connected with the book. The notes illustrating the text are full of delicate criticism, fine glowing insight, and apt historical allusion. An abler volume than Professor PLUMPTRE'S we could not desire."—*Baptist Magazine.*

Jeremiah, by A. W. STREANE. "The arrangement of the book is well treated on pp. xxx., 396, and the question of Baruch's relations with its composition on pp. xxvii., xxxiv., 317. The illustrations from English literature, history, monuments, works on botany, topography, etc., are good and plentiful, as indeed they are in other volumes of this series."—*Church Quarterly Review*, April, 1881.

"Mr STREANE'S **Jeremiah** consists of a series of admirable and wellnigh exhaustive notes on the text, with introduction and appendices, drawing the life, times, and character of the prophet, the style, contents, and arrangement of his prophecies, the traditions relating to Jeremiah, meant as a type of Christ (a most remarkable chapter), and other prophecies relating to Jeremiah."—*The English Churchman and Clerical Journal.*

Obadiah and Jonah. "This number of the admirable series of Scriptural expositions issued by the Syndics of the Cambridge University Press is well up to the mark. The numerous notes are excellent. No difficulty is shirked, and much light is thrown on the contents both of Obadiah and Jonah. Scholars and students of to-day are to be congratulated on having so large an amount of information on Biblical subjects, so clearly and ably put together, placed within their reach in such small bulk. To all Biblical students the series will be acceptable, and for the use of Sabbath-school teachers will prove invaluable."—*North British Daily Mail.*

"It is a very useful and sensible exposition of these two Minor Prophets, and deals very thoroughly and honestly with the immense difficulties of the later-named of the two, from the orthodox point of view."—*Expositor.*

"**Haggai and Zechariah.** This interesting little volume is of great value. It is one of the best books in that well-known series of scholarly and popular commentaries, 'the Cambridge Bible for Schools and Colleges' of which Dean Perowne is the General Editor. In the expositions of Archdeacon Perowne we are always sure to notice learning, ability, judgment and reverence.... The notes are terse and pointed, but full and reliable."—*Churchman.*

"**The Gospel according to St Matthew**, by the Rev. A. CARR. The introduction is able, scholarly, and eminently practical, as it bears on the authorship and contents of the Gospel, and the original form in which it is supposed to have been written. It is well illustrated by two excellent maps of the Holy Land and of the Sea of Galilee."— *English Churchman.*

"**St Matthew**, edited by A. CARR, M.A. **The Book of Joshua**, edited by G. F. MACLEAR, D.D. **The General Epistle of St James**, edited by E. H. PLUMPTRE, D.D. The introductions and notes are scholarly, and generally such as young readers need and can appreciate. The maps in both Joshua and Matthew are very good, and all matters of editing are faultless. Professor Plumptre's notes on 'The Epistle of St James' are models of terse, exact, and elegant renderings of the original, which is too often obscured in the authorised version."— *Nonconformist.*

"**St Mark**, with Notes by the Rev. G. F. MACLEAR, D.D. Into this small volume Dr Maclear, besides a clear and able Introduction to the Gospel, and the text of St Mark, has compressed many hundreds of valuable and helpful notes. In short, he has given us a capital manual of the kind required—containing all that is needed to illustrate the text, i.e. all that can be drawn from the history, geography, customs, and manners of the time. But as a handbook, giving in a clear and succinct form the information which a lad requires in order to stand an examination in the Gospel, it is admirable......I can very heartily commend it, not only to the senior boys and girls in our High Schools, but also to Sunday-school teachers, who may get from it the very kind of knowledge they often find it hardest to get."—*Expositor.*

"With the help of a book like this, an intelligent teacher may make 'Divinity' as interesting a lesson as any in the school course. The notes are of a kind that will be, for the most part, intelligible to boys of the lower forms of our public schools; but they may be read with greater profit by the fifth and sixth, in conjunction with the original text."—*The Academy.*

"**St Luke.** Canon FARRAR has supplied students of the Gospel with an admirable manual in this volume. It has all that copious variety of illustration, ingenuity of suggestion, and general soundness of interpretation which readers are accustomed to expect from the learned and eloquent editor. Any one who has been accustomed to associate the idea of 'dryness' with a commentary, should go to Canon Farrar's St Luke for a more correct impression. He will find that a commentary may be made interesting in the highest degree, and that without losing anything of its solid value. . . . But, so to speak, it is *too good* for some of the readers for whom it is intended."—*The Spectator.*

"Canon FARRAR's contribution to The Cambridge School Bible is one of the most valuable yet made. His annotations on **The Gospel according to St Luke**, while they display a scholarship at least as sound, and an erudition at least as wide and varied as those of the editors of St Matthew and St Mark, are rendered telling and attractive by a more lively imagination, a keener intellectual and spiritual insight, a more incisive and picturesque style. His *St Luke* is worthy to be ranked with Professor Plumptre's *St James*, than which no higher commendation can well be given."—*The Expositor.*

"**St Luke.** Edited by Canon FARRAR, D.D. We have received with pleasure this edition of the Gospel by St Luke, by Canon Farrar. It is another instalment of the best school commentary of the Bible we possess. Of the expository part of the work we cannot speak too highly. It is admirable in every way, and contains just the sort of information needed for Students of the English text unable to make use of the original Greek for themselves."—*The Nonconformist and Independent.*

"As a handbook to the third gospel, this small work is invaluable. The author has compressed into little space a vast mass of scholarly information. . . The notes are pithy, vigorous, and suggestive, abounding in pertinent illustrations from general literature, and aiding the youngest reader to an intelligent appreciation of the text. A finer contribution to 'The Cambridge Bible for Schools' has not yet been made."—*Baptist Magazine.*

"We were quite prepared to find in Canon FARRAR's **St Luke** a masterpiece of Biblical criticism and comment, and we are not disappointed by our examination of the volume before us. It reflects very faithfully the learning and critical insight of the Canon's greatest works, his 'Life of Christ' and his 'Life of St Paul', but differs widely from both in the terseness and condensation of its style. What Canon Farrar has evidently aimed at is to place before students as much information as possible within the limits of the smallest possible space, and in this aim he has hit the mark to perfection."—*The Examiner.*

The Gospel according to St John. "Of the notes we can say with confidence that they are useful, necessary, learned, and brief. To Divinity students, to teachers, and for private use, this compact Commentary will be found a valuable aid to the better understanding of the Sacred Text."—*School Guardian.*

"The new volume of the 'Cambridge Bible for Schools'—the **Gospel according to St John**, by the Rev. A. PLUMMER—shows as careful and thorough work as either of its predecessors. The introduction concisely yet fully describes the life of St John, the authenticity of the Gospel, its characteristics, its relation to the Synoptic Gospels, and to the Apostle's First Epistle, and the usual subjects referred to in an 'introduction'."—*The Christian Church.*

"The notes are extremely scholarly and valuable, and in most cases exhaustive, bringing to the elucidation of the text all that is best in commentaries, ancient and modern."—*The English Churchman and Clerical Journal.*

"(1) **The Acts of the Apostles.** By J. RAWSON LUMBY, D.D. (2) **The Second Epistle of the Corinthians**, edited by Professor LIAS. The introduction is pithy, and contains a mass of carefully-selected information on the authorship of the Acts, its designs, and its sources. ......The Second Epistle of the Corinthians is a manual beyond all praise, for the excellence of its pithy and pointed annotations, its analysis of the contents, and the fulness and value of its introduction."—*Examiner.*

"The concluding portion of the **Acts of the Apostles**, under the very competent editorship of Dr LUMBY, is a valuable addition to our school-books on that subject. Detailed criticism is impossible within the space at our command, but we may say that the ample notes touch with much exactness the very points on which most readers of the text desire information. Due reference is made, where necessary, to the Revised Version; the maps are excellent; and we do not know of any other volume where so much help is given to the complete understanding of one of the most important and, in many respects, difficult books of the New Testament."—*School Guardian.*

"The Rev. H. C. G. MOULE, M.A., has made a valuable addition to THE CAMBRIDGE BIBLE FOR SCHOOLS in his brief commentary on the **Epistle to the Romans**. The 'Notes' are very good, and lean, as the notes of a School Bible should, to the most commonly accepted and orthodox view of the inspired author's meaning; while the Introduction, and especially the Sketch of the Life of St Paul, is a model of condensation. It is as lively and pleasant to read as if two or three facts had not been crowded into well-nigh every sentence."—*Expositor.*

"**The Epistle to the Romans.** It is seldom we have met with a work so remarkable for the compression and condensation of all that is valuable in the smallest possible space as in the volume before us. Within its limited pages we have 'a sketch of the Life of St Paul,' we have further a critical account of the date of the Epistle to the Romans, of its language, and of its genuineness. The notes are numerous, full of matter, to the point, and leave no real difficulty or obscurity unexplained."—*The Examiner.*

"**The First Epistle to the Corinthians.** Edited by Professor LIAS. Every fresh instalment of this annotated edition of the Bible for Schools confirms the favourable opinion we formed of its value from the examination of its first number. The origin and plan of the Epistle are discussed with its character and genuineness."—*The Nonconformist.*

"**The Second Epistle to the Corinthians.** By Professor LIAS. **The General Epistles of St Peter and St Jude.** By E. H. PLUMPTRE, D.D. We welcome these additions to the valuable series of the Cambridge Bible. We have nothing to add to the commendation which we have from the first publication given to this edition of the Bible. It is enough to say that Professor Lias has completed his work on the two Epistles to the Corinthians in the same admirable manner as at first. Dr Plumptre has also completed the Catholic Epistles."—*Nonconformist.*

The Epistle to the Ephesians. By Rev. H. C. G. MOULE, M.A. "It seems to us the model of a School and College Commentary—comprehensive, but not cumbersome; scholarly, but not pedantic."—*Baptist Magazine.*

The Epistle to the Philippians. "There are few series more valued by theological students than 'The Cambridge Bible for Schools and Colleges,' and there will be no number of it more esteemed than that by Mr H. C. G. MOULE on the *Epistle to the Philippians.*"—*Record.*

"Another capital volume of 'The Cambridge Bible for Schools and Colleges.' The notes are a model of scholarly, lucid, and compact criticism."—*Baptist Magazine.*

Hebrews. "Like his (Canon Farrar's) commentary on Luke it possesses all the best characteristics of his writing. It is a work not only of an accomplished scholar, but of a skilled teacher."—*Baptist Magazine.*

"We heartily commend this volume of this excellent work."—*Sunday School Chronicle.*

"**The General Epistle of St James**, by Professor PLUMPTRE, D.D. Nevertheless it is, so far as I know, by far the best exposition of the Epistle of St James in the English language. Not Schoolboys or Students going in for an examination alone, but Ministers and Preachers of the Word, may get more real help from it than from the most costly and elaborate commentaries."—*Expositor.*

The Epistles of St John. By the Rev. A. PLUMMER, M.A., D.D. "This forms an admirable companion to the 'Commentary on the Gospel according to St John,' which was reviewed in *The Churchman* as soon as it appeared. Dr Plummer has some of the highest qualifications for such a task; and these two volumes, their size being considered, will bear comparison with the best Commentaries of the time."—*The Churchman.*

"Dr PLUMMER's edition of **the Epistles of St John** is worthy of its companions in the 'Cambridge Bible for Schools' Series. The subject, though not apparently extensive, is really one not easy to treat, and requiring to be treated at length, owing to the constant reference to obscure heresies in the Johannine writings. Dr Plummer has done his exegetical task well."—*The Saturday Review.*

THE CAMBRIDGE GREEK TESTAMENT
FOR SCHOOLS AND COLLEGES

with a Revised Text, based on the most recent critical authorities, and English Notes, prepared under the direction of the General Editor, THE VERY REVEREND J. J. S. PEROWNE, D.D.

"*Has achieved an excellence which puts it above criticism.*"—Expositor.

St Matthew. "Copious illustrations, gathered from a great variety of sources, make his notes a very valuable aid to the student. They are indeed remarkably interesting, while all explanations on meanings, applications, and the like are distinguished by their lucidity and good sense."—*Pall Mall Gazette.*

St Mark. "The Cambridge Greek Testament of which Dr MACLEAR'S edition of the Gospel according to St Mark is a volume, certainly supplies a want. Without pretending to compete with the leading commentaries, or to embody very much original research, it forms a most satisfactory introduction to the study of the New Testament in the original....Dr Maclear's introduction contains all that is known of St Mark's life; an account of the circumstances in which the Gospel was composed, with an estimate of the influence of St Peter's teaching upon St Mark; an excellent sketch of the special characteristics of this Gospel; an analysis, and a chapter on the text of the New Testament generally."—*Saturday Review.*

St Luke. "Of this second series we have a new volume by Archdeacon FARRAR on *St Luke*, completing the four Gospels....It gives us in clear and beautiful language the best results of modern scholarship. We have a most attractive *Introduction*. Then follows a sort of composite Greek text, representing fairly and in very beautiful type the consensus of modern textual critics. At the beginning of the exposition of each chapter of the Gospel are a few short critical notes giving the manuscript evidence for such various readings as seem to deserve mention. The expository notes are short, but clear and helpful. For young students and those who are not disposed to buy or to study the much more costly work of Godet, this seems to us to be the best book on the Greek Text of the Third Gospel."—*Methodist Recorder.*

St John. "We take this opportunity of recommending to ministers on probation, the very excellent volume of the same series on this part of the New Testament. We hope that most or all of our young ministers will prefer to study the volume in the *Cambridge Greek Testament for Schools.*"—*Methodist Recorder.*

The Acts of the Apostles. "Professor LUMBY has performed his laborious task well, and supplied us with a commentary the fulness and freshness of which Bible students will not be slow to appreciate. The volume is enriched with the usual copious indexes and four coloured maps."—*Glasgow Herald.*

I. Corinthians. "Mr LIAS is no novice in New Testament exposition, and the present series of essays and notes is an able and helpful addition to the existing books."—*Guardian.*

The Epistles of St John. "In the very useful and well annotated series of the Cambridge Greek Testament the volume on the Epistles of St John must hold a high position...The notes are brief, well informed and intelligent."—*Scotsman.*

CAMBRIDGE UNIVERSITY PRESS.

THE PITT PRESS SERIES.

⁎ *Many of the books in this list can be had in two volumes, Text and Notes separately.*

I. GREEK.

Aristophanes. Aves—Plutus—Ranæ. By W. C. GREEN, M.A., late Assistant Master at Rugby School. 3s. 6d. each.

Aristotle. Outlines of the Philosophy of. Compiled by EDWIN WALLACE, M.A., LL.D. Third Edition, Enlarged. 4s. 6d.

Euripides. Heracleidae. With Introduction and Explanatory Notes. By E. A. BECK, M.A., Fellow of Trinity Hall. 3s. 6d.

—— **Hercules Furens.** With Introduction, Notes and Analysis. By A. GRAY, M.A., and J. T. HUTCHINSON, M.A. New Ed. 2s.

—— **Hippolytus.** With Introduction and Notes. By W. S. HADLEY, M.A., Fellow of Pembroke College. 2s.

—— **Iphigeneia in Aulis.** By C. E. S. HEADLAM, B.A. 2s. 6d.

Herodotus, Book V. Edited with Notes and Introduction by E. S. SHUCKBURGH, M.A. 3s.

—— **Book VI.** By the same Editor. 4s.

—— **Book VIII., Chaps. 1—90.** By the same Editor. 3s. 6d.

—— **Book IX., Chaps. 1—89.** By the same Editor. 3s. 6d.

Homer. Odyssey, Books IX., X. With Introduction, Notes and Appendices by G. M. EDWARDS, M.A. 2s. 6d. each.

—— —— **Book XXI.** By the same Editor. 2s.

Luciani Somnium Charon Piscator et De Luctu. By W. E. HEITLAND, M.A., Fellow of St John's College, Cambridge. 3s. 6d.

Platonis Apologia Socratis. With Introduction, Notes and Appendices. By J. ADAM, M.A. 3s. 6d.

—— **Crito.** By the same Editor. 2s. 6d.

—— **Euthyphro.** By the same Editor. 2s. 6d.

Plutarch. Lives of the Gracchi. With Introduction, Notes and Lexicon by Rev. H. A. HOLDEN, M.A., LL.D. 6s.

—— **Life of Nicias.** By the same Editor. 5s.

—— **Life of Sulla.** By the same Editor. 6s.

—— **Life of Timoleon.** By the same Editor. 6s.

Sophocles. Oedipus Tyrannus. School Edition, with Introduction and Commentary by R. C. JEBB, Litt.D., LL.D. 4s. 6d.

Xenophon. Agesilaus. By H. HAILSTONE, M.A. 2s. 6d.

—— **Anabasis.** With Introduction, Map and English Notes, by A. PRETOR, M.A. Two vols. 7s. 6d.

—— **Books I. III. IV. and V.** By the same. 2s. each.

—— **Books II. VI. and VII.** By the same. 2s. 6d. each.

Xenophon. Cyropaedeia. Books I. II. With Introduction and Notes by Rev. H. A. HOLDEN, M.A., LL.D. 2 vols. 6s.

—— —— **Books III. IV. and V.** By the same Editor. 5s.

—— —— **Books VI. VII. VIII.** By the same Editor.

[*Nearly ready.*

London: Cambridge Warehouse, Ave Maria Lane.

23/6/90

II. LATIN.

Beda's Ecclesiastical History, Books III., IV. Edited with a life, Notes, Glossary, Onomasticon and Index, by J. E. B. MAYOR, M.A., and J. R. LUMBY, D.D. Revised Edition. 7s. 6d.

—— **Books I. II.** By the same Editors. [*In the Press.*]

Caesar. De Bello Gallico, Comment. I. With Maps and Notes by A. G. PESKETT, M.A., Fellow of Magdalene College, Cambridge. 1s. 6d. COMMENT. II. III. 2s. COMMENT. I. II. III. 3s. COMMENT. IV. V., and COMMENT. VII. 2s. each. COMMENT. VI. and COMMENT. VIII. 1s. 6d. each.

—— **De Bello Civili, Comment. I.** By the same Editor.
[*In the Press.*]

Cicero. De Amicitia.—De Senectute. Edited by J. S. REID, Litt. D., Fellow of Gonville and Caius College. 3s. 6d. each.

—— **In Gaium Verrem Actio Prima.** With Notes, by H. COWIE, M.A. 1s. 6d.

—— **In Q. Caecilium Divinatio et in C. Verrem Actio.** With Notes by W. E. HEITLAND, M.A., and H. COWIE, M.A. 3s.

—— **Philippica Secunda.** By A. G. PESKETT, M.A. 3s. 6d.

—— **Oratio pro Archia Poeta.** By J. S. REID, Litt.D. 2s.

—— **Pro L. Cornelio Balbo Oratio.** By the same. 1s. 6d.

—— **Oratio pro Tito Annio Milone,** with English Notes, &c., by JOHN SMYTH PURTON, B.D. 2s. 6d.

—— **Oratio pro L. Murena,** with English Introduction and Notes. By W. E. HEITLAND, M.A. 3s.

—— **Pro Cn. Plancio Oratio,** by H. A. HOLDEN, LL.D. 4s. 6d.

—— **Pro P. Cornelio Sulla.** By J. S. REID, Litt.D. 3s. 6d.

—— **Somnium Scipionis.** With Introduction and Notes. Edited by W. D. PEARMAN, M.A. 2s.

Horace. Epistles, Book I. With Notes and Introduction by E. S. SHUCKBURGH, M.A., late Fellow of Emmanuel College. 2s. 6d.

Livy. Book IV. With Introduction and Notes. By H. M. STEPHENSON, M.A. 2s. 6d.

—— **Book V.** With Introduction and Notes by L. WHIBLEY, M.A. 2s. 6d.

—— **Books XXI., XXII.** With Notes, Introduction and Maps. By M. S. DIMSDALE, M.A., Fellow of King's College. 2s. 6d. each.

Lucan. Pharsaliae Liber Primus, with English Introduction and Notes by W. E. HEITLAND, M.A., and C. E. HASKINS, M.A. 1s. 6d.

Lucretius, Book V. With Notes and Introduction by J. D. DUFF, M.A., Fellow of Trinity College. 2s.

Ovidii Nasonis Fastorum Liber VI. With Notes by A. SIDGWICK, M.A., Tutor of Corpus Christi College, Oxford. 1s. 6d.

Quintus Curtius. A Portion of the History (Alexander in India). By W. E. HEITLAND, M.A., and T. E. RAVEN, B.A. With Two Maps. 3s. 6d.

Vergili Maronis Aeneidos Libri I.—XII. Edited with Notes by A. SIDGWICK, M.A. 1s. 6d. each.

—— **Bucolica.** By the same Editor. 1s. 6d

—— **Georgicon Libri I. II.** By the same Editor. 2s.

—— —— **Libri III. IV.** By the same Editor. 2s.

—— **The Complete Works.** By the same Editor. Two vols. Vol. I. containing the Introduction and Text. 3s. 6d. Vol. II. The Notes 4s. 6d.

London: Cambridge Warehouse, Ave Maria Lane.

III. FRENCH.

Corneille. La Suite du Menteur. A Comedy in Five Acts.
With Notes Philological and Historical, by the late G. MASSON, B.A. 2s.

De Bonnechose. Lazare Hoche. With four Maps, Introduction and Commentary, by C. COLBECK, M.A. Revised Ed.tion. 2s.

D'Harleville. Le Vieux Célibataire. A Comedy, Grammatical and Historical Notes, by G. MASSON, B.A. 2s.

De Lamartine. Jeanne D'Arc. Edited with a Map and Notes Historical and Philological, and a Vocabulary, by Rev. A. C. CLAPIN, M.A., St John's College, Cambridge. 2s.

De Vigny. La Canne de Jonc. Edited with Notes by Rev. H. A. BULL, M.A., late Master at Wellington College. 2s.

Erckmann-Chatrian. La Guerre. With Map, Introduction and Commentary by Rev. A. C. CLAPIN, M.A. 3s.

La Baronne de Staël-Holstein. Le Directoire. (Considérations sur la Révolution Française. Troisième et quatrième parties.) Revised and enlarged. With Notes by G. MASSON, B.A., and G. W. PROTHERO, M.A. 2s.

―――― ―――― **Dix Années d'Exil. Livre II. Chapitres 1—8.**
By the same Editors. New Edition, enlarged. 2s.

Lemercier. Fredegonde et Brunehaut. A Tragedy in Five Acts. By GUSTAVE MASSON, B.A. 2s.

Molière. Le Bourgeois Gentilhomme, Comédie-Ballet en Cinq Actes. (1670.) By Rev. A. C. CLAPIN, M.A. Revised Edition. 1s. 6d.

―――― **L'École des Femmes.** With Introduction and Notes by G. SAINTSBURY, M.A. 2s. 6d.

―――― **Les Précieuses Ridicules.** With Introduction and Notes by E. G. W. BRAUNHOLTZ, M.A., Ph.D. 2s.

Piron. La Métromanie. A Comedy, with Notes, by G. MASSON, B.A. 2s.

Racine. Les Plaideurs. With Introduction and Notes, by E. G. W. BRAUNHOLTZ, M.A., Ph.D. 2s.

Sainte-Beuve. M. Daru (Causeries du Lundi, Vol. IX.). By G. MASSON, B.A. 2s.

Saintine. Picciola. With Introduction, Notes and Map. By Rev. A. C. CLAPIN, M.A. 2s.

Scribe and Legouvé. Bataille de Dames. Edited by Rev. H. A. BULL, M.A. 2s.

Scribe. Le Verre d'Eau. A Comedy; with Memoir, Grammatical and Historical Notes. Edited by C. COLBECK, M.A. 2s.

Sédaine. Le Philosophe sans le savoir. Edited with Notes by Rev. H. A. BULL, M.A., late Master at Wellington College. 2s.

Thierry. Lettres sur l'histoire de France (XIII.—XXIV.).
By G. MASSON, B.A., and G. W. PROTHERO, M.A. 2s. 6d.

―――― **Récits des Temps Mérovingiens I.—III.** Edited by GUSTAVE MASSON, B.A. Univ. Gallic., and A. R. ROPES, M.A. With Map. 3s.

Villemain. Lascaris ou Les Grecs du XVe Siècle, Nouvelle Historique. By G. MASSON, B.A. 2s.

―――――――

London: Cambridge Warehouse, Ave Maria Lane.

**Voltaire. Histoire du Siècle de Louis XIV. Chaps. I.—
XIII.** Edited by G. MASSON, B.A., and G. W. PROTHERO, M.A. 2s. 6d.
PART II. CHAPS. XIV.—XXIV. By the same Editors. With Three Maps.
2s. 6d. PART III. CHAPS. XXV. to end. By the same Editors. 2s. 6d.
Xavier de Maistre. La Jeune Sibérienne. Le Lépreux de
la Cité D'Aoste. By G. MASSON, B.A. 1s. 6d.

IV. GERMAN.

Ballads on German History. Arranged and annotated by
WILHELM WAGNER, Ph.D. 2s.
Benedix. Doctor Wespe. Lustspiel in fünf Aufzügen. Edited
with Notes by KARL HERMANN BREUL, M.A., Ph.D. 3s.
Freytag. Der Staat Friedrichs des Grossen. With Notes.
By WILHELM WAGNER, Ph.D. 2s.
German Dactylic Poetry. Arranged and annotated by
WILHELM WAGNER, Ph.D. 3s.
Goethe's Knabenjahre. (1749—1759.) Arranged and annotated by WILHELM WAGNER, Ph.D. 2s.
—— **Hermann und Dorothea.** By WILHELM WAGNER,
Ph.D. Revised edition by J. W. CARTMELL, M.A. 3s. 6d.
Gutzkow. Zopf und Schwert. Lustspiel in fünf Aufzügen.
By H. J. WOLSTENHOLME, B.A. (Lond.). 3s. 6d.
Hauff. Das Bild des Kaisers. By KARL HERMANN BREUL,
M.A., Ph.D., University Lecturer in German. 3s.
—— **Das Wirthshaus im Spessart.** By A. SCHLOTTMANN,
Ph.D. 3s. 6d.
—— **Die Karavane.** Edited with Notes by A. SCHLOTT-
MANN, Ph.D. 3s. 6d
Immermann. Der Oberhof. A Tale of Westphalian Life, by
WILHELM WAGNER, Ph.D. 3s.
Kohlrausch. Das Jahr 1813. With English Notes by WILHELM
WAGNER, Ph.D. 2s.
Lessing and Gellert. Selected Fables. Edited with Notes
by KARL HERMANN BREUL, M.A., Ph.D. 3s.
Mendelssohn's Letters. Selections from. Edited by JAMES
SIME, M.A. 3s.
Raumer. Der erste Kreuzzug (1095—1099). By WILHELM
WAGNER, Ph.D. 2s.
Riehl. Culturgeschichtliche Novellen. Edited by H. J.
WOLSTENHOLME, B.A. (Lond.). 3s. 6d.
Schiller. Wilhelm Tell. Edited with Introduction and Notes
by KARL HERMANN BREUL, M.A., Ph.D. 2s. 6d.
Uhland. Ernst, Herzog von Schwaben. With Introduction
and Notes. By H. J. WOLSTENHOLME, B.A. 3s. 6d.

London: Cambridge Warehouse, Ave Maria Lane.

V. ENGLISH.

Ancient Philosophy from Thales to Cicero, A Sketch of. By JOSEPH B. MAYOR, M.A. 3s. 6d.

Bacon's History of the Reign of King Henry VII. With Notes by the Rev. Professor LUMBY, D.D. 3s.

Cowley's Essays. With Introduction and Notes, by the Rev. Professor LUMBY, D.D. 4s.

More's History of King Richard III. Edited with Notes, Glossary, Index of Names. By J. RAWSON LUMBY, D.D. 3s. 6d.

More's Utopia. With Notes, by Rev. Prof. LUMBY, D.D. 3s. 6d.

The Two Noble Kinsmen, edited with Introduction and Notes, by the Rev. Professor SKEAT, Litt.D. 3s. 6d.

VI. EDUCATIONAL SCIENCE.

Comenius, John Amos, Bishop of the Moravians. His Life and Educational Works, by S. S. LAURIE, A.M., F.R.S.E. 3s. 6d.

Education, Three Lectures on the Practice of. I. On Marking, by H. W. EVE, M.A. II. On Stimulus, by A. SIDGWICK, M.A. III. On the Teaching of Latin Verse Composition, by E. A. ABBOTT, D.D. 2s.

Stimulus. A Lecture delivered for the Teachers' Training Syndicate, May, 1882, by A. SIDGWICK, M.A. 1s.

Locke on Education. With Introduction and Notes by the Rev. R. H. QUICK, M.A. 3s. 6d.

Milton's Tractate on Education. A facsimile reprint from the Edition of 1673. Edited with Notes, by O. BROWNING, M.A. 2s.

Modern Languages, Lectures on the Teaching of. By C. COLBECK, M.A. 2s.

Teacher, General Aims of the, and Form Management. Two Lectures delivered in the University of Cambridge in the Lent Term, 1883, by F. W. FARRAR, D.D., and R. B. POOLE, B.D. 1s. 6d.

Teaching, Theory and Practice of. By the Rev. E. THRING, M.A., late Head Master of Uppingham School. New Edition. 4s. 6d.

British India, a Short History of. By E. S. CARLOS, M.A., late Head Master of Exeter Grammar School. 1s.

Geography, Elementary Commercial. A Sketch of the Commodities and the Countries of the World. By H. R. MILL, D.Sc., F.R.S.E. 1s.

Geography, an Atlas of Commercial. (A Companion to the above.) By J. G. BARTHOLOMEW, F.R.G.S. With an Introduction by HUGH ROBERT MILL, D.Sc. 3s.

VII. MATHEMATICS.

Euclid's Elements of Geometry. Books I and II. By H. M. TAYLOR, M.A., Fellow and late Tutor of Trinity College, Cambridge. 1s. 6d.

—————— **Books III. and IV.** By the same Editor.
[*In the Press.*

Other Volumes are in preparation.

London: Cambridge Warehouse, Ave Maria Lane.

The Cambridge Bible for Schools and Colleges.

GENERAL EDITOR: J. J. S. PEROWNE, D.D.,
DEAN OF PETERBOROUGH.

"*It is difficult to commend too highly this excellent series.*—Guardian.

"*The modesty of the general title of this series has, we believe, led many to misunderstand its character and underrate its value. The books are well suited for study in the upper forms of our best schools, but not the less are they adapted to the wants of all Bible students who are not specialists. We doubt, indeed, whether any of the numerous popular commentaries recently issued in this country will be found more serviceable for general use.*"—Academy.

Now Ready. Cloth, Extra Fcap. 8vo. With Maps.

Book of Joshua. By Rev. G. F. MACLEAR, D.D. 2s. 6d.
Book of Judges. By Rev. J. J. LIAS, M.A. 3s. 6d.
First Book of Samuel. By Rev. Prof. KIRKPATRICK, B.D. 3s. 6d.
Second Book of Samuel. By Rev. Prof. KIRKPATRICK, B.D. 3s. 6d.
First Book of Kings. By Rev. Prof. LUMBY, D.D. 3s. 6d.
Second Book of Kings. By Rev. Prof. LUMBY, D.D. 3s. 6d.
Book of Job. By Rev. A. B. DAVIDSON, D.D. 5s.
Book of Ecclesiastes. By Very Rev. E. H. PLUMPTRE, D.D. 5s.
Book of Jeremiah. By Rev. A. W. STREANE, M.A. 4s. 6d.
Book of Hosea. By Rev. T. K. CHEYNE, M.A., D.D. 3s.
Books of Obadiah & Jonah. By Archdeacon PEROWNE. 2s. 6d.
Book of Micah. By Rev. T. K. CHEYNE, M.A., D.D. 1s. 6d.
Haggai, Zechariah & Malachi. By Arch. PEROWNE. 3s. 6d.
Book of Malachi. By Archdeacon PEROWNE. 1s.
Gospel according to St Matthew. By Rev. A. CARR, M.A. 2s. 6d.
Gospel according to St Mark. By Rev. G. F. MACLEAR, D.D. 2s. 6d.
Gospel according to St Luke. By Arch. FARRAR, D.D. 4s. 6d.
Gospel according to St John. By Rev. A. PLUMMER, D.D. 4s. 6d.
Acts of the Apostles. By Rev. Prof. LUMBY, D.D. 4s. 6d.
Epistle to the Romans. By Rev. H. C. G. MOULE, M.A. 3s. 6d.
First Corinthians. By Rev. J. J. LIAS, M.A. With Map. 2s.
Second Corinthians. By Rev. J. J. LIAS, M.A. With Map. 2s.

London: Cambridge Warehouse, Ave Maria Lane.

Epistle to the Ephesians. By Rev. H. C. G. MOULE, M.A. 2s. 6d.
Epistle to the Philippians. By Rev. H. C. G. MOULE, M.A. 2s. 6d.
Epistle to the Hebrews. By Arch. FARRAR, D.D. 3s. 6d.
General Epistle of St James. By Very Rev. E. H. PLUMPTRE, D.D. 1s. 6d.
Epistles of St Peter and St Jude. By Very Rev. E. H. PLUMPTRE, D.D. 2s. 6d.
Epistles of St John. By Rev. A. PLUMMER, M.A., D.D. 3s. 6d.

Preparing.

Book of Genesis. By Very Rev. the Dean of Peterborough.
Books of Exodus, Numbers and Deuteronomy. By Rev. C. D. GINSBURG, LL.D.
Books of Ezra and Nehemiah. By Rev. Prof. RYLE, M.A.
Book of Psalms. By Rev. Prof. KIRKPATRICK, B.D.
Book of Isaiah. By Prof. W. ROBERTSON SMITH, M.A.
Book of Ezekiel. By Rev. A. B. DAVIDSON, D.D.
Book of Malachi. By Archdeacon PEROWNE.
Epistle to the Galatians. By Rev. E. H. PEROWNE, D.D.
Epistles to the Colossians and Philemon. By Rev. H. C. G. MOULE, M.A.
Epistles to Timothy & Titus. By Rev. A. E. HUMPHREYS, M.A.
Book of Revelation. By Rev. W. H. SIMCOX, M.A.

The Smaller Cambridge Bible for Schools.

The Smaller Cambridge Bible for Schools *will form an entirely new series of commentaries on some selected books of the Bible. It is expected that they will be prepared for the most part by the Editors of the larger series (The Cambridge Bible for Schools and Colleges). The volumes will be issued at a low price, and will be suitable to the requirements of preparatory and elementary schools.*

Now ready.

First and Second Books of Samuel. By Rev. Prof. KIRKPATRICK, B.D. 1s. each.
Gospel according to St Matthew. By Rev. A. CARR, M.A. 1s.
Gospel according to St Mark. By Rev. G. F. MACLEAR, D.D. 1s.
Gospel according to St Luke. By Archdeacon FARRAR. 1s.

London: Cambridge Warehouse, Ave Maria Lane.

The Cambridge Greek Testament for Schools and Colleges,

with a Revised Text, based on the most recent critical authorities, and English Notes, prepared under the direction of the General Editor, The Very Reverend J. J. S. PEROWNE, D.D., DEAN OF PETERBOROUGH.

Gospel according to St Matthew. By Rev. A. CARR, M.A.
With 4 Maps. 4s. 6d.

Gospel according to St Mark. By Rev. G. F. MACLEAR, D.D.
With 3 Maps. 4s. 6d.

Gospel according to St Luke. By Archdeacon FARRAR.
With 4 Maps. 6s.

Gospel according to St John. By Rev. A. PLUMMER, D.D.
With 4 Maps. 6s.

Acts of the Apostles. By Rev. Professor LUMBY, D.D.
With 4 Maps. 6s.

First Epistle to the Corinthians. By Rev. J. J. LIAS, M.A. 3s.

Second Epistle to the Corinthians. By Rev. J. J. LIAS, M.A.
[*In the Press.*

Epistle to the Hebrews. By Archdeacon FARRAR, D.D. 3s. 6d.

Epistle of St James. By Very Rev. E. H. PLUMPTRE, D.D.
[*Preparing.*

Epistles of St John. By Rev. A. PLUMMER, M.A., D.D. 4s.

London: C. J. CLAY AND SONS,
CAMBRIDGE WAREHOUSE, AVE MARIA LANE.
Glasgow: 263, ARGYLE STREET.
Cambridge: DEIGHTON, BELL AND CO.
Leipzig: F. A. BROCKHAUS.

www.ingramcontent.com/pod-product-compliance
Lightning Source LLC
Chambersburg PA
CBHW021013240426
43669CB00037B/762